VILLAIN OR VICTIM?
A defence of Sir John Kerr and the Reserve Powers

Peter O'Brien

Connor Court Publishing

VILLAIN OR VICTIM? A defence of Sir John Kerr and the Reserve Powers

Published in 2022 by Connor Court Publishing Pty Ltd

Copyright © Peter O'Brien

All rights reserved. No part of this book may be reproduced or transmitted in any form or by any means, electronic or mechanical, including photo copying, recording or by any information storage and retrieval system, without prior permission in writing from the publisher.

Connor Court Publishing Pty Ltd
PO Box 7257
Redland Bay QLD 4165
sales@connorcourt.com
www.connorcourt.com
Phone 0497-900-685

Printed in Australia

ISBN: 9781922815101

Front cover design: Maria Giordano

Front Cover Picture: A6135, K3/9/74/20 - Governor General Sir John Kerr, 3 September 1974. Image courtesy of the National Archives of Australia. NAA: A6135, K3/9/74/20.

This book is dedicated to Winston Smith

ACKNOWLEDGEMENTS

Firstly, I would like to thank my wife Barbara for her uncomplaining support of my writing adventures.

Secondly, I thank Anthony Cappello of Connor Court Publishing for accepting my manuscript for publication.

I would like to acknowledge Roger Franklin, editor of Quadrant Online magazine, who encouraged me to embark on a writing career, if I may be permitted so grandiose a description of my humble efforts as a wordsmith. His support and guidance have been invaluable.

And finally, I sincerely thank Professor David Flint and Dr Michael Connor for their generous encouragement and valuable contributions to this project.

CONTENTS

Introduction		7
1	Kerr and The Queen – Dismay at the Palace	29
2	Kerr and Fraser – The Tip-off	63
3	Kerr and Whitlam – The Deception	75
4	Barwick, Mason and the High Court	89
5	Kerr's Journey: Dreaming of Menzies	103
6	The Guiding Stars: Evatt and Barwick	123
7	Fraser Strikes, Whitlam Resists	145
8	Kerr Turns Against Whitlam	165
9	Kerr's Fear of Recall	191
10	Whitlam's Blunders	213
11	Anthony Mason and the Arch of Opinion	231
12	Kerr's Decision	249
13	Manipulating a Willing Chief Justice	285
14	The Dismissal	303
15	Death in the Afternoon: The Second Crisis	327
Conclusion		347
Appendix		359
Index		365

INTRODUCTION

Unlike Britain, Australia has a written Constitution – well, most of it is written. But there is a significant element that is unwritten.

The Constitution prescribes the rules under which we are governed. It defines the limits of what each political entity can do and the relationship between them. It strives to cover any eventuality. However, no human-devised system is foolproof. Human nature often intervenes in the best laid plans in unexpected ways. So, there must be a mechanism (or mechanisms) to handle unforeseen problems. And it must necessarily *not* be over-prescriptive, otherwise it defeats its purpose. This, in turn, dictates that it will be susceptible to differing interpretations.

Our Constitution incorporates some conventions we inherited from Britain, and these are well understood. There are also what are known as the reserve powers of the Governor General. Although they are listed in the Constitution, the circumstances in which they may, or should, be used is not explicit. They are:

> The power to dissolve (or refuse to dissolve) the House of Representatives (section 5)
>
> The power to dissolve Parliament on the occasion of a deadlock (section 57)
>
> The power to withhold assent to bills (section 58)
>
> The power to appoint (or dismiss) ministers (section 64)

It is the use of these reserve powers that is at the centre of the ongoing, and dare I say it, artificial controversy surrounding the dismissal from the Prime Ministership of Gough Whitlam by the Governor General, Sir John Kerr, on 11 November 1975.

Over the years since 1975, partisan players have mounted an

ongoing campaign to vilify Sir John Kerr. They claim, variously, that the powers he invoked do not exist, or that they have become defunct, or that yes, they do exist but should never be used, or that yes, they exist but Kerr misused them. This cacophony of conflicting and, often self-contradictory, rodomontade has had the flow-on effect of discrediting the reserve powers and intimidating future Governors-General against their use. In fact, I believe that is the real intent behind the anti-Kerr campaign, although I'm not suggesting a conspiracy. The main, and most authoritative, protagonists in this campaign are Paul Kelly and Troy Bramston. Their 2015 book *The Dismissal – in the Queen's name* is the most comprehensive of the critiques of Kerr's actions, and that is the source I shall concentrate on.

At the outset, let me observe that *The Dismissal* is replete with *ad hominem* attacks on Sir John. It seems to me that Kelly and Bramston leave no stone unturned to paint the most unflattering portrait of him, which results in a rather grotesque caricature of an accomplished and successful man. Sometimes he is a pompous, self-seeking sycophant who revels in the trappings of high office. At others, he is a scheming Machiavellian figure who puts it all at risk for the dubious pleasure making his mark by dismissing a duly elected government. The two Kerrs that they offer us are mutually exclusive, as I hope to show. To be fair, both Whitlam and Fraser come in for a bit of criticism but nothing on the scale of character assassination to which Kerr is subject.

The Dismissal could be more aptly titled *The Trial of Sir John Kerr*. In his autobiography, *Matters for Judgement*, Kerr offers detailed explanations and defence of his actions. There is also a trove of personal papers held in the Australian Archives. Kelly and Bramston almost uniformly dismiss Kerr's explanations as 'self-justification'. Imagine if you will, a criminal trial in which one side presents the prosecution case and then the other side, representing the defendant, is called upon to present the 'self-justification' case. Not a great start for a fair trial, I am sure you will agree.

My purpose here is not only to defend Sir John Kerr for the sake of restoring his reputation, although I certainly hope my efforts will help in that respect. Ultimately, I believe history will judge him more kindly – and hopefully more objectively – than his contemporary critics have. This book is not a hagiography. I do not claim that Sir John was perfect or that he did not make mistakes or misjudgements. But those faults are comprehensively enumerated, and indeed exaggerated, within *The Dismissal*. As Kerr's self-appointed 'defence counsel', I do not see the need to place too much emphasis on them.

More importantly, by showing that Kerr was by no means the villain the Left have portrayed, I hope to help rehabilitate the status of the reserve powers, because I do not believe they are an anachronism but rather an important feature of our governance.

The Events of 1975

For the reader to understand the discussion that follows, it is helpful to have a short precis of the events that transpired on 11 November 1975.

The Labor government of Gough Whitlam, elected in 1972, had advised a double dissolution election in May 1974 when the opposition Liberal/Country coalition in the Senate had blocked a raft of important legislation and had threatened to deny the government supply i.e., reject its Budget. Labor won that election but did not gain control of the Senate. In March 1975, Malcolm Fraser became Leader of the Opposition.

Sir John Kerr, then Chief Justice of the NSW Supreme Court, had earlier been invited by Whitlam to take up the post of Governor-General upon the retirement of Sir Paul Hasluck. Kerr took some time to consider the offer, since it would entail him stepping down from a well-paid, secure and influential position to take up a post, largely ceremonial, that might last only five years. Eventually Kerr decided to take up the offer and was sworn in on 11 July 1974.

The second term of the Whitlam government was tumultuous and beset by a number of scandals. The major of these was known as the Loans Affair. Essentially, the Whitlam government attempted to borrow $4 billion, later revised downward to $2 billion, from a Pakistani financier, Tirath Khemlani. The loan was initially approved in the Executive Council for 'temporary purposes', although it was intended for national development projects and, according to Khemlani, was a 20-year loan with interest at 7.7% and a commission to Khemlani of 2.5%. Because this loan was ostensibly for temporary purposes, it was held that it need not be referred, for approval, to the Loans Council which comprised delegates from the Commonwealth and the States. Significantly, the meeting of the Executive Council which initially approved the loan, was scheduled at short notice when Sir John Kerr was not in Canberra. The meeting was held in his absence – not unusual, although he would always have given approval for the meeting in advance. In this case he was not even advised it had been scheduled. Following discussions, and despite some misgivings, he was persuaded to sign the Executive Council minute. This incident is covered exhaustively later so I will not go into further detail here. Eventually, the loan fell through but not before it had claimed the scalp of Minerals and Energy Minister, Rex Connor, for misleading Parliament. Although this affair does not directly impact on the dismissal (it was not the reason), it is significant in that it exemplifies the general dysfunction of the government which led to a serious erosion of public support during 1975 which, in turn, helped entrench the determination of the Opposition to adopt whatever means it could to remove the Whitlam government.

The crux of the crisis is based on the Senate's refusal, in 1975, to approve supply to the government, with the aim of forcing it to an early election, and Whitlam's understandable frustration at being forced to a third election in three years. In August, after the budget had been presented, Fraser indicated he would not block supply unless some unexpected and serious event occurred. Connor's resignation, and the revelation of the circumstance that had forced it, on 14 October gave Fraser his serious event. He determined that he would block supply until the government agreed to submit itself to the judgement of the people. Fraser, essentially, maintained that position throughout. Whitlam, on the other hand, proposed several compromises, but also made it clear he would not advise a full election under any circumstances, even though the funds available to government for its normal operation, wages etc, would be exhausted by 30 November. He said that he was determined to break forever the power of the Senate to frustrate a duly elected government. Kerr and Whitlam held numerous meetings to discuss the unfolding crisis and canvass possible solutions. Whitlam also gave Kerr permission to consult with Fraser – this became an issue after the dismissal. By 9 November, Kerr had determined that the impasse was unresolvable by compromise on the part of either Whitlam or Fraser, and that Whitlam's proposed solution of a half-Senate election on 13 December would not work. Specifically, it would not ameliorate the constitutional contravention of the government potentially governing without supply i.e., spending money that had not been appropriated by Parliament as required by the Constitution. It would mean that salaries and bills would not be paid for an indeterminate period of time, possibly in excess of two months. He determined to withdraw Whitlam's commission and invite Fraser to form a caretaker government.

On 11 November, Whitlam arrived at Government House to advise a half-Senate election. Before he could give that advice, after some brief initial discussion, Kerr presented him with the withdrawal of his commission. Kerr's and Whitlam's accounts of this meeting differ, and these differences will be discussed later. Kerr then summoned Fraser and invited him to form a caretaker government, subject to a number of conditions, which included that he would now grant supply and immediately advise a general election. This he did and, at the subsequent election held on 13 December, Fraser won a landslide victory – 91 seats to 36 seats for Labor.

Constitutional Provisions

If we look at the Constitution, Sections 61 to 64 provide:

Executive power

61. The executive power of the Commonwealth is vested in the Queen and is exercisable by the Governor-General as the Queen's representative, and extends to the execution and maintenance of this Constitution, and of the laws of the Commonwealth.

Federal Executive Council

62. There shall be a Federal Executive Council to advise the Governor-General in the government of the Commonwealth, and the members of the Council shall be chosen and summoned by the Governor-General and sworn as Executive Councillors, and shall hold office during his pleasure.

Provisions referring to Governor-General

63. The provisions of this Constitution referring to the Governor-General in Council shall be construed as referring to the Governor-General acting with the advice of the Federal Executive Council.

Ministers of State

64. The Governor-General may appoint officers to administer such departments of State of the Commonwealth as the Governor-General in Council may establish.

Such officers shall hold office during the pleasure of the Governor-General. They shall be members of the Federal Executive Council, and shall be the Queen's Ministers of State for the Commonwealth.

> Ministers to sit in Parliament
>
> After the first general election no Minister of State shall hold office for a longer period than three months unless he is or becomes a senator or a member of the House of Representatives.

It is clear that, in a strict interpretation of the Constitution, executive power resides with the Governor General. Ministers hold office at his pleasure. The convention that the Governor-General acts on the advice of his Ministers, recognises that the responsibility for the development and implementation of policy in the form of laws rests with the Parliament.

There is nothing in the Constitution about what we call 'the government'. There is nothing in the Constitution that refers to the Prime Minister. We imagine that when we go to the polls, we elect a government. But, constitutionally, that is only an indirect outcome of an election. What we elect is a Parliament. It is the Governor-General's role to appoint a government from within the ranks of that Parliament. There is nothing in the Constitution that says the Governor-General must appoint the leader of the party that has the majority of seats in the House of Representatives as Prime Minister. There is nothing in the Constitution that says the Governor-General must act on the advice of this person. There is nothing in the Constitution that says that a person appointed by the Governor-General must resign if he loses a vote of no-confidence in the House.

All these things form part of our governance, but they are not legally enforceable. They are conventions that, under normal circumstances, are applied to facilitate good government. Under normal circumstances they make sense. It makes sense for the Governor-General to appoint a Ministry from the ranks of those who, by virtue of their numbers, have the ability to implement a legislative program. But in certain circumstances – and 11 November 1975 was one such occasion – where the sitting Prime Minister is not able to implement his agenda without breaching the Constitution, the Governor-General has a duty to commission a Ministry which can and will resolve the situation. And this is the basis upon which Sir John Kerr acted.

A central premise of *The Dismissal* is that Kerr defied the convention that the Governor-General 'acts on the advice of his Ministers'. I will argue that this convention applies only to policy and related issues – the business of government. Once the Governor-General determines that a situation calls for him to invoke the reserve powers (which could include the dismissal of a Prime Minister) – that would be the province of governance – the convention does not, and in practical terms, cannot apply.

Kelly and Bramston argue that Sir John Kerr had a duty to 'advise and warn' Gough Whitlam that he might be forced to dismiss him if he persisted in his course of action. I believe that this convention means no more than that the Governor-General has a right, and maybe a duty, to advise the Prime Minister if he believes a certain policy initiative or course of action is possibly unconstitutional. He *may* proffer advice that he thinks a policy initiative may be illegal or ill-advised, but that would be a very rare occurrence.

These reserve powers, which only exist as conventions in Great Britain, were explicitly written into our Constitution a mere 75 years before the events of 11 November 1975. It can hardly be imagined that the drafters of our Constitution intended that these powers not be used, or that they would expire within such a short timeframe.

The Issues

The main issues that dominate this controversy are:

The existence of the reserve powers and constraints on their use,

The power of the Senate to block supply,

The question of the Governor-General acting contrary to the advice of the Prime Minister,

The question of the Governor-General seeking independent advice,

The charge that Sir John Kerr deceived Mr Whitlam,

The relationship of Sir John Kerr with the Palace.

These issues have been covered variously over the years but have been comprehensively examined in the 2015 book *The Dismissal – in the Queen's Name* by Paul Kelly and Troy Bramston. This book is devastatingly critical of Sir John Kerr, both personally and in respect of his momentous 1975 decision. In my critique I will examine most chapters of *The Dismissal*, with a view to providing an alternative viewpoint. For clarity, my chapters mirror those of *The Dismissal*. Readers will find my text somewhat repetitious, for which I apologise. The reason is that Kelly and Bramston themselves make the same few fundamental points over and over in different contexts. For completeness, I have responded accordingly.

Right at the outset, let me say that the very title of the subject book, *The Dismissal*, is tendentious although I do concede that it is probably the most obvious title. But, throughout the book, the dismissal is treated by the authors as the 'end-game' of Sir John Kerr's deliberations – that his aim was to 'dismiss' Prime Minister Gough Whitlam. That is not the case. Sir John's aim was to ensure that the government of the day had the funds it needed to carry out its functions and that it acquired them constitutionally. That outcome did not necessarily involve the withdrawal of Gough Whitlam's commission as Prime Minister – that came about because Whitlam failed to recognise the reality of his position. Even the book's sub-title – *in the Queen's name* – is misleading. Kerr did not dismiss Whitlam 'in the Queen's name' any more than he carried out any of his other functions in the Queen's name. In fact, he went out of his way to shield the Queen from any involvement in the crisis.

It might be said that the events of 1975 are now ancient history and of no interest to most of the modern generation. They are certainly history and for that reason we must ensure that the story of the removal of the Whitlam government 'is not written by the victors' but is written accurately.

The Dismissal purports to be the last word on the events of 1975 and many people believe that, with its release in 2015, the subject has been done to death. Not true. The only thing that has been done to death is the reputation of Sir John Kerr and, with it, the prospect of any balanced consideration of the reserve powers of the Crown in Australia.

At some point, sooner rather than later, we will be faced with a referendum on the so-called Australian Republic. Pivotal to that debate will be the role, if any, of the reserve powers. Readers can be sure that *The Dismissal* will be used, by those for whom the existence of the reserve powers is an anathema, to argue that whatever value they may have in theory is outweighed by the damage they can inflict in the hands of an unscrupulous President. Judging by the utterances of those currently in control of the Australian Republican Movement, this specious rhetoric is likely to find ready acceptance among its ranks. At the time of writing, the model proposed by the Australian Republican Movement had just been released. It proposes direct election of a President by the Australian people from a panel chosen by the State and Federal Parliaments. And it involves removing from the President, the power to dismiss a government, and, presumably, the other reserve powers as well. This represents a major change to our Constitution. It would render the Crown – that enigmatic entity that ultimately protects the interests of the people – impotent, a mere figurehead. If a referendum goes ahead, this is a complex debate that we must be prepared to have. And that debate must be based on a thorough and honest understanding of our current system. The misinformation that pervades *The Dismissal* will help to undermine that debate.

It is a deeply flawed book, at least in the way it treats Sir John Kerr – and my aim is to demonstrate that.

My first witness is Paul Kelly.

Writing in *The Australian* in September 2015, in the context of the failed ALP bid for the Senate to petition the Governor-General to dismiss Justice Dyson Heydon from the Trade Union Royal Commission, Kelly said:

> The principles here are exactly the same as in the 1975 crisis. On that occasion the governor-general, Sir John Kerr, acted on a motion passed by the Senate, defied the advice of the prime minister, broke the conventions surrounding his office and took a unilateral decision to preference the wishes of the Senate over the position of the executive government.[1]

Troy Bramston followed up a few days later:

> Gough Whitlam fought the 1975 election on the basis that the governor-general's decision to act on an opposition Senate motion was a fundamental breach of Australian democracy.

Both Kelly and Bramston would be correct to assert that if Kerr had acted in this fashion, it would have been in breach of our democracy and Constitution. But Kerr did not act in this way. There was no Senate motion calling for the Governor-General to dismiss the government, which is the way both statements read, taken in context. The Senate motion was to block supply to the government, an action which set in train a series of events that, eventually, led to the withdrawal of Whitlam's commission. The untutored reader may not understand this distinction.

I will now commence my appraisal with the Introduction to that book.

They begin:

> The dismissal is the most dramatic event in Australia's political history – the moment when our parliamentary institutions and constitutional system were put under their greatest strain ... Forty years later, when the passion and tumult have died, there is a fundamental truth: this was a highly unsatisfactory solution

---

[1] P. Kelly, 'Labor's zero-sum game over Dyson Heydon', *The Australian*, 2 September 2015, (online).

for Australian democracy.[2]

No, it wasn't. A grossly incompetent and dysfunctional government was replaced as a result of a general election. What could be more democratic than that? They continue:

> The dismissal was a monumental train wreck, in its prelude, its execution and its consequences. Neither inevitable nor necessary, it was inferior to other options available to resolve the four-week parliamentary deadlock.[3]

Kelly and Bramston make this claim throughout their book, that there were other options. And they quote others, such as Sir William Heseltine, to the same effect. But not one of them has been able to say what those options were. There were three scenarios that would have avoided the dismissal of Whitlam:

> Kerr could have somehow influenced Fraser to back down and pass supply, Kerr could have somehow influenced Whitlam to advise a double dissolution, or Kerr could have accepted Whitlam's advice for a half-Senate election.

Kelly and Bramston themselves, later in their introduction, describe the third option as 'a request no responsible governor-general would grant'.[4] If there were a fourth option no-one has been able to enunciate it beyond vague sentiments such as 'there must, or should, have been another way'.

So, we are left with either of the first two options. Firstly, Kerr could not advise or direct Whitlam or Fraser to act in any particular way. That would have been intruding into the politics. So, his influence would have to be more subtle or indirect. Whether Kerr had the personality to impose either his own views or the status of his office on these two headstrong men is problematical. In the end, events moved so quickly that he would have had very little time to develop the sort of dialogue that would have been required. His judgement was

---

[2] P. Kelly and T. Bramston, (2015). *The Dismissal – in the Queen's Name*, Ringwood: Penguin, p. ix..
[3] Ibid.
[4] Ibid., p. xiii.

that both men were immoveable, and he acted upon that belief.
And next:

> The rage and delight about 1975, depending on your perspective, has expired. But the story has not settled. The passage of four decades has not brought reconciliation over these events.[5]

Well, it certainly hasn't brought reconciliation on the part of Paul Kelly. Lt Hiroo Onoda, hiding out for nearly thirty years in the jungles of the Philippines, never backed his Emperor with the same level of devotion that Kelly has brought to the task of 'maintaining the rage'. Every few years it seems Sir John Kerr must be exhumed, dusted off and re-immolated upon our very own November bonfire – an antipodean Guy Fawkes. That may seem an unfortunate metaphor. I do not intend to imply that Fawkes was a victim of injustice, but that his actions were used, over centuries, to discredit Catholics in general. Kelly and Bramston use the same technique to discredit the reserve powers. Their real objection to Kerr's actions were not the way in which he exercised the reserve powers, but that they were used at all, as will become apparent later.

Let us continue:

> As the Queen, in blissful ignorance, slept in her bed in Buckingham Palace, the governor-general used the Crown's power to terminate the prime minister's commission in Canberra. Kerr acted in the Queen's name but one could not expect the Queen to have taken such action herself.[6]

That is essentially true, but not because she would have disdained Kerr's solution (although she may have) but because she simply does not have the power. The Governor-General may be the Queen's representative, but he is not her deputy. He is more like a regent. A regent is a ruler in all but name, such as the Prince of Wales was between 1810 and 1820, when his father King George III suffered from debilitating mental illness. He was known as the Prince Regent, and he exercised

---

[5] Ibid., p. ix.
[6] Ibid., pp. ix-x.

all the prerogatives of the Monarch. The Governor-General, although not officially designated a Regent, is in much the same position.

When the Queen comes to Australia, the Governor-General defers to her, but he does not relinquish his powers. They are given to him by the Constitution; specifically, ministers hold office during the Governor-General's pleasure, as detailed in Section 62 of the Constitution. Even if the monarchy were abolished in the United Kingdom and the Queen came to reside in Australia, that situation would still apply. What the Queen may or may not have done in similar circumstances in the United Kingdom is irrelevant. In the United Kingdom, the symbolic, ceremonial and executive roles of the Crown are embodied in the single person of the Queen. In Australia, the Queen is the custodian of the symbolic, she and the Governor-General share the ceremonial functions, and the executive function resides solely with the Governor-General.

The claim that the power was exercised *without warning* is specious. I will examine this issue in later chapters.

This theme continues:

> It was one of those rare occasions when the Crown's intervention was decisive in settling a great contest. The governor-general called his memoirs Matters for Judgement. This was Kerr's call, it was Kerr's test, it was Kerr's judgement. He had the power and the influence. Yet Kerr's solution – changing the government at the stroke of a pen – divided the nation, embittered the politics and compromised our institutions.[7]

Kerr did not 'change the government at the stroke of a pen'. He suspended government. It was the *people* who changed the government at the consequent election. It is doubtful that Kerr's action really divided the nation. There were those who supported Whitlam and those who supported Fraser. After the election, the vast majority of the populace got on with their lives. And as to compromising our institutions, if we are talking

---

[7] Ibid., p. x.

about conventions as institutions, it was Whitlam and Fraser who essayed whatever damage was done to them. If we are talking about actual institutions, Kelly and Bramston do not specify what institutions were compromised and in what way. I suspect they are referring to the High Court and the fact that Chief Justice, Sir Garfield Barwick, gave advice to Kerr. Kelly and Bramston deplore Barwick's intervention, but as we will see later, it is a complex and debatable point. For example, Barwick was able to point to several precedents for his involvement. Be that as it may, if anything was compromised it was not the High Court itself, but the reputation of the Chief Justice. Judges are often caught out in more explicit misdemeanours but there is never any suggestion that this compromises the court upon which they sit.

They summarise the crisis as follows:

> The originating conflict was between the Senate and the House of Representatives over the blocking of supply – the funding of general government services. This triggered the next conflict – whether the governor-general was obliged to follow the advice of his prime minister. In turn this provoked another issue – whether the governor-general was entitled to seek advice from the Chief Justice of the High Court. The final question became whether the governor-general in exercising the reserve powers of the Crown had an obligation to give Whitlam the choice of going to the election as prime minister.[8]

Two points emerge from this. As to Whitlam having the option of going to the election as Prime Minister, I will argue in a later chapter that he did, indeed, have that choice. Kelly and Bramston question whether the Governor-General had the right to not accept 'the advice of his prime minister'. The suggestion that the Governor-General must act on the advice of his Prime Minister pervades *The Dismissal*. However, a few pages later, Kelly and Bramston answer their own question:

> ... Whitlam misunderstood the battle he was facing. Because his government was denied funding, he had only a limited time

---
[8] Ibid.

in which to prevail. And he failed, the final proof being his absurd journey to Yarralumla on 11 November to seek a half-Senate election, without guarantee of supply for the election period, a request no responsible governor-general would grant.[9]

This clearly is an example of the Governor-General refusing to accept the advice of his Prime Minister. If it is acceptable in principle in this instance, then it can hardly be a matter of principle that the Governor-General *must always* accept such advice. This suggests that conventions, while useful, are not inviolate.

They continue:

> Whitlam and Fraser were titans from an era long passed. They were authentic leaders convinced of their mission, ready to invoke political violence for their cause and prepared to push the constitutional systems to breaking point in their rivalry. As governor-general it fell to Kerr – talented, ambitious and cunning – to manage the deadlock.
>
> It is a tribute to our politics and society that Whitlam and Fraser reconciled. Few participants and observers of the crisis would have imagined such an event.[10]

So, it seems the crisis was not such a divisive event after all. Perhaps Whitlam ultimately reconciled with Fraser because he recognised that had the situation been reversed, he would have acted in exactly the same way. As he, in fact, proposed to do on several occasions when he was Opposition Leader. But Kerr was not a member of this cosy politician's club, and he did not act in the way that Whitlam confidently expected him to. He therefore must be permanently shunned. The gratuitous and unflattering description of Kerr as 'talented, ambitious and cunning' sets a precedent that pervades the remainder of *The Dismissal*.

The next lengthy extract is telling. Bear with me:

> At the fortieth anniversary the power questions from 1975

---

[9] Ibid, p. xiii.
[10] Ibid, p. xi.

remain unresolved. The Senate can still block supply to force an election: a prime minister can still defy the Senate, precipitating a deadlock; and a governor-general can still sack a prime minister. In theory, it could happen again. In practice, that is extremely unlikely. The 1975 crisis was the product of three extraordinary personalities – Fraser, Whitlam and Kerr – unlikely to be replicated as individuals, let alone as a troika.

Predictions that the crisis would permanently undermine our democracy have proven unfounded. Other prophecies that none of this sequence of events can happen again are absurdly complacent.

But the 1975 crisis created a new set of 'understood' but undefined working rules – that the Senate should not again deny supply; that the High Court should not again advise the governor-general; and that the governor-general should represent the nation by shunning any repeat of Kerr-type interventions based upon the reserve powers of the Crown. This constitutes recognition that 1975 was an exercise in brinkmanship that went too far and did endanger the institutions and culture.[11]

The Dismissal is predicated on the idea that the events of 1975 were a cataclysm that shook the nation to its core and put our democracy at risk. No, they weren't. Kelly's and Bramston's own words – predictions that the crisis would permanently undermine our democracy have proven unfounded – attest to that. If it were, some attempt would have been made to remove or formally modify the offending provisions and practices. Notwithstanding the difficulty in amending the Constitution, if things were as serious as Kelly and Bramston claim, surely some attempt would have been made to, at the very least, remove the power of dismissal. But nothing of this nature was ever seriously suggested. And, contrary to their claim above, the High Court did not advise Kerr. Two of its members did, acting as private citizens. The Court itself never became involved. The Court can only be described as having done something when it sits, formally empanelled, hears legal

---

[11] Ibid.

argument and issues some form of judgement. This is a perfect example of the mischaracterisation of events that permeates *The Dismissal*. .

Their demand that a future Governor-General should shun the use of the reserve powers (presumably, specifically, the power of dismissal) lends credence to my earlier assertion that Kelly's and Bramston's fundamental objection is not to the way in which Kerr used the power, but that he used it at all.

And further:

> There were winners and losers in the 1975 power struggle but there were no heroes. This book exempts none of the three principals from blame.[12]

Indeed, they don't exempt any of the three. However, it is telling that of the first ten chapters, one each is devoted to Whitlam and Fraser and eight to Kerr. And later:

> This book rejects the view that Kerr was a victim of history, trapped between two fanatics on a collision course. This is the enduring falsehood of the crisis. Fraser and Whitlam would have had no option but to accommodate a persuasive governor-general who had the influence of the Crown at his disposal, had Kerr chosen to use that influence.[13]

If Kerr was a victim of history, it is because Kelly and Bramston have striven mightily to make it so. And, as I have observed earlier, Kerr had very little time in which to work the vice-regal magic.

Fraser was driven by a ruthless determination to have his way and Whitlam by a monumental ego. Kerr, rightly in my view, judged that neither was likely to back down. It is hard to imagine what argument he could put to either of them, in the febrile atmosphere that prevailed and in the very short time available to him, that would persuade them. Such an argument would have had to be developed over time to allow

---

[12] Ibid., p. xii.
[13] Ibid., p. xiii.

it to sink in. Time was one thing Kerr did not have. No-one, to my knowledge, has yet enunciated just what that persuasive argument might have been.

Now we have a gratuitous smear:

> For the rest of his life, Kerr delighted in outwitting and outlasting Whitlam. 'I felt he at all times did not think I would have enough guts to do it,' he wrote in his journal years later. He refers to Whitlam's 'euphoric megalomania' and his delusion 'that he was unassailable' – with the satisfaction of having shattered that psychology.[14]

I have not been able to access Sir John Kerr's journal, but I doubt it evinces much in the way of delight, although there may well be a touch of *schadenfreude* in hindsight. Which would be excusable in view of the vitriolic attacks to which he was subjected over the rest of his life. And, in fact, as we will discover, Whitlam did, indeed, believe that Kerr 'would not have the guts to do it'.

But moving on:

> Kerr operated as a judge, rather than a governor-general. He assumed his task, at some point was to pass sentence. His real responsibility, however, was the exact opposite: to use his influence to procure a political solution without recourse to the Queen's dismissal power.[15]

No, Kerr's responsibility was to procure a constitutional solution to a political problem and, it is true, to do that without recourse to the reserve powers, if at all possible. And it was not the Queen's dismissal power. It was Kerr's.

And further:

> The magic of monarchy is beauty concealing lethality. The Crown's influence is maximised not by using the reserve powers but by not using them – it is a golden rule arising from political and monarchical history missed typically by

---

[14] Ibid.
[15] Ibid., p. xiv.

clever lawyers.[16]

This sounds a bit like destroying a village in order to save it. It is a nonsensical argument. Unless a threat is believable it is ineffective. And if it is understood it must never be used, it becomes unbelievable. If a power is never used it must atrophy. And at some point, it must atrophy to the extent that it becomes moribund. That is the logic that opponents of the reserve powers use to deny their validity today. But if the power to dismiss a Prime Minister has atrophied to the extent that it has become moribund in the United Kingdom, the Australian founding fathers brough it back to life in Australia when they incorporated it into our Constitution.

Their Introduction concludes:

> The skeletons from 1975 still hang in the cupboard. At the fortieth anniversary it is time to get them out, dust them off and bring them to life. Their story will shock, astonish and provoke. It is a perpetual reminder of the strength of Australia's democracy. But it is also a reminder that institutions cannot be abused, and constitutional powers cannot be pushed to their limits. Political leaders must recognise this and governors-general must live with the obligation to rectify Sir John Kerr's legacy.[17]

In other words, the 1975 crisis did not damage Australian democracy in any way whatsoever but, because we (Kelly and Bramston) disagree with the way in which Sir John Kerr exercised his legitimate power to prevent a dysfunctional government from breaching the Constitution (by attempting to govern without supply), we must expunge that power from our system of governance, despite the combined wisdom of the founding fathers specifically including that power. And rather than go through the tedious process of sponsoring an amendment to the Constitution we'd rather just vilify Sir John Kerr and attempt to intimidate his successors to ignore the powers they undoubtedly have.

---
[16] Ibid.
[17] Ibid., p. xv.

Nothing in the current world of politics, either globally or here in Australia, fills me with confidence that we can safely dispense with the final protection of an independent constitutional protector, armed with appropriate powers and willing to use them where necessary.

1

Kerr and The Queen
– Dismay at the Palace

Kelly and Bramston cannot legitimately argue that the reserve power to dismiss a Prime Minister does not exist – although much of the emotive argument that we hear is based on that premise and that is still the position of many. What they argue is that Sir John Kerr acted too early and that he deceived or ambushed Whitlam. So, their argument is not really about whether or not Kerr had the power. It is about the way in which he used it.

And their principal technique is to mount a prolonged and vitriolic assassination of Sir John Kerr's character. It commences from the first chapter, which is titled 'Kerr and the Queen – Dismay at the Palace'. It postulates, firstly, that the Palace i.e., the Queen, disapproved strongly of Kerr's decision and, secondly, because of his subsequent behaviour, they wanted him gone as quickly as possible and put pressure to bear to bring his early resignation into effect. The book, which purports to present an objective assessment of the events of November 1975, begins with this:

> The Queen was keen to see the back of Sir John Kerr as governor-general and was relieved when he resigned as her representative in Australia in 1977. The Palace had worried about Kerr's behaviour, reliability, and his apparent pursuit of his self-interest, and believed the Kerrs, as a couple, were greedy. The decision that Kerr would quit as governor-general

became irrevocable at a meeting he had with the Queen on board the royal yacht Britannia at Fremantle, Western Australia, on 30 March 1977.[1]

It would be interesting to see how Kelly and Bramston know the inner mind of the Queen, a notably discreet lady. This claim, only tangentially relevant to the principal events themselves, is based on a private memorandum written by Sir Paul Hasluck, Kerr's immediate predecessor in the role:

> Hasluck wrote: 'It was also apparent that at some stage some pressure had been applied from the Palace to bring about his [Kerr's] resignation. Charteris – and by implication the Queen – had a poor opinion of the Kerrs'.[2]

Sir Martin Charteris was the Queen's Principal Secretary. The above observation is sourced to a memorandum of 10 August 1977, housed in the Hasluck Collection in Perth. Kelly and Bramston continue:

> Hasluck had also met Charteris on board the royal yacht Britannia when it docked at Fremantle in March 1977 as part of the Queen's Jubilee tour. From both these conversations Hasluck 'gained the impression that the Palace had brought pressure to bear on Kerr to retire'. Charteris told him the Palace's judgement had been to defer Kerr's retirement until after the Queen's visit to Australia and to accommodate Kerr's wish to visit London in mid-1977 for the Jubilee celebrations. Charteris said this gave 'the right public appearance' ahead of the resignation and Hasluck agreed.[3]

Hasluck is quoted again later in the chapter:

> In recording the views of the Palace, Hasluck wrote:
>
> We discussed the Kerrs, both man and wife, the conclusion being that it was a good thing they were going, that up to date it was a relief to know that his resignation was being handled smoothly, and that the Palace was fervently hoping

---

[1] Kelly and Bramston, *The Dismissal*, p. 3.
[2] Ibid., p. 4.
[3] Ibid.

that at the time he left office or immediately thereafter he did not doing (sic) anything that was improper, either in publication or in public activities. It was apparent that at the Palace the chief fear arose from a belief that the Kerrs and, especially, Lady Kerr, were 'very greedy'.

Has any recent governor-general inspired such a contemptible opinion from Buckingham Palace?[4]

Kelly and Bramston mean 'contemptuous', but I would contend that they inadvertently chose the correct word. The gratuitous and second-hand reference to the Kerrs being 'very greedy' – irrelevant in the context of Kerr's decision of November 1975 – certainly seems contemptible to my mind. But Kelly and Bramston can't get enough of it. They refer to it once on page three and twice on page five. (It also gets a run in their latest offering, *The Truth of the Palace Letters*.)

Let me make the point here, that, whatever Charteris's views were of Kerr as a person, they are irrelevant in the context of the events of 11 November 1975.

That 'the Palace was fervently hoping that at the time he left office or immediately thereafter he did not do anything that was improper, either in publication or in public activities' suggests that the Palace did not really know their man. Even if you accept the premise that the Palace disapproved of the sacking (which they may have done on public relations grounds), had Kerr committed any other transgression that might have given them cause for concern? Apart from one unfortunate incident in which a somewhat inebriated Kerr had made something of a fool of himself at the 1976 Melbourne Cup, had he not continued to act with the utmost propriety? Kelly and Bramston cite no examples of Kerr acting improperly.

A few paragraphs later, the authors quote Hasluck quoting Charteris to the effect that the Palace was worried about media reports 'that Kerr was going out of office with a book already written under his arm and that very high bids were being made

---

[4] Ibid, p. 5.

for the rights to publish it' and that the Palace had been in touch with him and reminded him of his assurances and the position of the Queen in respect of any communications to and from the Palace.[5] This is no doubt the source of the accusation of 'greed'. I will address this issue later. Charteris also said that the Queen and he 'had obtained assurances from Kerr not to publish any of the correspondence between himself and the Queen about Whitlam's dismissal'. 'This', the authors write, 'revealed not just the sensitivity of the Palace about the correspondence but its fears of Kerr's reliability and pursuit of his self-interest'.[6]

The Hasluck Memorandum, which is published in full as Appendix A, reveals that this assurance was sought when the Queen spoke to Kerr on the royal yacht Britannia in March 1977:

> One remark which Charteris made explicitly in talking with me in London was that in the talk on board the Britannia at Fremantle "we" (presumably The Queen in the presence of Charteris) obtained the assurance from Kerr that after his retirement he would not publish any of his dispatches or other communications to The Queen or Her communications to him concerning the dismissal of the Whitlam Government. He was told that these were The Queen's property.[7]

I suspect that Kerr might have felt greatly aggrieved at the suggestion he might do otherwise. Nothing in his letters to the Palace, either before or after 11 November, suggests he would be anything other than totally discreet as far as the Palace is concerned. And what Charteris told Hasluck seems odd because the issue of the Palace correspondence had been resolved well before March 1977. On 22 September 1976, Kerr wrote to Charteris concerning the disposal of his papers after he retired:

> We talked about this in London and you made the obvious point that this correspondence [between Kerr and the Palace] will

---

[5] Ibid.
[6] Ibid., pp. 5-6.
[7] Paul Hasluck, *The Hasluck Memorandum*, 10 August 1977.

have to be under embargo for a very long time.[8]

As a result of this letter Kerr and Charteris agreed the Palace correspondence would be embargoed for 60 years. Kerr was hardly likely to breach that agreement. And, indeed, he never did. And, as it turns out there was nothing detrimental to either Kerr or the Palace in these letters. Possibly the sensitivity of the Palace simply related to a desire that Kerr not create a precedent. That the mystique of the Monarchy be preserved.

During 1976, Kerr advised the Palace that he had been approached to write an autobiography. He said, explicitly, that there was no question of him writing anything about his time in office while he was still in office, but he floated the idea of an autobiography of his earlier life. He was chafing under the barrage of vitriolic criticism to which he had been subjected and clearly wanted to respond in some way. He probably thought such a book might soften his image or give some indication of his values and character. He was dissuaded from this course by Charteris. But the Palace could have had no doubt that he would write a book, once he left office. And if they were concerned about a book, why would they want him to leave office earlier rather than later? He had given his undertaking to the Palace that he would not do so while in office and it can hardly be doubted that he would keep his word on that, such was his devotion to the Monarchy. He was itching to put his side of the story. Kelly and Bramston describe Kerr's book as self-justification or self-interest. I would describe it as a defence.

His autobiography, *Matters for Judgement*, was published in 1978, after his retirement as Governor-General. The book contains nothing critical of, or injurious to, the Palace. So, in effect, Charteris, and, for all we know the Queen, were proved quite wrong in their assessment of Sir John Kerr in respect of his unreliability and pursuit of self-interest. Why then should their thoughts occupy such a prominent place at the beginning of *The Dismissal*? Obviously, it didn't matter to Kelly and Bramston,

---

[8] Letter from Sir John Kerr to Sir Martin Charteris, *The Palace Letters*, 22 September 1976, https://www.naa.gov.au/explore-collection/kerr-palace-letters.

that Kerr did *not* act as Charteris and others purportedly feared — it was enough that they thought he might.

Let me address the issue of the Kerr's 'greed'. It is clear from the Hasluck Memorandum that this accusation appears quite late in the piece, in August 1977 (at least that is when Hasluck first heard it). This was some six months after Kerr had been 'pressured' to resign and no doubt sprang from the proposed memoir which was, naturally, attracting serious offers. I imagine that Kerr, having been 'pressured' into relinquishing a well-paid position, would not have felt himself particularly greedy if he were to recoup some lost income? In fact, Sir Paul Hasluck did not believe he was motivated by greed:

> I said that Kerr would know what was discreet and proper and I did not think he would wish to appear to act dishonourably even for a good price. He had shown some weakness for "self-justification" but his experience as a judge should have taught him that there are some positions in which one had to forego the pleasures of self-justification. The Governor-Generalship was one of them. I thought that self-justification might be his strongest temptation.[9]

I must take issue with Hasluck's contention that Kerr, simply as a former Governor-General, should have to maintain a dignified silence in the face of the continuing vitriolic attacks upon him. Particularly, as I noted earlier, considering the shabby treatment he had apparently received from an institution he had served loyally. Here is Kerr's 'self-justification' on that point:

> My book is, in part, a defence which I am entitled to make now, in bare justice to myself, against an extreme and bitter attack upon me and my actions. More importantly, the book should be published now because in the public interest the facts of my role in the happenings of 1975 should be known — in the interests of truth and of maintaining freedom of discussion and the development of knowledge on matters of great public importance. In relation to these matters there is a gap due to the silence I have maintained until now. That gap is being filled by

---

[9] Hasluck, op.cit.

gossip, rumour, error, bogus history, falsehood and invention.[10]

It is worth remembering that among that catalogue of misinformation were preposterous but, nonetheless, damaging claims that Kerr was in league with the CIA to get rid of Whitlam because of his communist sympathies, and that Kerr conspired with the Palace to get rid of Whitlam because of his republican sympathies. The latter still has some vestigial support among a small coterie of diehards today.

Finally on the subject of greed, Charteris did not specifically say that the Queen thought the Kerrs greedy. Neither did he specifically say that the Queen had a low opinion of the Kerrs. However, Hasluck inferred that the latter criticism did include the Queen:

> Charteris – and by implication the Queen – had a low opinion of the Kerrs.[11]

Hasluck did not infer, at least not in the Memorandum, that the Queen shared Charteris's view that the Kerrs were greedy. Nonetheless, the whole impression of this discourse, particularly Kelly's and Bramston's rendition of it, is that she did. If that is so, you would have to wonder at the chutzpah of someone born to immense wealth and privilege criticizing a 'working class boy made good' for being greedy. What yardstick would she use, I wonder? To be honest, I find it hard to imagine the Queen would have expressed this view, even to Charteris. This may seem a trivial point, but *The Dismissal* is littered with this sort of smear. It's death by a thousand cuts to Sir John Kerr's reputation and I intend to apply dressings to as many of them as I can.

Set in the middle of this discourse, Kelly and Bramston say:

> By early 1977, not only Buckingham Palace but Australia's prime minister, Malcolm Fraser, whom Kerr had installed in office, saw Kerr as a chronic liability. ...

---

[10] John Kerr, (1979). *Matters for judgment : an autobiography*. London: Macmillan, from the Preface.

[11] Hasluck, op.cit.

> Interviewed for this book, Fraser's senior adviser ... David Kemp said: 'Fraser did not have regard for Kerr and welcomed his departure.' Official Secretary to Kerr ... Sir David Smith said of Fraser: 'How many governors general did he have? Kerr, Cowan and Stephen. My impression of Fraser was that he was always ready to treat them with disrespect if it suited his purposes. He had no particular respect for them and he expected them to do what he wanted' ... Fraser confidant Tony Staley, who saw a lot of Kerr as governor-general said: 'He made it plain to me that he felt un-liked by Malcom ... I think in a way, Malcolm despised him'.[12]

And later:

> The strain on Kerr had been immense. Fraser finally came to the view that he was a broken man. There would be no political peace over the office of the governor-general until Kerr left the stage. Fraser's support for Kerr lasted for as long as it was useful to have him in place and no longer.[13]

That speaks volumes about Fraser's character and behaviour, but doesn't shed a lot of light on Kerr's.

In fact, Kerr had repeatedly canvassed the possibility of his retirement as early as the immediate aftermath of the dismissal. He clearly wanted to be dissuaded, both from the fact that he valued the job (having originally negotiated with Whitlam, who appointed him, to have a tenure of ten years) and from a completely natural desire to have his actions vindicated. But of course, he was not unaware that healing would be slower the longer he remained in office. As the authors note:

> David Smith said he discussed the issue of resignation with Kerr. Interviewed by the authors, Smith conceded the office was 'inevitably' damaged by the dismissal because anything that 'brings the governor-general into public controversy damages the office in the minds of some people'.[14]

Kerr was well aware of, and anticipated, this before he made

---

[12] Kelly and Bramston, op.cit., p. 4.
[13] Ibid., p. 9.
[14] Ibid.

his decision. I will argue later that this awareness does not sit well with the character and motivation that Kelly and Bramston have devised for him.

It may well be that the Palace wanted Kerr gone sooner rather than later, but I contend that if this is so, it is more a manifestation of path-of-least-resistance political expediency rather than a reaction to Kerr's 'unreliability and pursuit of self-interest', of which no evidence has been presented by the authors.

I would now like to turn to the Hasluck Memorandum and cover some points not raised in *The Dismissal*. It is clear that at the first meeting between Hasluck and Charteris in March 1977, nothing derogatory was said about Kerr. Hasluck merely noted that he had been told the decision had been made that Kerr would retire and that he gained the impression pressure had been brought to bear. All the disparaging commentary occurred in the August meeting.

On 21 September 1976, Kerr wrote a personal letter direct to the Queen, in which he expressed, *inter alia*, his desire that nothing he did would hurt the monarchy and:

> I appreciate from what Sir Martin has said that no question has yet arisen as to which I should be feeling the need to set a different course in Your Majesty's interest but should the occasion arise I should like to give you my humble assurance that, as new Governors General can always be found, my desire would be to assist in accordance with your judgement.[15]

If that is not an invitation for the Queen to ask him to resign if she were so inclined, I don't know what is. Does that suggest he would need to be 'pressured' to resign?

On 29 September, Charteris replied, on behalf of the Queen:

> In anything to do with your future as her representative, Her Majesty, like you, must be guided by the advice she receives from the Prime Minister: this, as you know is the constitutional

---

[15] John Kerr, Letter to Martin Charteris, *The Palace Letters*, 21 September 1976, pp. 5-7.

reality. None the less, I think you can rest assured that Her Majesty has no disposition to ask you to follow any course different from that on which you are now set.[16]

Earlier in this chapter, Kelly and Bramston claim, referring to the Hasluck Memorandum:

> These are remarkable admissions. The governor-general is appointed and removed by the Queen only on the advice of the prime minister. That the Palace wanted Kerr gone suggests an unusual degree of dissatisfaction. By early 1977, not only Buckingham Palace but Australia's prime minister, Malcolm Fraser, whom Kerr had installed in office, saw Kerr as a chronic liability. It had been a rapid, sad and divisive descent.[17]

So, what changed between October 1976 and March 1977? Well, not much. Up to late January it was business as usual with Kerr writing long detailed letters and Charteris writing chatty replies. There is no hint of reserve in Charteris's letters of this time, such as you might expect if the Palace were desperate to see Kerr go.

And what might have emerged in Kerr's conduct during that period that would have caused the Queen to reverse her quite firm opinion, expressed in October via Charteris, that Kerr's future was matter for the Prime Minister? Again nothing. The angst over the dismissal was diminishing. The anniversary of 11 November passed without major incident. Plans were underway for the Queen's visit in March during which Kerr had undertaken to keep a low profile.

In my view the only thing that had changed, or at least crystallised, was that Fraser now thought it was time for Kerr to go.

My belief is that the 'pressure' for Kerr to go, came not from the Palace itself but from Fraser via the Palace. Fraser met the Queen and, separately, Charteris in Canada on 24 July 1976. Shortly after that, rumours started to emerge that

---

[16] Sir M. Charteris Letter to John Kerr, 29 September 1976, *The Palace Letters*, p. 227.
[17] Kelly and Bramston, op.cit.., p. 4.

Fraser was pressuring the Governor-General to resign. On 4 August 1976, *The Bulletin* published an article by David Marr titled 'November 11 in Retrospect – Was Kerr Right?'. In its introduction it noted:

> Tempers aren't getting any cooler. Once or twice a week the police are out sheltering Sir John Kerr from hostile crowds. Rumours abound that Prince Charles will take over his job and Prime Minister Fraser has to deny he's pressuring the Governor-General to resign.[18]

This would accord with Kelly and Bramston's view that Fraser wanted Kerr gone.

I now return to the Hasluck Memorandum and the views of Sir Paul Hasluck. Hasluck was scrupulous during his lifetime to make no criticism of Kerr. But clearly, he had reservations as expressed in the Memorandum, about Kerr's conduct. Of particular interest and, strangely not mentioned, in *The Dismissal*, is his feeling that Kerr acted 'politically':

> I offered the opinion that Kerr had acted politically because I thought he may have helped to produce the situation in which it was possible for him to act "judicially" ... Again I did not know all the material facts but it seemed to me that in the period leading up to crisis the Governor-General had either acted politically or had been neglectful.[19]

It is important to understand that Hasluck was not talking about acting politically in a party-political sense, but something more in the nature of power politics. Tactics and manoeuvring, in other words. Since that is what Kelly and Bramston accuse him of throughout their book, I am surprised they didn't jump on this. Kerr addressed this aspect in *Matters for Judgement*, but as that had not been published in August 1977, we cannot know whether, after having read it, Hasluck might have changed his opinion on this matter. Possibly not, but Charteris, who did know the facts, despite his poor opinion of the Kerr's, accepted

---

[18] D. Marr, 'November 11 in Retrospect – Was Kerr Right?', *The Bulletin*, 4 August 1976.
[19] Hasluck, op.cit.

that Kerr had acted judicially.[20] Hasluck's judgement on Kerr should also be considered in the light of this:

> We then agreed that part of the situation was that Whitlam had a poor opinion of Kerr. I recalled remarks Whitlam made to me about Kerr at the time he was recommending his appointment. Neither of us was quite sure whether or not Whitlam intended Kerr to be his puppet but it was clear that he had a poor opinion of him and consequently this lessened any influence that Kerr might have had in the role of Governor-General as counsellor and one able to give advice and warning to the Prime Minister. I said that I myself had found Whitlam very responsive to a question or a cautionary word.
>
> Unfortunately, as we both agreed, Whitlam had publicly expressed his low opinion of Kerr. He was also reported to have said as the crisis was approaching, "The Governor-General will do what I tell him." This would understandably have stiffened Kerr and possibly put him into a frame of mind - political rather than judicial - of showing the Prime Minister who was master and perhaps (again with a motive that was political rather than judicial) of trying to outwit him by producing the situation in which he could dismiss him.[21]

The first thought that occurs to me is what on earth would Whitlam be doing appointing as Governor-General someone of whom he had a low opinion, unless setting him up as a puppet was exactly his intention. And the second thought is that Hasluck probably believed that he would have handled the situation better. And he may well have been right. But one has to remember that Whitlam's relationship with Hasluck would have been conditioned by fact that he and Hasluck had been fierce adversaries in the House of Representatives. He knew that Hasluck was a formidable man, who had been in the office since 1969 and had grown comfortable in his role. He had honed his style as Governor-General on Liberal Prime Ministers John Gorton and William McMahon and would have cut neither of them any slack, particularly McMahon. Whitlam would have

---

[20] Ibid.
[21] Ibid.

known better than to try to treat Hasluck as a puppet. On the other hand, Kerr was in office barely six months before he 'tried it on' with him. (This refers to the Loans Affair which will be covered in another chapter.) So, perhaps not too much blame can be attached to Kerr if he was forced to play by Whitlam's rules rather than Hasluck's.

As to Hasluck's thought that Whitlam's attitude towards Kerr may have motivated him to produce a 'situation in which he could dismiss him', this is nothing but speculation.

Hasluck, in an interview with former Labor Minister Clyde Cameron in 1985, stuck to his policy of not criticizing Kerr. He did say he thought the problem arose through a lack of dialogue between Kerr and Whitlam, which seemed to apportion the blame equally between the two.

Which brings us to the issue of the Palace's reaction to the dismissal itself – the second theme of this chapter:

> The reality, however, is that the Palace and the Queen wanted a 1977 departure. Their concerns about Kerr arose far earlier. They originate with the dismissal itself.[22]

Most of the evidence they amass is based on personal interviews that the authors had with Sir Martin Charteris, Principal Private Secretary, and Sir William Heseltine, Assistant Private Secretary. Charteris was interviewed in 1995 and Heseltine in 2015.

Here is Heseltine's story:

> It was Heseltine and Charteris who broke the news of the dismissal to the Queen. When David Smith, as official secretary, rang the Palace during the afternoon of 11 November, Australian time, it was Heseltine who took the call in the middle of the night in London:
>
> > 'I was asleep in my virtuous bed in an apartment in St James' Palace when the telephone rang. It was an extension from the Buckingham Palace switchboard and the operator told me that

---

[22] Kelly and Bramston, op.cit., pp. 9-10.

'Mr David Smith was on the telephone. I said "Hello, David, what on earth are you ringing for at this time of the night?" And he said, "Well, the Governor-General has dismissed the Prime Minister." The double take of all time. I can't remember what I said to him, but the reaction was stunned surprise because in all the lead-up to this I personally and I don't think my colleagues had any indication it was happening.'

'I deliberated wondering whether I should try and call the Queen and tell her the news. Well, I thought, 2.30 in the morning I wouldn't be a very popular caller and there was nothing she could do about it. I resolved the sensible thing was to get up and get to the Palace before she would be awakened listening to the news. I think I even went back to sleep again for a while digesting this news.'

The decisive encounter at the Palace came in the early morning. Heseltine said:

'It would have been the eight o'clock news I knew she listened to. So, it was probably about half past seven in the morning and I found that Martin Charteris was already there. He had no immediate explanation of why he hadn't been available at two in the morning but I knew he had been at the Lord Mayor's banquet that night. Anyway, he was seething with rage when I got there.'

Charteris already knew of the dismissal – he had been told by Whitlam.[23]

Two observations occur to me at this point. Firstly, if Heseltine had no indication whatsoever that Kerr might dismiss the Prime Minister, he could not have been paying particular attention to Kerr's letters to the Palace. I will develop more on this later. And secondly, the observation, in this context that Charteris was 'seething with rage', suggests quite clearly that Charteris was incensed by Kerr's decision to dismiss Whitlam. That is certainly the impression I got when I read it. Later, the authors offer the following clarification:

---

[23] Ibid., pp. 11-12.

Heseltine said that 'Martin was very cross at being taken unawares.'[24]

Charteris was not angry because he was taken unawares by the decision, but because he heard the news from Whitlam and not Kerr. The following extract from one of his letters to Kerr, immediately after the dismissal, makes this clear:

> David Smith will have reported to you that Mr Whitlam telephoned me at 4.15am (our time) on 11th November. I had been out and not heard the news which David passed to Bill Heseltine sometime before. Mr Whitlam ... spoke calmly and did not ask me to make any approach to the Queen, or indeed, do anything other than the suggestion that I should speak to you and find out what was going on. I said I knew you would be reporting what had happened, to the Queen, not realizing at that time that you had already done so.[25]

As regards the Palace reaction to the dismissal itself, the authors quote Heseltine:

> Asked how he felt about Kerr's dismissal of Whitlam, Heseltine said: 'I didn't think it was very prudent. I thought with a little bit more subtlety he could have delayed the event for a few more days when it was my impression the Senate would have caved in.' Heseltine said that at the Palace 'we talked about virtually nothing else for the next few days'. He was sure that Charteris had the same reservation: 'I think we both felt exactly the same about it.'
>
> In an earlier interview, Heseltine said that if the governor-general had sought the Queen's advice – which he didn't – obviously he could not 'say categorically' what the Queen would have advised but he had a view on what she was likely to have said. 'My own feeling is that she would have advised him to play out the situation a little longer,' Heseltine said. 'I do suspect that in the course of another day or two a political solution rather than this drastic imposed solution would have been found.'[26]

That may have been his view from the comfort of his apartment in St James' Palace, but Heseltine was not the man on the ground,

---

[24] Ibid., p. 12.
[25] M. Charteris, Letter to John Kerr, *The Palace Letters*, 17 November 1975, p. 36.
[26] Kelly and Bramston, op.cit., p. 10.

facing the implacability of two arrogant political warlords against a cacophonous background of media speculation and comment. Heseltine's impression, formed in London, that the Senate would 'cave in' can hardly weigh against Kerr's own carefully considered judgement, based on conversations with both Whitlam and Fraser. One wonders what subtlety he imagines Sir John Kerr could or should have brought to bear on the situation or what political solution, short of either Whitlam or Fraser backing down, might have been found. If he had any constructive thoughts on this, he has apparently decided to keep them to himself – even to the present day. In fact, as we will see, it was Whitlam that brought matters to a head. And the suggestion that Kerr could or should have sought the Queen's advice runs counter to the fact that it was not the Queen's decision. Kerr was exercising his own prerogative.

Heseltine is quoted to similar effect later in the chapter. But notably, Charteris, who figures prominently in the Kelly/Bramston narrative, as also disapproving Sir John Kerr's action, is not quoted directly in the book on this issue – even though Kelly interviewed him in 1995. He is only quoted indirectly via either Hasluck or Heseltine, and generally it is in the form of speculation – something in the nature of 'Charteris gave the impression that …'.

There is one other curious reference quoting Charteris:

> A few weeks after the dismissal the official secretary at Australia House, London, Tim McDonald, had a discussion with Charteris whom he knew well. … In 1995 he relayed this conversation with Charteris to Paul Kelly and John Menadue in separate notes:
>
> 'It was a few weeks after the dismissal that I asked him for his personal view of events. What, I asked, would have been his advice to the Queen in a comparable situation. His reply suggested that the Palace shared the view that Kerr acted prematurely. He said that if faced with a constitutional crisis which it appeared likely to involve head of state his advice would have been that she should only intervene when a "clear sense of inevitability" had developed in the

public that she must act. This had been Kerr's mistake.'

McDonald said the comment from Charteris 'made such an impression on me at the time that I am confident that the recollection is accurate'. He said the import was that the head of state must only act 'independently' and 'in accordance with public opinion' not 'as the instrument of political forces'.[27]

Two thoughts emerge from this. Firstly, the suggestion that the Governor-General of Australia would act 'in accordance with public opinion' is extraordinary. Politicians act in accordance with public opinion. The Governor-General does not. Kerr had to act when a 'clear sense of inevitability' became evident to him, not to the public. Although, that said, there was certainly a growing sense in the public mind that something must be done and for many observers that meant an intervention on the part of the Governor-General. Newspaper extracts from that time make this perfectly clear.

The other thought is that Charteris would have been acting quite out of character, and extraordinarily indiscreetly, to have made these observations to an Australian public servant, particularly so soon after the event. McDonald's account seems highly improbable, particularly as it is merely a recollection of a conversation twenty years earlier.

The authors do quote Charteris directly to the effect that he spoke to Whitlam and that Whitlam asked nothing of him. He is quoted directly as saying to Paul Kelly that 'The Queen did appreciate Sir John's desire to ensure she was not involved.' And he did, apparently, say in 1995 (presumably to Kelly) 'there was plenty of drama in Buckingham Palace after it became known.' None of these statements are critical of Kerr. There is no doubt that, if Charteris had been critical of Kerr during his interview with Kelly, then Kelly would have had no hesitation in including such material. And there is no doubt Kelly would have quizzed Charteris on his view of the dismissal. Charteris, out of discretion, could have been noncommittal. But if Charteris were so free with his confidences with Tim McDonald in 1975,

---
[27] Ibid., pp. 13-14.

why would he be so reticent with Kelly in 1995?

In fact, Kelly's mining expedition with Sir Martin Charteris yielded no pay dirt whatsoever. Apart from Chapter One, he gets only one further reference in the whole of *The Dismissal*, and that relates to the question of Whitlam dismissing Kerr. I will cover that in due course but suffice to say now that this reference is not critical of Kerr either.

It is possible that Charteris felt that Sir John had been precipitate. He may even have strongly disapproved, but if we consider that he represents the official face of the Palace, then a study of his letters to Kerr is instructive.

Let me begin this short review of the Palace letters by returning to the question of why it should be so that the Place was surprised, shocked even, that Sir John dismissed Mr Whitlam. On 20 October, Kerr wrote to Charteris:

> The situation here changes from day to day but it appears to be crystallizing in an unexpected way. I shall mention first, the leaders on the Opposition side. They are openly asserting that I have a duty to act very soon to force an election, that it is open to me to dismiss the Prime Minister and call upon someone else (Mr Fraser, of course) willing to advise a dissolution of the House of Representatives, or both houses. They see the Governor General, as having a duty to get them all to the people.[28]

He goes on to say that he is 'not yet making up my mind about ultimate and final decisions', but he is clearly canvassing the possibility of dismissal, since he does not categorically rule it out. He also talks about the 'Ellicott memorandum'. He tells the Palace that he has asked the Prime Minister to provide advice on it. This is an opinion written, and made public, by the Opposition's Shadow Attorney General, Bob Ellicott QC. In it he opines that the Governor General has the power to dismiss the Prime Minister and that he should do so straight away. Kerr says, in a letter of 22 October:

> Yesterday I carefully considered the Ellicott memorandum and

---

[28] J Kerr, Letter to Martin Charteris, *The Palace Letters*, 20 October 1975, p. 118.

decided to ask the Prime Minister to obtain for me an opinion of the law officers of the Crown on the proposition set out in it. He agreed to do this on his own behalf with the intention of passing it on to me. I realize that the law officers will profoundly disagree with what Mr Ellicott said and may even go so far as to say there is nothing left of any substance in the reserve powers. But it does not follow that in an extreme constitutional crisis I would accept that. I have of course, on any view, little room to move contrary to the Prime Minister's advice.[29]

Here again, is a clear indication that Kerr is contemplating the use of the reserve powers.

On 27 October, commenting on an opinion expressed by Sir Paul Hasluck, in his 1972 Queale Memorial lecture, Kerr wrote:

It could easily happen that Parliament will, by the end of November, have finally and unequivocally denied supply and the government will be attempting to govern without it. ... In such a situation it will become necessary to consider whether the Prime Minister and his government should resign or recommend a dissolution. I should have to consider whether I should ask for this.
I do not have to spell out the problems involved in such a course of action if the Prime Minister refuses to do either of these things as he says he will. On these questions, some opinions by Sir Paul Hasluck in his Queale Memorial Lecture in 1972 have been widely canvassed. ...
Not everyone agrees with Sir Paul Hasluck but in conditions of momentous deadlock over supply, the question whether the Hasluck doctrine should be accepted and a final constitutional crisis precipitated by Vice Regal act will have to be thought about. This would force an election.[30]

And towards the end of the letter:

I appreciate that, except on such matters as those upon which the Prime Minister advises Her Majesty direct, that she would be anxious – or at least I assume so – for this crisis to be worked out in Australia. However, anything I may do or not do could indirectly affect the Monarchy in Australia and I should welcome any obser-

---

[29] Ibid., p. 105.
[30] Ibid., pp. 75-76.

vations on a private and personal basis which you may care to make and which, as you see it, should be taken into account in the interests of the Monarchy in Australia.[31]

This seems, to me, like an invitation for the Palace to give its views on the use of the reserve powers.

In an addendum to the letter dated 29 October, Kerr notes that according to the latest Gallup poll, Fraser had lost ground, presumably giving hope that he may finally back down.

On 6 November, in the last letter he would write to the Palace prior to the dismissal, Kerr wrote:

> The crisis is now a very serious one and, if both parties and their leaders remain adamant, an important decision one way or the other may have to be made by me this month.[32]

My purpose in providing the above extracts is not to argue the rights and wrongs of Kerr's decision, but to support my earlier point that if Palace officials were stunned by Kerr's decision, then they were not paying close attention to his letters. The only point upon which they might justifiably have been surprised was the timing, since Kerr had earlier foreshadowed that he thought the crisis would come to a head in late November.

Charteris's response to these later letters, dated, 4 and 5 November would have arrived at Yarralumla too late to have influenced Kerr's decision, however it is worth noting that in the latter he says:

> It is of course true that anything you may do could indirectly affect the Monarchy in Australia. This places you in what is, perhaps, an unenviable, but is certainly a very honourable position. If you do, as you will, what the constitution dictates, you cannot possibly do the Monarchy any avoidable harm.[33]

Here Charteris is allowing the possibility that some action by the Governor-General may cause some *unavoidable* harm, but

---
[31] Ibid., p. 77.
[32] Ibid., p. 69.
[33] M Charteris, Letter to John Kerr, *The Palace Letters*, 5 November 1975, p. 55.

it would not be unjustified on that basis alone. Significantly, he also wrote:

> Just in case you do not know it, I should like to quote to you Arthur Meighan's splendid phrase about the role of the Crown/Governor-General in the Canadian Constitution ... I think it is good stuff:
>
>> 'The sphere of discretion left to a Governor-General under our constitution, and under our practice, is a limited sphere indeed, but it is a sphere of dignity and great responsibility. Within the ambit of discretion residing still in the Crown of England and residing in the Governor General in the Dominions, there is a responsibility as great as falls to any estate of the realm or to any House of Parliament ... Within the sphere of that discretion the plain duty of the Governor-General is not to weaken responsible government, not to undermine the rights of parliament ... it is to make sure that responsible government is maintained, that the rights of Parliament are respected, that the still higher rights of the people are held sacred. It is his duty to make sure that parliament is not stifled by government, but that every government is held responsible to parliament and every parliament held responsible to the people.'[34]

And that is precisely what Kerr did. You may argue that Kerr went about it the wrong way, that he deceived Whitlam, that his timing was precipitate (all subjects to be covered later in this book) but, based on Charteris's own words, you cannot argue that he would have justifiably been unduly surprised by Sir John's ultimate decision or that he essentially disagreed with it. Further extracts from his letters to Kerr confirm this latter point.

In his first letter after the dismissal, dated 17 November, he said:

> It seems to me, as a very interested observer, though one not very well versed in the Australian Constitution, that your action, buttressed as it is by the opinion of the Chief Justice, cannot easily be challenged from a constitutional point of view however much the politicians will, of course, rage.[35]

---

[34] Ibid.
[35] M Charteris, Letter to John Kerr, *The Palace Letters*, 17 November 1975, p. 36.

and

> As you can imagine the crisis in Australia has been on everybody's mind and on everybody's lips here during the last day or two. There have been some who have questioned what you have done but I have, as yet, found no-one who has been able to tell me what you ought to have done instead to have resolved the crisis: and this is something which I think your critics have an obligation to do.[36]

Of course, the latter comment was made well in advance of the avalanche of analysis and opinion that the dismissal engendered, but my point here is that, at this stage – now that the unavoidable damage to the Monarchy (such as it was) was a *fait accompli* – Charteris seemed quite at ease with the decision.

In a letter dated 2 March 1976, Kerr mentioned to Charteris that he had received some supportive letters from Eugene Forsey, an eminent Canadian jurist, and a copy of his book *Freedom and Order*, which had been inscribed 'HE Sir John Kerr with respect and admiration from Eugene Forsey 19th February 1976'. This was clearly an attempt by Kerr to reinforce his position within the Palace, and he was quite upfront about that, writing: 'I value this very much and know you will not be too critical about me letting you know how he sums up his attitude.'[37] In his 8 March reply to that letter, Charteris said: 'I am glad my friend, Eugene Forsey, sent you a copy of his book "Freedom and Order". The inscription he wrote in it is exactly what I would have expected from this stalwart upholder of the prerogative of the Crown'.[38]

Kelly and Bramston claim that the concerns of the Palace about Kerr had originated at the time of the dismissal and, from that point, that they wanted him gone as soon as possible. Had that been the case – had they decided to exert subtle pressure on Kerr to leave without actually saying so – it is likely that Charteris would have been considerably more non-committal – much less effusive, for example, in his response to the mention

---

[36] Ibid., p. 37.
[37] J Kerr, Letter to Martin Charteris, *The Palace Letters*, 2 March 1976, p. 154.
[38] M Charteris, Letter to John Kerr, *The Palace Letters*, 8 March 1976, p. 140.

of the Forsey gift – and deliberately formal in his responses to Kerr's letters. In fact, by this time it was 'My dear Martin' and 'My dear John'.

There is no doubt that the Palace would have preferred the dismissal not to have taken place and it may well be that they would have welcomed the departure of Sir John Kerr at a suitable interval after the fuss had died down, but there is no suggestion in these letters that they actively wanted him gone or that pressure from the Palace was exerted to induce him to resign.

In support of my position, I offer the following extracts of letters from Charteris to Kerr, right up to the time of his resignation.

From 21 April 1976, Charteris to Kerr:

> ... may I say how delighted I am that the Queen awarded you the GCMG. I know it is an award that will give a great deal of pleasure to your many friends in Australia and in Britain. Many Governors-General get this award before they have had a chance to earn it in office: no-one can say that about you. My colleagues in the Royal Household join me in sending you our warm congratulations.[39]

From 23 April 1976, Kerr to Charteris:

> It recently came to my knowledge that in all probability, Mr Menadue, the Permanent Head of the Prime Minister's Department, had been turning his attention to the question whether, having regard to the developing situation, it might become necessary for me to consider going from this position before the [Queen's proposed 1977] visit takes place.
>
> In the circumstances I got the Prime Minister to come and see me and I said to him, quite frankly, that, if by any chance his views were that, as the year developed, the question of my departure from this office might have to be considered, I should like him to tell me now because I would find it necessary to consider my position from a position of relative strength rather than one of possible weakness ... He gave his long-standing answer to the effect that he and his government and the members of the coalition parties were

---
[39] Ibid., p. 41.

unanimously of the view that I must remain here and carry on. He indicated, indeed, that politically speaking, it would be a serious disadvantage for him and his government if I were to go. This was said altogether apart from the question of the justice of the situation and what ought to be done on general grounds.[40]

One suspects that Fraser didn't give a fig for the 'justice of the situation' and that Kerr knew this very well.

From 28 April 1976, Charteris to Kerr:

> I agree with the view that academic opinion among constitutional lawyers in England is that what you did last year was correctly done. It must be said, however, that political opinion is not quite so unanimous; here the question is asked "could it not have been done differently?" I think this sort of questioning is inevitable amongst those whose business is politics and who are not fully acquainted with all the facts.[41]

This is the only occasion on which Charteris makes an implied criticism of the way Kerr handled the matter. It is hardly condemnatory.

From 6 May 1976, Charteris to Kerr:

> You do not ask for any observations from me on your situation and at 12,000 miles distance it would not only be unwise but impertinent to give any. I believe, however, that it would not be irresponsible for me to say that you would be justified in taking some comfort from the recent poll of which you quote the figures. Things could look even brighter in two or three months' time, and I very much hope they will.[42]

From 17 May 1976, Charteris to Kerr:

> In a previous letter I said that my impression was that legal opinion in this country was very much on your side and this impression was much fortified the other night when I attended Grand Night at Gray's Inn and also when I had luncheon with the Judges at the Old Bailey. At both places I found a very robust attitude.

---

[40] Ibid., p. 49.
[41] Ibid., pp. 39-40.
[42] Ibid., p. 24.

In your letter of 4th May you refer to our correspondence with particular reference to the book written by Paul Kelly in which he says that you kept the Queen informed in great detail of what was happening, "even voluminously" and I detect a feeling on your part that you may have written too much to me for the Queen's information. I can give you an absolute assurance that this is not so ... You have absolutely no need to be sensitive about the personal quality which has, to some extent, appeared in this correspondence: in the circumstances it could not and should not be otherwise. In other words "keep at it."[43]

From 9 June 1976, Charteris to Kerr:

It must surely be right to discourage pro-Governor-General demonstrations, welcome as they would be in many ways, which could only inflame matters. I feel sure that the energy in the anti-Governor-General demonstrations, if they are left alone and allowed to be seen for what they are, will fade away. This passive attitude which you are forced to adopt must be exasperating but I am sure it is wise.

This brings me naturally to the audience for which Mr Whitlam has asked ... Her Majesty's attitude to this audience can be plainly stated. She made it clear that she would only receive Mr Whitlam with positive advice from Mr Fraser to do so and that such advice must reach her through you. The Queen will be aware of the sort of campaign Mr Whitlam has mounted against you and I do not believe he will get any change out of Her Majesty at all.[44]

From 30 June 1976 – Charteris to Kerr following Whitlam's audience:

The actual audience with the Queen seems to have gone very well and Her Majesty told me she had spoken very firmly about the use of violence. [This refers to a demonstration in which Kerr's Air Force ADC was injured].

Your second letter gives me some encouragement and I was glad to learn from David Smith that you are receiving a full and supporting mail. You must nonetheless be living under considerable tension ...

---

[43] Ibid., pp. 22-23.
[44] M Charteris, Letter to John Kerr, *The Palace Letters*, 6 June 1976, p. 243.

These are difficult times for you but I remain convinced that it is indeed right for you to "stand fast". All who know you admire your courage and determination.[45]

From 5 August 1976, Charteris to Kerr:

I think I should begin this letter by saying that whatever Mr Menadue may think about the desirability of your leaving Yarralumla before the Queen's visit, I could detect no sign of a wish that you should do so in Mr Fraser's mind. [Fraser met the Queen in Montreal while on a visit to Canada.] Nor is there any disposition on the Queen's part to wish you to resign.[46]

From 29 September 1976, Charteris to Kerr (responding to handwritten letter of 21 September):

In anything to do with your future as her representative, Her Majesty, like you, must be guided by the advice she receives from the Prime Minister; this, as we know, is the constitutional reality. Nonetheless, I think you can rest assured that Her Majesty has no disposition to ask you to follow any course different from that on which you are now set.[47]

From 8 October 1976, Charteris to Kerr, referring to the disposal of Palace correspondence:

If you agree to this solution it remains to be decided for what period of time your papers should be placed under embargo. The figure we usually specify nowadays is 60 years from the end of the appointment concerned. In 1968, when the National Library of Australia tracked down the papers of the first Lord Stonehaven (Governor General of Australia 1925-30), his son and successor offered to hand them over to the Library subject to the Queen's wishes. On Her Majesty's instructions, we stipulated, and the Library accepted, that they should remain closed until 60 years after the end of the appointment.[48]

The embargo on the Palace letters was a severe irritant to certain journalists and was cited as a self-serving arrangement

---

[45] Ibid., p. 193.
[46] Ibid., p. 127.
[47] M Charteris, Letter to John Kerr, *The Palace Letters*, 29 September 1976, p. 227.
[48] Ibid., pp. 225-226.

to conceal discreditable facts. But now we know it was just common practice. And, in the event, the letters reveal nothing discreditable about either party.

From 18 November 1976, Charteris to Kerr:

> ... let me say how pleased everyone is here that 11th November passed off so successfully ... I think 11th November was an important milestone to get behind us, and this having satisfactorily passed, I hope we may be able to look to the future with increasing confidence.[49]

From 4 January 1977, Kerr to Charteris:

> You may like to know that I have had some offers from publishing companies to publish my 'memoirs' or 'autobiography'. I have been doing some writing but, of course, have made no decisions or commitments about publication. Certainly, I cannot publish anything about my Governor-Generalship while still in office. One question that has arisen is whether I can write autobiographical material dealing with earlier stages of my life and publish it while still in office. I shall not make any decision about this until I have a chance to speak with you when you are in Australia.[50]

To which Charteris replied on 21 January 1977:

> We will discuss this matter further when we meet in Australia, in the meanwhile I think all I can usefully say is the obvious: that it would be clearly improper for you to publish anything about events that have taken place during your term of office whilst you remain Governor-General.
>
> I cannot, personally, see anything wrong in your publishing autobiographical material from a period before you assumed office, but I think one must recognize that almost anything you publish now will be scrutinized with November 1975 in mind if only to discover how your past life may have influenced your later actions. I can visualize commentators avidly going back to your childhood and school days for "leads".[51]

---

[49] Ibid., p. 154.
[50] John Kerr, Letter to Martin Charteris, *The Palace Letters*, 4 January 1977, p. 113.
[51] M Charteris, op.cit., p. 92.

Shortly after this, the letters dry up.

The Queen's visit to Australia in April 1977 had been a success, partly because Kerr had kept a low profile, only being seen with Her Majesty on two occasions. It is clear that during this time, the decision was made that Kerr would retire. There would have been three players in this negotiation – Kerr himself, the Palace and Malcolm Fraser. Kerr insists it was his decision to do so, and, of course, he has not been contradicted by the other two. If it became known that either had pushed Kerr out, that would have alienated that half of the population which by then supported him. However, I do believe there was pressure and that it came from Fraser.

Here is an extract from Charteris's letter of 15 June 1977:

> By the same bag I am sending you a formal reply to your letter to the Queen of 10th June in which you ask to be relieved of your appointment as Governor General.
> There is, however, so much that cannot be said in formal letters! I am sure, nonetheless, how greatly the Queen respects the honourable motives which have led you to your decision to resign as Governor General. She fully understands that you are doing this to serve the best interests of Australia and the office you hold.[52]

Sir John Kerr's resignation took effect on 14 July 1977, and he left office on 8 December of that year.

I now return to the import of the Palace letters, apparently supportive of Sir John. These were not available to Kelly and Bramston in 2015 but are covered in some detail by them in *The Truth of the Palace Letters*.

Their thesis now is that, far from wanting an early retirement from Sir John, who had, in fact, been agonising over such a decision, they were desperate to keep him from doing so, on the basis that an early resignation would be seen as an admission he had made the wrong decision. And, more importantly from their perspective, that the Queen's representative had appointed an illegitimate Prime Minister. And in this premise, they are no

---

[52] Ibid., p. 58.

doubt correct. That does not, of itself, indicate that the Palace actually believed he had made the wrong decision.

Kelly and Bramston argue, in *The Truth of the Palace Letters*:

> After the dismissal, Sir John Kerr was trapped in a psychological conflict – anxious to publicly defend the dismissal but fearful that the divisions unleashed might require his early resignation as Governor-General.[53]

And:

> In his time of need, the Palace was supportive of the Queen's representative ... This established the position of the Palace in dealing with Kerr post dismissal: it would support the Governor-General and urge him to stay calm and silent. The Queen and the Palace had no choice. But the overly friendly tone and exaggerated endorsement of Kerr's action by Charteris, a recurring theme after the dismissal, was neither appropriate nor necessary. It is understandable but it exposed the Palace to the charge, in retrospect, of supporting Whitlam's dismissal. Having made clear it was Kerr's constitutional responsibility to deal with the crisis, the Palace could not turn around afterwards and censure him. Kerr had signalled he could use the reserve powers and that is what he did ...[54]

Let me deal with the suggestion that Kerr 'was fearful that the divisions unleashed might require his early retirement'. Firstly, no doubt, Kerr would rather stay on in his role, but he recognised that circumstances might prevent that. However, if he were fearful of this possibility, one imagines he would be devising ways of avoiding it. But in fact, reading the Palace letters, it is clear he is actively canvassing the possibility of his resignation.

Kelly and Bramston also say:

> After the dismissal, Kerr was desperate to win the Palace's approval. Craving to win assurance he wrote five letters in seventeen days, the most intense period of correspondence in his time as Gover-

---

[53] Paul Kelly, Troy Bramston & Paul Keating. (2020). *The truth of the palace letters: deceit, ambush and dismissal in 1975*. Carlton, Victoria: Melbourne University Press, p. 129.
[54] Ibid., pp. 129-130.

nor-General. Six days after the dismissal, in a letter to Charteris of 17 November, Kerr began to unburden himself. He was a troubled and confused man – confused over his responsibility to the nation while wrestling with self-interest. Kerr was alarmed at the prospect of Whitlam being vindicated at the December poll.[55]

This is a gross mischaracterisation. The authors themselves reveal that in the passage immediately following the above:

> Reflecting on how he had wished Whitlam 'good luck' at the moment of dismissal, Kerr told Charteris: 'Nevertheless it would be impossible for me to work with him or for him to work with me if he wins the election. My probable best course of action would be to stay to commission him and to hand to him, at the same time, a letter of resignation which I would have already despatched to the Palace. The other school of thought is that I should make him dismiss me. As things stand, I do not favour this.'[56]

Kerr was quite aware of the prospect of a Whitlam victory at the time of the dismissal. It would be natural that he would canvass his options with Palace. The polls at that time were in Whitlam's favour. But there is nothing of confusion or alarm evident in Kerr's letters of this time. As to the frequency of his letters, certainly Kerr wished to make clear to the Palace the basis of his decision, and that could not be accomplished with a cursory note – the issues were much too complex, and the rapidly evolving situation required that he write often and in detail. In fact, Kerr's natural inclination was to write voluminously, both before and after the dismissal. He himself was aware of this and, on several occasions, asked Charteris if he was sending too much. And, of course, he was anxious to justify his actions. He could hardly leave the Palace in any doubt as to the probity, from his perspective, of his actions. That could rightly be termed 'justification'. But Kelly and Bramston's frequent use of the terms 'self-justification' or 'self-interest' is nothing more than a cheap ploy to undermine a perfectly natural process. If you read Kerr's letters with an open mind, by which I mean at face value, they are dispassionate yet

---

[55] Ibid., p. 131.
[56] Ibid.

vehement in his belief that he did the right thing. There is no self-pity or confusion. Throughout the saga he was scrupulous to send the Palace much background material, as much of it critical of himself as supportive.

As to the question of resignation, there were two phases. The first was in the immediate aftermath of the dismissal, and the second was after the Fraser victory. Kerr recognised, and accepted, that in the event of a Whitlam victory, his position would be untenable. His concern was not how he could avoid a departure from office, but how he could manage it in a manner that best protected his own legacy. That is not unnatural. The options were to commission Whitlam and then immediately resign, or force Whitlam to dismiss him. In his first letter on this subject, he inclined towards the former. Later he shifted the other way. The other possibility that he canvassed was to announce before the election that he would remain to commission the new Prime Minister, whoever it was, and then resign.

In the event, both Fraser and the Palace strongly advised him to make no announcement on this subject before the election. Being human, no doubt he was relieved to accept this advice. The reason both Fraser and the Palace wanted him to remain was the possibility that a resignation would be seen as an admission of error. On the other hand, an announcement before the election, that he would resign either way, could also be taken as a sign of good faith – that Kerr had not acted out of self-interest and was prepared to accept the same fate he had handed to Whitlam. I cannot help thinking that it was a shame he did not take this option. Had he done so, his life would have been much easier, and his reputation would not have suffered to the extent that it has. That he didn't is probably down to the fact that the Palace asked him not to. Kerr was nothing if not loyal to the Monarchy, as his letters continually attest, and would acquiesce in anything they asked.

In the event, Fraser won the election, the moment for a grand healing gesture had passed and Kerr then took the view that he would remain as long as it suited the Palace. The subject of his resignation did come up frequently in subsequent correspondence. One incident concerned the machinations of John Menadue, the Permanent Head of the Prime Minister's Department, a Whitlam loyalist and former Labor parliamentary candidate. Kerr became aware that Menadue was lobbying among senior public servants that he should resign before the anniversary of the dismissal. He became somewhat obsessed by this and sought assurances from Fraser which were given. My point is that from the December 1975 election, Kerr never again suggested he should resign. He remained untroubled by the logic of and justification for his decision, but was of course concerned at the consequences of it, particularly as it pertained to the position of the Monarchy in Australia. As it emerged that support for the Monarchy remained high, he became more entrenched in his view that he need not resign. So, apart from the initial few weeks, the Palace had no fear that he would resign and had no need to flatter him to keep him in the tent, as suggested by Kelly and Bramston.

As regards the supportive tone of the Palace letters, Bramston and Kelly have this to say:

> Anne Twomey, drawing on her knowledge of vice-regal relationships in various realms, said (in an interview with Paul Kelly): it is standard practice to support a vice-regal officer after he or she has exercised a reserve power. Once the deed is done and the vice-regal officer is swamped with criticism and media attacks, the Palace sees its role as one of support and comfort, usually with lashings of praise included.[57]

The import of this, in the case of Kerr, is that, if it is *standard practice* to support the Vice Regal officer with 'lashings of praise', how does one tell, in any particular case, whether or not the Palace accepts that the officer made the right decision – unless, of course, the contention is that the use of reserve powers is always wrong. So, we can draw no conclusions from the effusive support of the Palace as to its attitude to the legitimacy of the dismissal itself.

---

[57] Ibid, p. 130.

In the event, it is clear that, despite his face-saving explanation, Kerr was prevailed upon, after the Queen's visit, to resign. At that stage things had pretty much calmed down, the Queen's visit had been a success and it would seem to me that the Palace had no particular imperative to see Kerr depart the scene. So, I suspect that the driving force behind the resignation was Malcolm Fraser. He wanted to dissociate himself from the controversy of the dismissal before the next election and one way to help achieve that would be to not have Kerr in the public eye any longer than he need be. He would not have wanted to recommend officially to the Queen that she withdraw Sir John's commission, but a quiet word from him to Charteris might do the trick.

And this brings me to my main point. It matters not what the Palace thought of Kerr's motives or character. The Palace, viz., the courtiers and officials that surround the Queen, had their own agenda which did not primarily concern itself with the issue of good governance in Australia. No doubt the Palace would have preferred the dismissal not to have happened. But the Monarchy is not a sinecure. If it is not prepared to accept some political controversy from time to time, it should look for another job.

I don't know if the Kerrs were 'very greedy'. I don't know if the Queen believed that. But whatever the truth of that, it has absolutely no bearing on Kerr's decision of 11 November 1975.

What matters is, did Kerr do the right thing? That question is not addressed in Chapter One of *The Dismissal – in the Queen's name*. In the following chapters I will attempt to rebut the specious case that Kelly and Bramston have mounted against Sir John Kerr, primarily to discredit the use of the reserve powers.

2

Kerr and Fraser – The Tip-off

On the morning of 11 November, Sir John Kerr agreed to see Prime Minister Whitlam later that day. He knew that Whitlam would come to advise a half-Senate election.

Over the prior weekend, Kerr had formed the view that Whitlam was unshakeable in his determination to break the Senate, and that, in agreeing to a half-Senate election, he would be facilitating a breach of the Constitution. The government would be attempting to govern without having 'supply' – the funds that it needed to pay its bills. Kerr's estimate was that the money would run out at the end of November but a half-Senate election, at which Whitlam had high hopes of achieving a majority, could not deliver this result until at least one month, possibly more, after that. Tight Senate elections are notoriously lengthy affairs. And, of course, Kerr had also to consider the possibility that Whitlam might fail to gain control of the Senate, in which case the stand-off would continue. In that case, it is possible that Fraser, having earned a degree of opprobrium for forcing this situation, would fold and agree to pass supply. But the damage would have already been done, and speculation as to what *might* happen could not form part of Kerr's calculations. He had to deal with what he knew and that was that a half-Senate election would definitely result in a period in which the Government could not pay its bills.

Whitlam had explored a solution whereby the banks would lend money to the Government to tide it over that period, but there was considerable doubt as to whether the banks would come to the party or that the scheme was, in fact, lawful. And, in any case, the Government would have to commit to paying interest to the banks. To do that it, would need legislation to that effect, passed by both Houses. It is highly unlikely that Fraser would have agreed to pass this legislation in the Senate. I will cover this in more detail later.

Kerr also believed that Fraser would hold firm and continue to block supply. Over that weekend, Kerr determined that the only way to resolve the deadlock, unless Whitlam was prepared to advise an election of at least the House of Representatives, was to dismiss him and appoint Fraser caretaker Prime Minister on the condition that he would approve supply and then immediately advise an election of both Houses.

Kerr's aim was not to dismiss Whitlam *per se*, as Kelly and Bramston would have you believe. That was merely a means to Kerr's end, which was to procure supply to the Crown.

And this is where the 'tip-off' comes in. One of the major transgressions that Kelly and Bramston hold against Kerr is that he 'tipped Fraser off' in a phone call on the morning of 11 November and before he had confronted Whitlam.

In his memoir, *Matters for Judgement*, Kerr claimed that the purpose of his call to Fraser was to determine if he was still firm in his resolve:

> I next spoke to Mr Fraser who confirmed that the position and the Opposition policy remained the same. I said nothing else to him about the situation. Mr Fraser's statement that things remained the same confirmed that temporary supply would not be available for a half-Senate election ...[1]

Kelly and Bramston claim that there was more to it than that:

> In this call Kerr tipped off Fraser about his plan to dismiss Whitlam that afternoon. The extraordinary feature of the dismissal is not just that Whitlam did not know he was going to be dismissed – it is also that Fraser was forewarned. Kerr was not just defying the advice

---

[1] Kerr, *Matters for Judgement*, p. 355.

of his Prime Minister. The Governor-General was in collusion with the opposition leader over his intention to commission Fraser that afternoon and gift him victory in the greatest political contest in the nation's history.[2]

This characterisation is based on a version of the phone call that emerged in 1987 in which Kerr is alleged to have said to Fraser, words to the effect, that if he were to dismiss Whitlam, would Fraser be prepared to accept the commission as caretaker Prime Minister under certain conditions. These were that Fraser would agree to pass supply, to recommend a double dissolution, to act as a caretaker prime minister, to instigate no police charges in relation to the Loans Affair, and to not establish a Royal Commission into the Loans Affair.

Apart from the two relating to the Loans Affair, these are the same conditions that Kerr stated that he first put to Fraser later that afternoon at Government House before he commissioned him.

Kerr always denied this version of the phone call, but Fraser insisted it was true. Initially he referred to a memo he had handwritten at the time, but he was unable to locate it, even as late as 1995 when Kelly interviewed him. Eventually, Fraser found the memo amongst his papers in the early 2000s and he gave a copy of it to Troy Bramston in 2013.

There is some doubt about the provenance of the memo. Fraser claimed he wrote the memo while talking to Kerr on the morning of 11 November. Coalition members Reg Withers and Vic Garland, who were in his office at the time, confirmed this. Kelly and Bramston quote Withers in 1997:

> 'He took up his big felt pen,' ready to make his note, Withers said. 'Vic and I could read it upside down. It was the four or five points Kerr had laid down ... he [Fraser] agreed when Kerr said they'd be the conditions ... Anything that Kerr and Fraser said since has been ... none of them told the truth about that.' Withers said that 'Malcolm was so excited he didn't realise we were there' but 'he came

---

[2] Kelly and Bramston, *The Dismissal*, p. 17.

to and took the paper aside'.[3]

Despite this confusing and incomplete rendition of what Withers apparently said, readers may feel that his account is given a degree of verisimilitude by virtue of the fact that he clearly remembers Fraser writing the memo with 'his big felt pen'. A copy of the memo is reproduced in *The Dismissal*. It is obvious that it is not written with a big felt pen, although the signature, clearly added later, could well have been. So, strike one against Withers. It is also worth noting here that the date was originally written as '1985' and then over-written to read '1975'. That is the sort of mistake that is more likely to have been made after the event. But this raises another question. If Fraser was just jotting down the points that Kerr raised with him, why would he feel the need to, later in the day, sign and date such a prosaic document? Normally, once it had served its purpose, it would go in the bin.

Here is some more 'evidence':

> Withers believes Kerr had previously rung Fraser on his private line. He recalls being in Fraser's office a number of days before the dismissal when Fraser took a call, had a short conversation and told Withers: 'You never heard that.' Withers had initially thought it might be his wife, Tamie, but Fraser said, 'No, no, it wasn't.'[4]

So here are Kelly and Bramston intimating that the 'tip-off' actually occurred even before the morning of 11 November. Is it likely that Withers would have thought a conversation with Kerr was actually with Fraser's wife? Especially after being told 'you never heard that'? A more likely explanation would be that it was Fraser's mistress. As evidence against Kerr, this alleged phone call is absolutely worthless. It is nothing more than innuendo.

Getting back to the 11 November phone call and the alleged note, just when did it surface? Here is Kelly's and Bramston's version of events:

---

[3] Ibid., p. 21.
[4] Ibid.

The doubts about Fraser's account of this phone call were given weight because Fraser, over many years, could not find the note he made of this conversation. Indeed, in 1995, Fraser told Kelly he had lost the handwritten note. Eventually, the note was rediscovered. Fraser told Troy Bramston he had found the note when he began sorting his papers in the 2000s and gave Bramston a copy of it in 2013.

The weight of evidence overwhelmingly supports Fraser's view against Kerr. Fraser argued that of all the discussions in his political career this is the one he would be least likely to forget. He has no ulterior motive since the revelation is a potential embarrassment for him as well.[5]

I'm not sure why Fraser would regard this revelation as a potential embarrassment for himself, firstly as he didn't originate the call and, secondly because he himself argued that Kerr did nothing improper (as Kelly and Bramston note). It seems that the note emerged via Fraser in 2013.

However, later in the chapter, the authors tell us:

> In the afternoon of November 11, Dale Budd, Fraser's Principal Private Secretary, saw the note scrawled at 9.55am sitting on Fraser's desk. It was already signed and marked by Fraser's bold pen in the bottom right-hand corner. Budd had not been in the room during the phone call. But he describes the call as Kerr indicating to Fraser 'the provisions applying to a caretaker government, should Fraser be commissioned in that role'. Budd told the authors he photocopied the note that afternoon. 'I thought it was an interesting and potentially historical document,' he said. The authors have a copy of Budd's photocopy.[6]

If Budd were not in the room during the phone call, his version of it carries no weight whatsoever. I will return to this extract shortly. In the meantime:

> During 2005 and 2006 a public dispute arose between Sir David Smith and Dale Budd about some of the events and phone calls between them on the morning of 11 November, including the 9.55

---

[5] Ibid., p. 20.
[6] Ibid., p. 22.

a.m. Fraser-Kerr phone call. ... Budd decided to contact Fraser. He asked Fraser to provide him a letter to substantiate the position Budd had been taking against Smith and to verify the note. 'To my surprise instead of giving me a letter he sent a statutory declaration,' Budd said. He told Fraser he didn't want to use the statutory declaration in his dispute with Smith. He didn't want to create a bigger public event. Budd just sat on the statutory declaration.[7]

Now here's a mystery. Budd was engaged in a public debate on this issue with Sir David Smith and sought confirmation of his position from Fraser in the form of a letter, which he presumably intended to make public. A letter would provide a certain degree of corroboration, but a statutory declaration would carry considerably more weight. The declaration was Fraser's version of the 11 November phone call. So why would Budd be prepared to rely on a letter but not use a statutory declaration? Because he 'didn't want to create a bigger public event'? He wanted to win small but not big? Or was he less sure of his facts than he let on, and did not want to put his former boss in the position of making a false declaration? Kelly and Bramston reproduce the declaration, but it does not prove anything one way or the other.

Later, Kelly and Bramston refer to author Philip Ayres 1987 biography of Fraser:

> The Ayres account has Kerr putting the four questions that Fraser lists in his statutory declaration.[8]

Just to further cloud the issue, the note produced in 2013 lists six conditions, not four, and the statutory declaration lists five.

But the bigger mystery is what happened, in all those years, to the photocopy that Budd made for historical purposes? Are we to believe that Fraser's original *and* Budd's photocopy disappeared for 25 or more years, both to resurface at roughly the same time? Did the authors ask Budd what he had done with the photocopy at the time that he made it? Presumably, he would have put such a potentially historical document in

---

[7] Ibid.
[8] Ibid., pp. 23-24.

an official file. He clearly didn't have it in 2006, during his dispute with Sir David Smith. So how and when did it come to light?

Professor David Flint, in his Neville Bonner Oration of 2015, postulates that:

> If Fraser made some notes during the conversation they were not necessarily a record of the conversation. If I make notes during a telephone conversation they are either of the conversation, or an aide-memoire for what I want to say, or of matters which are triggered in my mind by the conversation although they were not mentioned in the call. Given the insertion of material never required by Kerr—that about not holding royal commissions—they were more likely to have been Fraser recalling a list of six conditions he and his staff would have thought were those Kerr was likely to impose.[9]

That is more plausible than the Garland/Withers account.

And on this topic, a telling point in favour of the Kerr version, is that he left copious notes and diaries, which Kelly and Bramston have meticulously trawled in order to dig up as much dirt as they can. For example, we will learn the details of discussions Kerr had with High Court judge Sir Anthony Mason, of previously undisclosed phone calls to the Chief Justice, Sir Garfield Barwick, and even of a private *tete-a-tete* with Malcolm Fraser during which Kerr revealed his fear of his own dismissal by Whitlam. Kerr was remarkably candid and thorough in his own private documentation. And yet the Fraser version of this call does not appear. That strongly suggests it didn't happen.

Historian Michael Connor has forensically dissected this issue in *Quadrant Magazine* and has come to a different conclusion – that Kelly and Bramston have confused the notes which Fraser made for his address to the Parliament on the afternoon of the dismissal with notes he supposedly took when talking with Kerr that morning. Connor says that these are the numbered points for a speech. That this list includes the two items relating to the

---

[9] David Flint, 'Blame Whitlam and Fraser, Not Kerr', *Quadrant Magazine*, 1 January 2016.

Loans Affair that Fraser committed to in his speech, *but* which did not appear in the agreement he signed at his commissioning, lends considerable credence to this interpretation. As does the fact that Dale Budd did not find the note until the *afternoon* of 11 November.[10]

Thus, there are two alternative explanations for the note, both more plausible than the Fraser version.

Earlier I pondered why Fraser would bother to sign and date a cryptic short-term *aide-memoire* rather than just throw it in the bin after it had served its purpose. Budd apparently believed it might have historic significance, so he made a copy. Maybe Fraser also felt it might be needed for posterity. But if that were the case, why did he not have his staff type the note up as a formal memorandum for inclusion in an appropriate file? And why did he not make any other contemporaneous notes about the whole affair?

Nonetheless, despite the doubtful provenance of the note, for the purposes of my argument I will proceed from here on the basis that the phone call took place as described by Fraser.

In fact, as I will now argue, this note is inconsequential in terms of the propriety, or otherwise, of Kerr's actions. Earlier, I noted that Kelly and Bramston claim that Kerr and Fraser were 'in collusion'. That suggests a conspiracy, particularly if you couple that assertion with a later claim that:

> Kerr's motive was obvious. He was worried the sacking of Whitlam might be undone that afternoon. Kerr wanted a quick execution. This meant preparing the pathway with Fraser.[11]

Kerr did not want a quick 'execution'. He wanted a quick and clean resolution of the political impasse by virtue of a general election. Whitlam's political 'execution', if you wish to think of it that way, was a necessary precursor to that resolution. Fraser did not collude – he merely co-operated with Kerr in implementing a solution that Kerr had already decided upon.

---

[10] M. Connor, 'Inventing the Dismissal', *Quadrant Magazine*, 21 October 2017.
[11] Kelly and Bramston, op.cit., pp. 17-18.

Kelly and Bramston expand on this theme:

> Fraser said he now knew this 'was the day Kerr intended to act'. Clearly, he knew this as a fact, unlike Whitlam. Fraser, however, tries to excuse Kerr as well. He said Kerr made it clear no final decision had been made. He says he could not be certain from this call that Kerr would dismiss Whitlam. '[I] still wasn't certain that, once faced with an ultimatum, Whitlam would not back down and choose to go to an election as Prime Minister', Fraser said. But this is wordplay on Fraser's part.[12]

Why is it wordplay on Fraser's part? It seems eminently logical to me. In fact, repeatedly throughout this chapter, the authors refer to the fact that Kerr needed to be sure of Fraser before he presented his ultimatum to Whitlam, and they note that all on the Coalition side believe this was perfectly reasonable. For example:

> Fraser now knew what Kerr was planning. The conditions Kerr was imposing on Fraser's caretaker commission were vital and he wanted to ensure they would be accepted in full without problems or negotiations. Fraser understood this ... The scenario Kerr put to Fraser that morning played out in this exact manner in the afternoon. There can be no other conclusion: Fraser was tipped off in order to make the operation as smooth as possible.[13])

And what is wrong with that? Should Kerr have left Fraser's reaction to chance? Here is Fraser's response to that:

> This call made by Kerr to Fraser was first revealed by Philip Ayres in his book Malcolm Fraser – A Biography, published in 1987 ... The Ayres account has Kerr putting the four questions that Fraser lists in his statutory declaration. 'He can't go to the end of the road with Whitlam,' Fraser told Ayres, 'and find that he's got an unacceptable situation as far as I'm concerned.' Fraser's biographer concluded that 'although he now felt sure of the outcome' Fraser 'did not yet have knowledge of it.'
>
> There is validity in this fine distinction. But it cannot disguise the

---

[12] Ibid., p. 19.
[13] Ibid., pp. 19-20.

reality: Kerr had tipped off Fraser.[14]

It might be a fine distinction, but, nonetheless, Kerr had a very real issue to deal with here. You might ask why would Kerr doubt Fraser accepting a caretaker commission, which is what he had been angling for all along. The answer may lie in the two conditions relating to the Loans Affair. And, if Fraser's account is true, this is one area in which I would question Kerr's judgement. What right did he have to put obstacles in the way of the pursuit of what might have been an illegal operation? In this one area he was clearly doing Labor a favour, and, in my view, going outside of his remit to do so. Regardless of that, had he not bedded these two conditions down beforehand – had he dismissed Whitlam before speaking to Fraser – all the aces would have been with Fraser, who might well have rejected those two conditions, knowing that Kerr had nowhere else to go. In fact, neither of the Loans Affair conditions appeared in the final letter that Fraser signed on accepting his commission, although this could be because Kerr did not want them in writing and was happy to accept Fraser's word on them. On the whole though, I am inclined to believe that someone with Kerr's judicial background would never have been so injudicious as to make these two demands. David Flint's theory makes more sense, in that Fraser may have been contemplating offering them as an inducement if Kerr evinced any hesitancy in finalising his decision. It must also be remembered that Kerr also required a double dissolution, not just an election for the House of Representatives. That could also be a reason he would need to sound Fraser out early. That is, if you accept Fraser's account.

As to Kerr's denial of the substance of the call, it is noteworthy that Fraser also initially concurred with Kerr's version of the call until 1987, when he then, for some unknown reason (possibly to discredit Kerr), decided to reveal it. Kelly and Bramston concede that prior to 1987, Fraser had assured political journalist Alan Reid that he had no prior knowledge of Kerr's intentions. So, it's a bit rich of Fraser to then claim,

---

[14] Ibid., pp. 23-24.

as he is quoted in *The Dismissal*:

> ...Fraser is scathing of Kerr's version of events: 'Look, denying it was a sign of weakness,' Fraser said of Kerr. 'There are many signs of weakness in his character, and that is probably true of most of us. It was an error of judgement and it was a weakness not to explain it how I've explained it.'[15]

No doubt, being human, Kerr thought it wiser not to reveal the full substance of the phone call (if it happened that way), probably because he suspected that some partisan journalist would hang it around his neck as a 'tip-off'.

But, even if it occurred as Fraser claimed, was it a tip-off? I would argue not. A tip-off necessarily involves conferring some improper advantage on one party in a transaction. But what advantage did Fraser get from this tip-off? In what way did he act differently on that day to the way he would have acted in the absence of this hint of Kerr's intentions?

Fraser's biggest danger was that wavering back-benchers would insist he back down. But according to Kelly and Bramston:

> After the phone call Fraser went into the joint party meeting. If anything was to go wrong, this was the moment. It was a strange event. They stood silent for two minutes to honour Armistice Day. Fraser and his deputy, Phil Lynch, had taken a tactical decision – they would say nothing to the party room about their earlier meeting with Whitlam and nothing about Whitlam's decision to call a half-senate election. Indeed, they wanted no discussion of the crisis. Their greatest fear would be expressions of alarm and unrest within the party room suggesting Fraser might not be able to hold his troops together.[16]

What better way to calm the troops than to let slip that they were on the verge of victory? But Fraser did not do that. He honoured Kerr's request that the phone call be treated as confidential. He derived no advantage from the morning phone call, which therefore could, in no way, be characterised as a

---

[15] Ibid., p. 21.
[16] Ibid., p. 27.

'tip-off'. When you weigh Kerr's imperative to have Fraser's agreement in place before confronting Whitlam, against the fact that Fraser would have had an inkling he was on the verge of victory – something he would, in any case, have suspected even from the more innocuous call that Kerr claims he made – this 'tip-off' claim is nothing but a storm in a teacup. It did not materially, if at all, affect the outcome.

3

Kerr and Whitlam – The Deception

The main premise of Kelly and Bramston's condemnation of Kerr is that he deceived or ambushed Whitlam. In other words, he did have the power to dismiss Whitlam, but he did it in an underhand way, which denied Whitlam the opportunity to rescue his Prime Ministership. They get to this point right away:

> Sir John Kerr said in his memoirs that by Thursday, 6 November, with Gough Whitlam and Malcolm Fraser on a collision course, he had to take a decision. His guiding principle was to keep this decision secret from the prime minister. The reason was that Kerr feared dismissal by Whitlam if the prime minister had any inkling of his plans. Kerr was frank about concealing his plans from Whitlam – it is the first stage in a process legitimately called deception.[1]

In support of their position that Kerr deceived Whitlam, Kelly and Bramston cite Sir Anthony Mason, a friend of Kerr, and a High Court judge at the time of the dismissal. Mason and Kerr discussed the dismissal during the crisis, a fact that did not come to light until 2012, and for which Sir Anthony was subject to considerable criticism. This aspect is covered in detail later in the book, but his involvement is cited here:

> In fact, the governor-general was damned by his closest friend during the crisis, High Court Judge Sir Anthony Mason. ... Mason said he told Kerr that 'if he did not warn' Whitlam then 'he would run the risk that people would accuse him of being deceptive'. It was a prophecy of startling accuracy. Whitlam hung the charge of

---

[1] Kelly and Bramston, *The Dismissal*, p. 28.

deception around Kerr's neck.[2]

This is somewhat disingenuous. In the wording above, Mason does not accuse Kerr of being deceptive but merely warns him that others might think that. In other words, it is a question of tactics and public relations. On the other hand, I must point out that Sir Anthony did say:

> I said to Sir John that he should warn the prime minister that he would terminate his commission if he did not agree to hold a general election. The warning was not heeded.
>
> In his writings since 9 November 1975, Sir John has strongly defended his decision not to warn Mr Whitlam. Although he did not discuss his reasons for that decision with me before or after the dismissal, my impression is that Sir John thought that warning the prime minister might lead to Her Majesty becoming embroiled in the Australian constitutional controversy and that he wanted to avoid such an outcome ...
>
> Despite my disagreement with Sir John's account of events and his decision not to warn the Prime Minister, I consider that Sir John was subjected to unjustified vilification for making the decision which he made. I consider and have always considered that Sir John acted consistently with his duty except in so far as he had a duty to warn the Prime Minister of his intended action and he did not do so.[3]

But again, this falls short of accusing Kerr of deception. Mason believed Kerr had a duty to warn the PM, but Kerr had a different view, viz., that his duty demanded that he not take steps that might cause the Palace to become embroiled in a catfight between the Governor-General and the Prime Minister. I will return to both these questions later.

Back to Kelly and Bramston:

> Kerr was explicit about his decision and his motive: 'I believed, quite starkly, that if I had said anything to Mr Whitlam about the possibility that I might take away his commission I would no longer

---

[2] Ibid
[3] A. F. Mason, 'Text of statement by Sir Anthony Mason', *The Sydney Morning Herald*, 27 August 2012.

have been there. I conceived it to be my proper behaviour in the circumstances to stay at my post and not invite dismissal ... if Mr Whitlam or any other minister was deceived, he deceived himself.'

It is true that Whitlam deceived himself but it is also true that Kerr, by what he said and failed to say, encouraged this deception. The heart of the crisis was Kerr's decision to deny Whitlam access to his judgement of the situation. He treated the prime minister as a dangerous potential adversary. In the end, he sacked Whitlam in what is correctly described as a constitutional ambush. This violated the convention and practice whereby the governor-general acts on the advice of the prime minister and engages frankly with the prime minister.[4]

Here we have the first example of a glib misrepresentation of the convention that the Governor-General 'acts on the advice of the prime minister'. That convention has a specific meaning. It is true that, in the normal course of events, the Governor-General gets his riding instructions from the prime minister. The form of words – acts on the advice of – means that the prime minister is 'advising' the Governor-General that whatever instrument he is asking him to sign is constitutional and has been appropriately endorsed by Parliament. As will be covered later, what Whitlam was advising in this case was unconstitutional.

If we look at the Constitution, Sections 61 to 64 provide:

Executive power
61. *The executive power of the Commonwealth is vested in the Queen and is exercisable by the Governor-General as the Queen's representative*, and extends to the execution and maintenance of this Constitution, and of the laws of the Commonwealth.

Federal Executive Council
62. There shall be a Federal Executive Council to advise the Governor-General in the government of the Commonwealth, and the members of the Council shall be chosen and summoned by the Governor-General and sworn as Executive Councillors, *and shall hold office during his pleasure.*

---
[4] Kelly and Bramston, op.cit., pp. 28-29.

Provisions referring to Governor-General
63. The provisions of this Constitution referring to the Governor-General in Council shall be construed as referring to the Governor-General acting with the advice of the Federal Executive.

Ministers of State
64. The Governor-General may appoint officers to administer such departments of State of the Commonwealth as the Governor-General in Council may establish. *Such officers shall hold office during the pleasure of the Governor-General.* They shall be members of the Federal Executive Council, and shall be the Queen's Ministers of State for the Commonwealth.

Ministers to sit in Parliament
After the first general election no Minister of State shall hold office for a longer period than three months unless he is or becomes a senator or a member of the House of Representatives.

It is clear that in a strict interpretation of the Constitution, executive power resides with the Governor-General. Ministers hold office at his pleasure. The convention that the Governor-General acts on the advice of his Ministers recognises that the responsibility for the development and implementation of policy in the form of laws rests with the Parliament. It also means that he cannot accept advice from someone who is not a Minister. It does not mean that he *must* accept the advice of his Ministers.

But in the case where the Governor-General has decided to exercise the reserve power to dismiss a prime minister, we are not talking about policy or laws but about governance, and the convention does not apply. The Constitution makes no provision that the Governor-General *always* acts on the advice of his Ministers, as is often cited.

In fact, Whitlam's intended advice on the fateful day was for a half-Senate election on 13 December, at which he hoped to achieve a majority in the Senate. Kerr had already assessed that this would not resolve the problem, which was that Whitlam was intending to govern without supply, for possibly as long as three months. I cover this aspect in more detail later, but effectively Whitlam's 'advice' would have been 'allow me to resolve this political impasse in my own way'. But to act on this advice would effectively neuter the Governor-General and render him merely a cipher, a role that Kerr specifically, and rightly in my view, rejected. It would also mean that the Prime Minister need not trouble the Palace to rid himself of this meddlesome Governor-General, but simply 'advise' him to resign his own commission. That would mean that the reserve powers do not exist.

Once the Governor-General has decided to act against the prime minister, the convention – and that is all it is – no longer applies.

The discourse continues:

> Central to Kerr's strategy was his conditioning of Buckingham Palace. He devoted countless hours writing letters to the Palace designed to keep the Queen informed of events. These letters, despite their importance to Australian history, are still secret forty years later, in a self-serving deal negotiated between Government House and the Palace that mocks Australia's sovereignty.[5]

This is a classic example of the deceptive technique employed throughout book to disparage Kerr. The implication of the first sentence – the use of the word 'strategy' – is that Kerr was planning the dismissal all along, even before the crisis began. Kerr began writing letters to the Queen from the moment he assumed the post. It is ludicrous to suggest he was planning a 'coup' from the word go, although throughout their book Kelly and Bramston are at pains to give this impression. The crisis commenced with the presentation of the budget in August 1975 and speculation in the media that Fraser might block it. This was what we might call the 'phoney crisis'. The real crisis commenced on 16 October, when the Opposition formally committed to block the budget, and lasted less than one month. There were 212 letters (only roughly half of which were from Kerr) released in 2020 covering almost the entirety of Kerr's tenure. In fact, if we look at the period 15 August 1974 to 8

---

[5] Ibid.

October 1975, Kerr wrote some 29 letters to the Palace and received 30 in reply. So, Kerr wrote roughly twice a month. Admittedly most of his letters were quite voluminous but, still, that doesn't sound like countless hours. So, was this obsequious sycophant Kerr or manipulative schemer Kerr at work here? Or was it just a conscientious man doing his duty – keeping the Queen informed on matters upon which he represented her and upon which he knew she took a keen interest?

This might seem a trivial point, but Kelly and Bramston have used the letters as one of their main weapons in their character assassination of Kerr. This aspect will figure prominently in the pages ahead. In fact, following the release of the Palace letters, they wrote another book, *The Truth of the Palace Letters*.

As to the embargo on the letters being a self-serving deal, we have already seen in a letter from Charteris on 8 October 1976 that it was just normal practice:

> If you agree to this solution it remains to be decided for what period of time your papers should be placed under embargo. The figure we usually specify nowadays is 60 years from the end of the appointment concerned.[6]

There was no 'self-serving' deal.

The authors go on to describe a 20 October 1975 letter:

> On 20th October 1975, Kerr wrote to the Palace: 'The Prime Minister's position has hardened and changed considerably in the last forty-eight hours. He has now decided that he will advise no election of any kind whatsoever. On Saturday he told me that he is determined to break the alleged power of the Senate to force an election, at its whim, of the House of Representatives by denying supply ... He has, so he says finally and irrevocably decided never to take the House of Representatives to the people because the Senate denies it power to govern, by cutting off money. He will not do this now, not next May, not ever. He has said something along these lines publicly and has been accused by Mr Anthony, the Leader of the National Country Party, of attempting to stand over the Governor-General.'

---

[6] M. Charteris, Letter to John Kerr, *The Palace Letters*, 8 October 1976, pp. 225-226.

In short, Kerr was telling the Queen that Whitlam was seeking to intimidate him. There is no doubt he felt this. His conditioning of the Palace, however, was subtle. A constitutional ambush conceived in secret would be a remarkable event, but Kerr could not foreshadow any dismissal, since that would implicate the Queen.[7]

Kelly and Bramston seem to be suggesting that Kerr was planning a 'constitutional ambush' as early as 20 October i.e., that he had already made up his mind to dismiss Whitlam and was 'covering his backside' by suggesting to the Palace that the issue was that the standing of the Queen's representative was under threat from the Prime Minister. The use of the term 'constitutional ambush' in the context of this passage is simply a gratuitous slur. And the suggestion that he concealed from the Palace the possibility that he might dismiss Whitlam is ludicrous, since the very first paragraph of the letter says:

> They (the Opposition) are openly asserting that I have a duty to act very soon to force an election, that it is open to me to dismiss the Prime Minister and call on someone else (Mr Fraser, of course) willing to advise a dissolution of the House of Representatives, or both houses. As to that, whilst not yet making up my mind about ultimate and final decisions necessary at a time of really final, constitutional crisis, my present disposition is to say that ... the crisis ... is not at this stage at the constitutional brink.[8]

So, Kerr is openly canvassing with the Palace the possibility that he might dismiss the Prime Minister. It is true he is merely quoting the Opposition's opinion that he can do so, but significantly, he does not disavow that possibility. It was not the possibility that he might dismiss the Prime Minister that he needed to conceal from the Palace. It was just his final decision to do so. That must be made without advice from or knowledge of the Palace. So, there is no question here of him 'conditioning the Palace'.

We now return to the question of advice:

> Not only did Kerr omit to inform Whitlam of his views but he se-

---

[7] Kelly and Bramston, op.cit., pp. 29-30.
[8] J Kerr, Letter to Martin Charteris, *The Palace Letters*, 20 October 1975, p. 119.

lected his own constitutional, advisers from outside the government. His principal personal adviser was his old friend Mason and his ultimate constitutional adviser became the Chief Justice, Sir Garfield Barwick. Kerr's separate and initial contacts with Mason and Barwick came before the blocking of supply in mid-October. Whitlam was in complete ignorance that the governor-general, supposed to take advice from the government, had initiated his own advisory arrangements within the High Court.[9] (emphasis added)

Here we have a conflation of two separate issues. We have already examined the convention that the Governor-General acts on the advice of his Ministers. That convention applies to the political process of giving effect to laws, regulations and other instruments of government e.g., giving Royal Assent to bills. That is not what we are talking about here.

Here we are talking about a potential conflict between the Governor-General and his Ministers i.e., the government. Advice from the government would come from the Solicitor General, who is the chief legal adviser and represents the government in legal matters. He is not a member of Parliament. Taking advice from the government is certainly a worthwhile exercise but as we will discover later, Sir John Kerr had great difficulty in getting such advice. And in a conflict between the Governor-General and his government it is not unreasonable for the former to seek independent advice, particularly if, unlike Sir John Kerr, he is not legally trained. The fact of a Governor-General seeking advice from two judges of the High Court is certainly contentious but, as Kelly and Bramston concede later in the book, it is not unprecedented. And it is only contentious in respect of the public office held by the advisers, not in respect of getting advice independent of the government *per se*. This is discussed in more detail in the following chapter.

The remainder of this chapter deals with the relationships and discourse between Kerr and various Labor figures (including Whitlam) and senior public servants. It postulates that they all believed that Kerr was on their side and that he encouraged them in that belief, principally by not disabusing them of that notion.

---

[9] Kelly and Bramston, op.cit., p. 30.

John Menadue, then head of the Prime Minister's Department, is quoted as saying that:

> There was no doubt that Mr Whitlam believed that the governor-general was sympathetic to his position and the problems with the Senate. In conversation also with me the gave the very clear impression that he regarded the course proposed by the Opposition as being quite improper. This arose during discussions I had with him at briefing sessions in the months leading up to the crisis.[10]

Firstly, an 'impression' no matter how clear, is not evidence of anything. Impressions are subjective things. We don't know what Kerr said to Menadue, or exactly when he said it, but whatever inference Menadue drew from those remarks is neither here nor there as regards Kerr's intentions. Kerr may or may not have thought that Fraser's course was improper, but he also knew it was not unconstitutional. And it would not have been improper 'in the months leading up to the crisis' as Menadue claims, because it was not until 16 October that Fraser announced his decision to block supply. Kerr probably was sympathetic to Whitlam's position. But that is irrelevant to his role as Governor-General. What is relevant is that Menadue had been Whitlam's private secretary when he was Deputy Opposition Leader and had also stood unsuccessfully as Labor candidate in 1966 for the Federal seat of Hume, so it is clear where his loyalties lie. His recollections after the event must be treated with caution.

In Mid-October, just days prior to the formal denial of supply, Kerr had a meeting with Whitlam:

> I said to him, on the subject of governing without supply, 'Do you think that is the wisest course? Wouldn't it be better to go to an election even if you lose? Your opponents will have a difficult time next year if they win, and provided we do not have chaos over supply you would have a very good chance of coming back as Wilson did in England. You are still young and, even if you lose now, if you play your cards right you could easily have a second term as Prime Minister.' In saying this I was going as far, as Governor-General,

---

[10] Ibid, pp. 30-31.

as I could go in the exercise of my right to advise and warn.' The Prime Minister rejected this approach out of hand.[11]

This does not suggest that Kerr thought the actions of the Opposition so improper as to outweigh Whitlam's proposed course of governing without supply.

The remainder of this chapter is littered with similar reminiscences, all after the event, from Labor politicians of the time, and all couched in terms of a narrative that Kerr had, all along, planned to dismiss Whitlam:

> A minister who actually opposed Whitlam's 'tough-it-out' tactic of not going to an election, John Wheeldon, said 'I was at Government House chatting to Kerr ... He said to me, "How are we going?" It struck me at once – how are we going? When I got back to Parliament House I bumped into Jim McClelland and said to him, "Well, your good friend Kerr is onside alright" ... McClelland replied. "I'm just on my way to see Gough, so I'll tell him."'[12]

Firstly, the use of 'we' in this context might not necessarily mean that Kerr was aligning himself politically with Labor but might simply reflect the fact that Kerr saw himself as part of the Government, which he most certainly did. And we don't know at what point in the crisis, this statement was made. Since Kerr had left the Labor Party many years earlier and was now more ideologically aligned with the Liberals, it is hardly likely he would declare himself as part of a Labor team. This incident, if it occurred, was reported after the dismissal, and looks more like clutching at straws in a *post hoc* attempt at bolstering the 'ambush' narrative.

One more example, from former Minister Jim McClelland:

> McClelland ... spoke with Kerr several times during the crisis 'I wouldn't have held it against Kerr if he had just been honest. If he had said to Gough "Prime Minister, I'm in a dilemma and I might soon have no option but to dismiss you." But he didn't. Instead, he planned an ambush. He did his best to deceive us and mislead us

---

[11] Kerr, *Matters for Judgement*, p. 254.
[12] Kelly and Bramston, op.cit., p. 31.

about his intentions on the reserve powers'.[13]

There are other examples, that I won't go into here, but they all amount to the fact that, in the weeks leading up to the crisis, Sir John Kerr, in his personal interactions with government members, acted as if it were business as usual. But what else would he do? Are they suggesting he should have dropped hints to various Ministers that he might act the way he eventually did? That would be a very indiscreet Governor-General, indeed. If he had a 'duty to warn', and this topic will be covered in more detail later, it would be confined to the Prime Minister and take place in the Governor-General's office.

The attitude seems to be 'we misread Kerr, so he must have misled us'. The possibility that Kerr might dismiss Whitlam had been bruited about for weeks. It can hardly have escaped the notice of every influential member of Whitlam's caucus. Did not one of them think it might eventuate, or did wishful thinking rule the day?

In fact, Kerr could not dismiss the Prime Minister unless and until Whitlam gave him a reason to do so. Kerr was planning for the eventuality that he might have to dismiss Whitlam – a responsible course of action – but he had not, at any stage up until about 6 November, decided to act. The implication – a theme that runs throughout the book – that he planned it all along, deliberately deceiving the Prime Minister and his Ministers so that they would not deviate from their position, and therefore they would inevitably hand him the reason he needed, is ludicrous. It is a conspiracy theory developed to vilify Sir John Kerr as to his motives and tactics simply because his actions were constitutionally unchallengeable.

Kelly and Bramston report selectively here:

> (On 21 October) Kerr rang Whitlam, who left a caucus meeting to take the call. The governor-general raised the publicly released opinion by Opposition front bencher, Bob Ellicott QC, on whom Fraser was relying, arguing for Kerr to dismiss Whitlam because

---

[13] Ibid.

he could not obtain supply. Ellicott's opinion went right to the heart of the crisis. 'This Ellicott opinion ... it's all bullshit, isn't it?' Kerr asked. Whitlam could only be encouraged. He took great hope from this remark – yet it proved a false hope.[14]

This incident is referenced to Kelly's earlier 1995 book *November 1975*. This sounds unlikely. Since it is no more than a claim by Whitlam after the event, it can be accorded little credibility. Kerr would not have thought the opinion 'all bullshit' since it aligned with his own view that he had the power to dismiss the Prime Minister. Where he disagreed with Ellicott was on the question of timing, the latter having opined that the Governor-General had the power to, and should, act immediately, subject to certain conditions. And he certainly thought the opinion credible enough to seek advice on it from the Government. And that fact alone should have tempered Whitlam's 'great hope'. This aspect will be covered in more detail later.

The following extracts from Chapter Three go to the heart of the matter:

> Fundamental to these political and social exchanges Labor Ministers describe with Kerr is the absence of any direct comment by the governor-general in which he rejects dismissal as an option.[15]

As I have argued earlier, it would be quite improper for the Governor-General to comment on these matters in casual conversation, and other than in the privacy of his office i.e., in confidence. And of course, if he had rejected dismissal as an option, he *would* have been acting deceptively, as Kelly and Bramston concede:

> He did not rule out dismissal because dismissal was an option. Kerr did not lie to Whitlam. He did not have to lie because Whitlam never engaged him directly on the key issues. This aversion to any intimacy with Kerr was Whitlam's blunder and turned their interaction into a flawed psychological drama.[16]

---

[14] Ibid., p. 34.
[15] Ibid., p. 34.
[16] Ibid., pp. 34-35.

The authors seem to have discounted the possibility that Whitlam's blunder might actually have been a tactical ploy. I will explore this possibility later. Continuing:

> Having decided not to speak frankly with Whitlam, Kerr said that 'any guesses' the prime minister made about the governor-general's thinking were Whitlam's own responsibility. This is far too cute. Kerr was encouraging Whitlam and his ministers. He did not lie but he did mislead.[17]

This is just sophistry. Bramston and Kelly have provided no evidence that Kerr *encouraged* Whitlam and his Ministers to believe that he was 'on their side'. Had he done so he would have been in breach of his fundamental duty. The indictment continues:

> The evidence is overwhelming from minister after minister. So is the behaviour pattern – it fits with Kerr's character as a social being who liked to chatter. Labor assumed he was its friend and that assumption was correct – Kerr was its friend until he dismissed the government.[18]

It's difficult to see how the fact that Kerr was sociable and engaged with the Whitlam ministers – according to his nature as the authors admit, and in accordance with his status as a member of the Executive – clashes with the fact that he was contemplating the possibility that he might have to dismiss them. Did they expect him to avoid them, or treat them with unaccustomed reserve? A sort of 'nod, nod, wink, wink' relationship? And what has friendship to do with duty, as Kelly and Bramston acknowledge in the very next paragraph:

> But being governor-general in the 1975 crisis was not about friendship. It was about responsibility.[19]

In other words, their preceding paragraph is irrelevant and can only have been included to bolster the idea that Whitlam and his Ministers felt betrayed *after the event* and that therefore

---

[17] Ibid.
[18] Ibid.
[19] Ibid.

Kerr must have acted dishonourably and deceived them. They continue:

> This reveals the shallowness of Whitlam's thinking. As prime minister, Whitlam was officially Kerr's adviser. He should have engaged Kerr on the fundamentals of the crisis: his view of the situation, his role as governor-general and of the reserve powers. 'It could perhaps have been different if he had asked me,' Kerr said. 'Mr Whitlam's failure to ask my view of the Reserve Powers must, I have always believed, have been deliberate avoidance.' This is Kerr's strong point: it is where Whitlam deceived himself as much as Kerr deceived him.[20]

Kelly and Bramston refer to the shallowness of 'Whitlam's thinking' and his 'greatest blunder', attributing Whitlam's contribution to the crisis as merely mistakes, rather than the deception they have hung around the neck of Sir John Kerr. They ignore Kerr's belief, quoted above, that Whitlam's failure to ask his views was deliberate. As I outline in Chapter Six, former Labor Minister Clyde Cameron told Sir Paul Hasluck that this was Whitlam's style. It is hard to engage with someone if they refuse to engage with you. And it would seem to me that the incumbency on one of the parties to initiate a discussion on the reserve powers rested with Whitlam, who would be most affected by their application, rather than Kerr.

> In the end, however, the issue of deception turns on Kerr's refusal to counsel or warn Whitlam before resorting to the reserve powers.[21]

As we shall see, Whitlam often referred to the possible use of the reserve powers. And there I will leave Chapter Three, as the question of the 'warning' is fundamental to Kelly's and Bramston's case against Sir John Kerr, and it will be covered in detail in later chapters.

---

[20] Ibid., p. 35.
[21] Ibid.

4

Barwick, Mason and the High Court

This chapter examines the question of the propriety of the Governor-General seeking advice other than from the Prime Minister. And, in particular, from a High Court judge. It is a confused chapter. There are three villains. Sir John Kerr – because he sought advice from two sitting High Court judges and that he used this advice to bolster his position after the event. Chief Justice Sir Garfield Barwick – because he gave the advice requested. And Sir Anthony Mason – because he also advised Sir John Kerr, in informal discussions for some weeks leading up to the decision, and that he concealed his involvement for many years.

In their coverage of this issue, Kelly and Bramston again conflate the two separate concepts of 'advice' to the Governor-General, viz., the convention that the Governor-General 'acts on the advice of his Ministers' – which I have argued refers to political advice tendered in the normal course of events – and independent advice to inform his decision making, sought in exceptional circumstances such as pertained in November 1975.

Sir John Kerr sought official advice from the Chief Justice, Sir Garfield Barwick, on Sunday 9 November 1975, which advice was tendered on the morning of 10 November. Following the dismissal, neither Kerr nor Barwick sought to conceal the fact of this advice, which suggests that neither man thought this course of action was improper.

Kelly and Bramston argue that in similar circumstances now,

recourse to the Chief Justice for advice would not happen because 'after the events of 1975, the separation of powers doctrine and the imperative for the court to be impartial have gained fresh intensity'.[1] I will examine this claim shortly but let me reiterate a point I made earlier. The advice Kerr received was not advice from the High Court. It was advice from the Chief Justice.

Their premise is essentially that Barwick's involvement brought the High Court into disrepute.

They quote former Chief Justices, Sir Gerard Brennan and Robert French, in support of this view. French is quoted:

> 'There is nothing in the Constitution to suggest it is part of the function of the Chief Justice to provide independent advice to the governor-general in relation to the powers of the governor-general or the discharge of those powers.'[2]

To which I would respond, neither is there anything in the Constitution to suggest that the Governor-General must accept the advice of his Ministers, or that he must appoint his Ministry from the ranks of the party that holds a majority of seats in the House of Representatives. So, the lack of a specific prerogative in the Constitution does not, of itself, preclude a Chief Justice from giving advice. As an example of incisive judicial thinking, French's observation leaves something to be desired.

Much of this chapter is devoted to the opinions of subsequent Chief Justices – principally Brennan, Gleeson and French – as to the propriety of Barwick's involvement. Most agree that it would not happen today – according to Kelly and Bramston because the application of the doctrine of separation of powers has gained 'fresh intensity'. In fact, the major reason advanced by the above judges was because of the adverse reaction, in some quarters, to Barwick's involvement. Gleeson noted he had never been consulted in similar circumstances but that may have been because no crisis had arisen. And he says:

---

[1] Kelly and Bramston, *The Dismissal*, p. 38.
[2] Ibid., p. 39.

But another reason, I think, would be that there would be caution about it because of the reaction to what Barwick did.[3]

He also said:

> If the governor-general can't go to the chief justice, to whom can the governor-general go? It can't be the case that the governor-general is legally bound to rely only on the advice of his ministers.[4]

Barwick made the same point, particularly in relation to a Governor-General who is not legally trained.[5]

There are two questions that are relevant here. The first is the right of Sir John Kerr to seek advice independent of the government of the day. And the second is the advisability of seeking it from Sir Garfield Barwick, who was not only the Chief Justice at the time but also a former Minister in the Menzies government and, arguably, politically biased. I am not saying his advice *was* politically biased, but it could, and indeed was, regarded that way by many.

Kelly and Bramston commence their coverage of this issue thus:

> Barwick made little effort then, or later, to conceal his enthusiasm for a role in dispatching the Whitlam government. While the advice he provided was a legal opinion on the constitutional powers of the governor-general, Barwick believed he had an influence on Kerr's action. Barwick knew that Kerr shunned conflict and tended to 'temporise'. He believed he 'stiffened' Kerr to the task. The Chief Justice became, in the public's mind, an authorising agent for the governor-general.
>
> This is exactly what Kerr wanted – his resort to the chief justice invested the dismissal with constitutional weight and the perception of High Court consent, which was intended to increase his leverage over public opinion. Kerr did not need Barwick's opinion to act. Yet Kerr, a prudent man despite this audacity, wanted to implicate the High Court in his decision – and Barwick, eyes wide open, was

---

[3] Ibid., p. 40.
[4] Ibid.
[5] Ibid., p. 49.

> a willing participant in this collaboration. It is absurd to believe
> Barwick did not strengthen Kerr's personal resolve.[6]

This passage is a great example of the skill with which Kelly and Bramston invest the most benign circumstance with a sinister overtone. To begin with, Kerr – who the authors describe as a prudent man and quote Barwick as describing him as prone to 'temporise' – was about to make the most momentous decision of his life. It would have taken someone with Gough Whitlam's boundless self-assurance to make that decision without seeking a second opinion, regardless of how confident Kerr himself was in his assessment. As Kelly and Bramston note, Kerr did not need Barwick's opinion to act, but in acting entirely alone, Kerr could arguably have been described as an arrogant and reckless maverick.

And, again, we see the distortion of Kerr's aim, which was not to 'dispatch the Whitlam government' but to avoid a situation in which Whitlam attempted to govern without supply. Whitlam could have avoided his own dispatch by advising a general election. The only other way in which Whitlam could have survived was if Fraser had backed down. That was something beyond Kerr's control – he did not have the prerogative to insist that Fraser back down. And as to Barwick being unable to conceal 'his enthusiasm' for his role, this is merely emotive clickbait without any evidence to support it. A perusal of Barwick's *Sir John Kerr Did His Duty* reveals a dispassionate explanation of the constitutional issues.

Kelly and Bramston never miss an opportunity to use terminology that demonises Kerr. Hence, they say that 'Kerr wanted to *implicate* the High Court in his decision.' This wording suggests some form of shared guilt. It would be more appropriate to say that Kerr wanted the *imprimatur* of the High Court, although even that is misleading because the High Court *per se* had nothing to do with this decision. It would be fair to say it had the imprimatur of the Chief Justice. As I have opined earlier, it was a natural and prudent act on the part of

---

[6] Ibid., pp. 38-39.

the Governor-General to demonstrate that, at least, one other eminent legal authority agreed with his course of action. He could have chosen to ask a retired judge, but no doubt felt that the current Chief Justice would carry most weight. The propriety of Sir Garfield Barwick providing advice was not Kerr's concern. Presumably, he believed that Sir Garfield would satisfy himself on that issue.

Kerr knew his decision would be contentious. He knew it would divide Australians. He was entitled, indeed had a duty, to ameliorate that division in any way he could. That meant he had to disarm (as far as possible) his opponents, inform the untutored and buttress his supporters by demonstrating that he had not acted on an impulse and had, at least one, other learned opinion on his side. And what better opinion to have than that of the most senior judge in the land?

Which brings us to the separation of powers. Here is an explanation of the doctrine from the Australian Parliamentary Education Office:

> Parliament
> The Parliament makes and amends the law.
> Parliament (also referred to as the Legislature) is made up of the Queen (represented by the Governor-General), the Senate and the House of Representatives.
>
> Executive
> The Executive puts the law into action.
> The Executive is made up of the Queen (represented by the Governor-General), Prime Minister and ministers.
>
> Judiciary
> The Judiciary makes judgements about the law.
> The Judiciary is made up of the High Court of Australia and other federal courts.

Essentially, the doctrine of separation of powers is the avoidance of conflicts of interest, a concept that pervades our governance. It means that the courts cannot make the law. Courts, properly empanelled, make judgements, which are enforceable, and sometimes issue advice, which is not. Judges, acting on their own account, can issue advice but not make judgements.

Kelly and Bramston argue that the separation of powers doctrine and the imperative for the court to be impartial have gained fresh intensity. This suggests that Barwick, at best, treated the doctrine of the separation of powers in a cavalier way. I would argue the opposite. Barwick was well aware of the doctrine and took it into account when he made his decision to provide advice to Kerr. The doctrine could only be violated by Barwick's provision of advice if the matter had the potential to come before the High Court i.e., if it was justiciable.

On this subject, Kelly and Bramston say:

> Barwick advanced a core principle to justify his involvement as chief justice. He was sure the issue was not 'justiciable': that is, the question of any dismissal could not come before the court. That meant, he said, his advice 'would in reality not be advice given in a judicial capacity'. It would rank 'no higher than personal advice' though it might carry more weight because of his office. He argued that 'if I were asked for advice on a justiciable question or matter, I would decline to give it', and, therefore the issue was clear cut: to give the governor-general advice on a non-justiciable question did not compromise the independence of the chief justice. 'I did not breach the strictest view of the separation of powers,' Barwick said.[7]

Kelly and Bramston quote former Chief Justice French:

> Despite the confidence of lawyers, 'someone might bring a challenge to the court which might be required to determine whether the action was justiciable'. And a chief justice who had provided advice in relation to the action 'could hardly sit in judgement even on the question whether the action was justiciable'.[8]

What Barwick effectively did was to anticipate an action and decide what his ruling on justiciability would be.

Barwick maintained that it was not justiciable, and he was

---

[7] Ibid., pp. 45-46.
[8] Ibid., pp. 49-50.

supported in that view by both his eventual successors Sir Harry Gibbs and Sir Anthony Mason. In fact, as Kelly and Bramston report:

> Gibbs said the governor-general 'was entitled to seek advice from Sir Garfield and Sir Garfield was entitled to give it'.[9]

We don't know the view on this issue of the other High Court judges of the time. The other judges were Lionel Murphy, Sir Kenneth Jacobs and Edward McTiernan. The first two certainly opposed Kerr's action and the provision of advice by Barwick. This is made clear in *The Dismissal*, which also observes that, in the view of Michael Sexton, Judge McTiernan's associate 'It's more a matter of speculation, I think, but he certainly would have disapproved of any involvement by any members of the court.'[10] So, from what we know, at least, three members of the Court believed the matter was not justiciable. The remaining members explicitly or implicitly disapproved of the dismissal and of Barwick's involvement, but we don't know their views on the justiciability question.

The fact is no action was brought, even in the febrile aftermath of Kerr's decision. So, this whole question of justiciability is just kite flying.

Barwick did not have the power to compel or to prevent Kerr from acting as he did, and nor did he attempt to coerce Kerr. He issued no 'judgement' and therefore did not breach the separation of powers doctrine. His advice, which Kelly and Bramston describe as 'contentious and, in the view of many, flawed'[11] was, as shown below, dispassionate and objective:

> In response to Your Excellency's invitation, I attended this day at Admiralty House. In our conversations I indicated that I considered myself, as Chief Justice of Australia, free, on Your Excellency's request, to offer you legal advice as to Your Excellency's constitutional rights and duties in relation to an existing situation which, of its nature, was unlikely to come before the Court. We both clearly

---

[9] Ibid., p. 46.
[10] Ibid., p. 49.
[11] Ibid., p. 41.

understood that I was not, in any way, concerned with matters of a purely political kind, or with any political consequences of the advice I might give.

... I respectfully offer the following.

The Constitution of Australia is a federal Constitution which embodies the principal of Ministerial responsibility. The Parliament consists of two houses, the House of Representatives and the Senate, each popularly elected and each with the same legislative power, with the one exception that the Senate may not originate nor amend a money bill.

Two relevant constitutional consequences flow from this structure of the Parliament. First, the Senate has power to refuse to pass a money bill; it has power to refuse supply to the government of the day. Secondly, a Prime Minister who cannot ensure supply to the Crown, including funds for carrying on the ordinary services of Government, must either advise a general election (of a kind which the constitutional situation may then allow) or resign. If, being unable to secure supply, he refuses to take either course, Your Excellency has constitutional authority to withdraw his commission as Prime Minister.

There is no analogy in respect of a Prime Minister's duty between the situation of the Parliament under the Federal Constitution of Australia and the relationship between the House of Commons, a popularly elected body, and the House of Lords, a non-elected body, in the unitary form of Government functioning in the United Kingdom. Under that system, a Government having the confidence of the House of Commons can secure supply, despite the recalcitrance of the House of Lords. But it is otherwise under our Federal Constitution. A Government having the confidence of the House of Representatives but not that of the Senate, both elected Houses, cannot secure supply to the Crown.

But there is an analogy between the situation of the Prime Minister who has lost the confidence of the House of Commons and a Prime Minister who does not have the confidence of the Parliament i.e., of the House of Representative and the Senate. The duty and responsibility of the Prime Minister to the Crown in each case is the same;

if unable to secure supply to the Crown, to resign or to advise an election.

In the event that, conformably to this advice, the Prime Minister ceases to retain his Commission, Your Excellency's constitutional authority and duty would be to invite the Leader of the Opposition, if he can undertake to secure supply, to form a caretaker government (i.e. one which makes no appointments or initiates any policies) pending a general election, whether of the House of Representatives, or of both Houses of the Parliament, as that Government may advise.

Accordingly, my opinion is that, if Your Excellency is satisfied in the current situation that the present Government is unable to secure supply, the course upon which Your Excellency has determined is consistent with your constitutional authority and duty.[12]

Certainly, Barwick's advice, as opposed to the fact of his giving it, was contentious, in that not everyone agreed with it, but the fact that 'many' viewed it as 'flawed' is neither here nor there. Kelly and Bramston do not specify who or in what respect(s) it was viewed as flawed.

The Constitution is quite clear that Ministers serve at the pleasure of the Governor-General. A black letter reading of the Constitution allows no other conclusion than that the Governor-General has the power to withdraw a commission and it imposes no conditions on this power:

> 64. The Governor-General may appoint officers to administer such departments of State of the Commonwealth as the Governor-General in Council may establish.
>
> Such officers shall hold office during the pleasure of the Governor-General.

Even if there were some previous incident establishing a precedent that did impose some conditions, that would still not make the matter justiciable. There *was* a precedent for dismissal of a head of government in Australia, but it held no

---

[12] Kerr, *Matters for Judgement*, pp. 342-344.

implications for 1975, other than to establish that, under the Westminster system, the reserve power of a governor to dismiss a government leader who had the confidence of the lower house, exists. It came, in 1932, when NSW Governor, Sir Philip Game, dismissed NSW Premier Jack Lang for defying valid Federal government legislation in relation to the management of State funds. As a result of this action, a state election was called, and Lang was soundly defeated. Interestingly, Game is quoted as saying:

> Still with all his faults of omission and commission I had and still have a personal liking for Lang and a great deal of sympathy for his ideals and I did not at all relish being forced to dismiss him. But I felt faced with the alternative of doing so or reducing the job of Governor all over the Empire to a farce.[13]

That is the same mindset that informed Sir John Kerr's decision and which, I contend, has been weakened – to our detriment – by the ongoing and unjustified vilification of him. Kelly and Bramston have built a specious picture in *The Dismissal*, that Kerr positively relished the idea of sacking Whitlam. Nothing could be further from the truth. I will examine this aspect in the next chapter.

Sir Anthony Mason comes under fire for the fact that, as a sitting High Court judge, he discussed Kerr's options and advised him on the matter over a period of some weeks. Both he and Kerr concealed this fact. It came out, officially, in 2012 when Mason made a short statement. As to the propriety of Mason giving advice, the same considerations apply as for Barwick, so I don't intend to address this aspect. Where legitimate criticism might be applied to Mason is in relation to the secrecy. Kelly and Bramston devote a considerable portion of this chapter covering the views of various Hawke/Keating ministers, all of whom predictably say that, had they known of Mason's involvement, they would never have countenanced him being appointed Chief Justice. That's as to be expected, but it says nothing about the substantive issue – the withdrawal

---

[13] Letter by Sir P Game to Mrs Eleanor Hughes-Gibb, 2.7.1932, ML MSS 2166/5.

of Whitlam's commission and his replacement by Malcolm Fraser.

Mason essentially confirmed Kerr's account of their meetings, with the exception that Mason claimed he advised Kerr that he should warn Whitlam that he might be dismissed and give him the opportunity to go to an election as Prime Minister. We have only Mason's word for that, and I will examine this question in a later chapter.

As to the suggestion that adherence to the doctrine of separation of powers has strengthened in recent years, I would contend that the opposite is true. As far as the judiciary is concerned, separation of powers essentially means that the courts do not make law. However, in 1992, the High Court, under Sir Anthony Mason, discovered, in the common law, a previously unknown concept that came to be known as Native Title. Their judgement was based, to a large extent, on a repudiation of the doctrine of *terra nullius* which was claimed, erroneously, to have been the basis of the British assumption of sovereignty. Many (among them Justice Daryl Dawson who wrote the dissenting opinion) view this as judicial over-reach. The Mabo decision essentially confirmed that a small group of Meriam Islanders had the right to ownership of their land. There were several factors that justified this decision. The Meriam Islands were not annexed by the Colony of Queensland until 1879. The islanders were known to occupy permanent villages and they did conduct agriculture in the form of gardening. It is hard to argue with this decision. But the Court then extended the same logic to the entire Australian continent, where the above considerations did not apply. That is a massive over-reach. Their decision resulted in the Australian Parliament enacting a law to give force to the High Court ruling. That seems like the High Court effectively making law to me. Historian Michael Connor comprehensively explores this issue in his book *The Invention of Terra Nullius*.[14]

Ironically, it was Sir Anthony Mason who presided over the

---

[14] Michael Connor (2005). *The invention of Terra Nullius: historical and legal fictions on the foundation of Australia*. Paddington, N.S.W: Macleay Press, pp. 188-230.

High Court which made this judgement. And that is why, as Kelly and Bramston point out, many judges are reluctant to criticise Mason for his role in the events of 1975. Here is one example of this double standard, from a 2015 interview of Justice Jacobs by former High Court judge, Michael Kirby:

> Jacobs told Kirby he was 'extremely shocked' by Whitlam's dismissal ... Jacobs said he did not know in advance of Barwick's role and learned of the dismissal during the court's lunch break on 11 November. Kirby said: 'He believed that the court should not get involved in the slightest way in such matters because they were deeply divisive and politically partisan.' When Kirby offered an excuse for Barwick's action, Jacobs said he was being 'very kind'. Kirby wrote that 'by "kind" I took him to mean "naïve"'. Jacobs said 'he felt that he would be tarnished if he had anything whatever to do with the provision of advice' ... Kirby said such criticism as Jacobs voiced was directed 'solely' at Barwick's action. Jacobs was 'very fond' of Mason and 'did not criticize him'. Indeed, Jacobs had told Kirby on many occasions for his high regard for Mason's subsequent service as chief justice.[15]

However, despite their condemnation of Barwick, Kelly and Bramston have to concede that there were many precedents for his action. Barwick cited the case of the first Chief Justice, Sir Samuel Griffith, advising the then Governor-General over the 1914 double dissolution. Other examples include the Governor of Victoria receiving advice from both the Chief Justice of the High Court and the Chief Justice of Victoria in 1952 over the blocking of supply and the method of granting a dissolution of Parliament.[16]

Kelly and Bramston concede:

> The best academic authority on this issue is Professor Anne Twomey from Sydney University. Her research identified eighteen occasions before 1975 when judges advised vice-regal officers. In short, the practice was not unusual.[17]

---

[15] Kelly and Bramston, op.cit., pp. 47-48.
[16] Ibid., pp. 51-52.
[17] Ibid., p. 52.

Following from this:

> According to Barwick, precedent meant there was 'no impropriety' in him giving advice. It is true he had both precedent and learned opinion on his side.[18]

If Barwick had the right to provide advice, it would therefore seem logical that Kerr had the right to seek it. And that would mean that the whole of this chapter of *The Dismissal* is merely 'sound and fury, signifying nothing'. But no:

> However, Kerr sought Barwick's advice in defiance of Whitlam's views.[19]

The implication is that, therefore, Kerr did not have the right to consult the Chief Justice. This is a nonsensical argument. The Prime Minister is not the Governor-General's boss. Whitlam had no power to tell Kerr what or what not to do. Kerr's freedom of action was governed by the terms of the Constitution and various long-standing conventions. The convention that the Governor-General acts on the advice of his Ministers does not apply when the Governor-General is in conflict, or potentially in conflict, with his Ministers. That is, when he is contemplating the use of the reserve powers.

They then say:

> The reality is that political and personal ties were pivotal to the advice Kerr sought and got from Barwick. Those ties are a theme of this book. It was part of Kerr's plan to involve the High Court in any dismissal and he did that to protect himself.[20]

In fact, Justice Murray Gleeson told Kelly and Bramston that he did not think Barwick's action had compromised the High Court. He also believed that if the Governor-General needed advice, it was better that it come from the Chief Justice rather than from any unofficial professional associate of Kerr.[21] This claim that Kerr involved the High Court to protect himself is

---

[18] Ibid., p. 53.
[19] Ibid.
[20] Ibid., pp. 54-55.
[21] Ibid., pp. 53-54.

nonsense, as I will argue in a later chapter.

In summary, Barwick was entitled to provide advice, Kerr was entitled to seek it, and, in the end, it had no substantive bearing on Kerr's decision or the outcome.

5

Kerr's Journey: Dreaming of Menzies

Chapter Five of Kelly and Bramston's *The Dismissal* commences with this:

> John Kerr found his liberation when he deserted the Labor Party.[1]

That is a pretty brutal statement. It is designed to set the tone of the chapter, which ostensibly traces Kerr's early years and shows how they formed the character that he brought to bear on the events of 1975. Throughout this chapter alone we have the following statements:

> As a man, Kerr was an adroit opportunist, a beneficiary of patrons and a man who liked running with the winning team. (p. 59)
> Prone to pomposity too early in life, his ability carried him to the epicentre of events and this was where he thrived. (p. 60)
> Whitlam never grasped that Kerr was capable of a single act of pure ruthlessness. (p. 61)
> He was a vain man. I think he wanted to go down in history as a man who made a decisive action. (p. 61 quoting Sir Laurence Street).
> But ambition and pretension would constitute a fatal chemistry in Kerr's character. (p. 62)
> Kerr's true character now emerged ... Kerr was not a man to make such a sacrifice. He wanted to be with winners. His friends misjudged him. (pp. 65-66)
> The nakedness of his turn against Labor was startling. P 66.
> His rejection of the ALP was comprehensive: intellectual, self-interested and visceral. (p. 67)
> Sir Roden Cutler was unimpressed, saying 'to be frank, I thought

---

[1] Kelly and Bramston, *The Dismissal*, p. 59.

his understanding of politics was weak ... I often found that his judgement was wrong'. (p. 69)
Kerr's opportunism, his ambition to make his mark and be on the winning side, a consistent theme in his career. (p. 72)

This extensive catalogue of Kerr's vices and frailties is leavened by only one approving reference:

> At his peak, in the late 1950s and early 1960s, Kerr was an imposing figure ... A classical face, thick maze of white hair and roving intellectual range vested Kerr with a standout physical presence that made only more improbable his incongruously high-pitched voice. Kerr was never a narrow legal technician but a man of diverse interests and social charm.[2]

and even that is qualified by the gratuitous reference to Kerr's voice.

They continue:

> Prone to pomposity too early in life, his ability carried him to the epicentre of events and this is where he thrived.[3]

I am not sure how Kelly and Bramston know that Kerr was 'prone to pomposity too early in life', since he predated Kelly by some 33 years and Bramston by even longer. I am also curious to know what is the acceptable age for pomposity to kick in. When is it not too early? And how does it relate to one's achievements?

Much of the analysis of Kerr's character and motivations outlined in Chapter Five of *The Dismissal* is sourced to 'John Kerr, Oral History Interview, 1974-1976, ORAL TRC 440, National Library of Australia'. The authors note that, although they obtained access to it in 2013, it is not available for public access until 2041 without written permission from Kerr's executor. Of the 45 citations in Chapter Five, 25 of them are to this interview. So, for much of this character assessment of Kerr, readers are totally reliant on whatever interpretation the authors wish to inflict upon this one source, which is unavailable

---
[2] Ibid., p. 60.
[3] Ibid.

to them. This is the basis of most of the character assassination that pervades this chapter of *The Dismissal*.

I will examine the more damaging of these claims but let me begin with Kerr as an 'adroit opportunist, beneficiary of patrons' and a liking for running with the winning team. Kerr liked running with the winning team? Does anyone enjoy running with a losing team? Is that somehow more virtuous? Apart from the fact that Kerr resigned from the Labor Party, in circumstances that I will outline later, what other examples are there of Kerr abandoning one losing cause in order to jump on a winning bandwagon? Kelly and Bramston provide none. And as to him being an 'adroit opportunist' – as opposed, presumably, to being a clumsy one – the same question arises. An opportunist is defined as one who exploits immediate opportunities, especially regardless of planning or principle. So, opportunism is not necessarily reprehensible. It might be admirable, provided that principle is not abandoned. We are often advised to *carpe diem*. So, the question remains, in what circumstances did Kerr abandon his principles in order to take advantage of some opportunity to benefit himself. And again, Kelly and Bramston provide no examples. These vague characterisations are lumped together simply to prejudice the reader against Kerr and the most egregious of the three is that he was 'a beneficiary of patrons'. This suggests someone who advanced not on his own merits but by virtue of monetary support from others. To address this slight, it is necessary to know something of Sir John Kerr's life.

Kerr was born in 1914 into a working-class family in Balmain Sydney. His father, a boilermaker, was at one time a workmate of William McKell, later to become the Labor premier of NSW and finally Governor-General. The family naturally gravitated towards the Labor side of politics and became active in support of Herbert Vere Evatt (later Labor Minister and eventually Opposition Leader in the Federal Parliament, Judge of the High Court and President of the United Nations General Assembly) when he was a candidate, in 1925, for the NSW Legislative Assembly. Evatt won that election, was expelled from the

Labor Party by Premier Jack Lang, and recontested the seat as an Independent in 1927, when he won again. He sent a letter thanking all those who had actively supported him, including Kerr's father. Evatt was a barrister and had attended Fort St High School (from which many later prominent and successful Australians graduated, including Sir Garfield Barwick). The young Kerr decided he too would follow that path and this he did.

When he was at Fort St he won an essay prize donated by Evatt, the subject of which that year was 'Australia should be more enterprising in the Pacific'. That became significant in Kerr's later career, both during the war and after it. When he graduated from school, as Vice-Captain, in 1931, Kerr wanted to study law but realised that the family finances would not support such a choice. As a first step he applied for what was termed an Exhibition in Arts – this would entitle him to pay no fees. He was also awarded a bursary that would pay him eight shillings a week, but he knew that would not be enough on its own and that it would be a major struggle for the family to support him beyond that. According to Kerr, a friend, the son of a solicitor, told him it would be madness to attempt to study law under those conditions without having some legal connections. So, he hit upon the idea of seeking the advice of Evatt, who was, by then, a High Court judge. Armed with the letter Evatt had sent his father, Kerr knocked, unannounced, on Evatt's Mosman front door. Evatt's wife advised Kerr to call her husband later that night, which he did. He was invited back to the house for an interview, during which Evatt advised him that the best way would be to study Arts first and then Law, but he recognised this would not be amenable to Kerr. So, he then suggested that Kerr apply to have his Exhibition transferred from Arts to Law and, with his bursary, attempt to find articles. Kerr was doubtful about the latter course, however, Evatt then came to the rescue. According to Kerr:

> He then said, 'I would like to do something myself. I would like to give you, personally, a scholarship to enable you to do Law. I said 'That's not what I've come for.' He said, 'I have no doubt it's

not what you came for but you've got to consider your parents if you're going to do this. You're fully entitled to what I'm offering. If there had been a scholarship around you would probably have won it.' He added 'I will give you a scholarship of fifty pounds a year.' I was amazed at this offer, indeed overwhelmed, and thanked him with some emotion, but said that I would like to think about it and that I would not want it interpreted by him that I had come seeking financial help. He asked me to think it over and discuss it with my parents and take their advice. His view was that they would advise me to accept which they did. So I made a compromise. I got in touch with him again and said I would accept his scholarship for one year only until I could work things out, but he said it was, subject to performance, available for the whole course. He agreed to limit it, for the time being, to one year.[4]

In the event, Kerr kept to his word and relinquished the scholarship after the first year. And that concludes his illustrious career as a 'beneficiary of patrons', unless you include the influence that well-connected friends and mentors may have, from time to time, exerted on his behalf. The sort of influence, by the way, which has helped smooth the way for almost all successful men.

In Kerr's case, it was Evatt again who was influential in this way, offering him an associateship when he graduated – an offer which Kerr declined. Eventually, Evatt advised him to go early to the Bar and was instrumental in placing him in a set of chambers occupied exclusively by Labor lawyers.

Kerr, comparing himself to Garfield Barwick and Percy Spender, former Fort St students who were both doing very well, said of himself at this time:

> My own desire was not well worked out although I wanted to become a Labor lawyer. I was a supporter of the Labor Party; I wanted to identify myself with the Labor Party and the trade unions and for a number of years I did. This was largely due to my association and friendship with Evatt.[5]

---

[4] Kerr, *Matters for Judgement*, pp. 39-40.
[5] Ibid., p. 45.

During his time at University, Kerr became interested in Trotskyism but in his own words once he 'read beyond it' he became 'a strong anti-Stalinist social democrat'.

After some years practicing, he found that his practice was growing increasingly reliant on workers compensation cases, and he did not see this as a field of law in which he would be content to remain. In his own words:

> I believed that I was on the wrong track – not politically but professionally. Having the type of academic record I had at the Law School ... the point to which I had narrowed my activity was more and more evident to me ... I was giving up all that beckoned me in the great sweep of the Law. I rationalized this was something I was doing for the Labor Party, but came increasingly to see that I had limited excessively the legal challenge I could have been meeting.[6]

So, Kerr left his chambers and joined another that was engaged in equity law. Again, in his words:

> I wanted to go my own way politically as a Labor man, but to be freer as a barrister, to develop an all-round practice. I continued to do Labor work ... The Labor label stuck for a long time and nothing I did at that stage constituted an abandonment of the Labor Party politically.[7]

But then the war intervened. As it did for many who served, the experience broadened and modified Kerr's outlook. He was called up in April 1942 and spent the first few months of his military service as a private soldier at a base supply unit at Parkes in NSW. He was then invited, via the good offices of a friend who had recommended him, to join a small research section, headed by Alfred Conlon and established at Land Headquarters, under the command of the then Adjutant-General VPH Stantke. Possibly this was one example of Kerr being the 'beneficiary of patrons' but his 'adroit opportunism' failed him on this occasion because he declined the offer. Nonetheless, he was overruled and received orders to join the unit. It was designed to provide specialist advice to Army commanders on

---

[6] Ibid., p. 89.
[7] Ibid., p. 90.

unusual situations that might arise in the course of the war – interaction with civil authorities was part of its remit. It later morphed into the Directorate of Research and Civil Affairs reporting directly to General Blamey. One of its major areas of research was the re-establishment of civil control over Papua New Guinea after the war. There was concern that military government imposed during the war might have engendered discontent and unrest among the local population.

Kerr's involvement gradually changed from research into practical problem handling, as result of which he travelled to both England and the United States. He developed an interest in international affairs and in civil government, particularly in regard to PNG. And he developed skills in problem solving. After the end of the war, rather than return immediately to legal practice, he stayed on as Chief Instructor of the Land Headquarters School of Civil Affairs. In this role he was promoted to Colonel, although he had not volunteered for the position. He had intended to return to civilian life but, as he tells it, he was press-ganged into the job by his chief Alfred Conlon and presented with a *fait accompli*. His initial reaction was hostile but he decided on reflection to accept the job, as he believed it was an important initiative. He was demobilised in 1946 but remained at the School as it transitioned into the Australian School of Pacific Administration, a civilian institution. During his three years at the School, he was asked to organise the South Pacific Commission and was part of the Australian delegation, under HV Evatt, to the United Nations General Assembly in 1947. He flirted with idea of becoming a diplomat but in the end decided to return to the Bar, which he did at the end of 1948.

He found that he was still regarded as a Labor lawyer – although his political commitment had waned somewhat during the war years – and much of his income derived from Labor work. For example, during this time he represented Labor Minister Eddie Ward, as junior counsel, in a Royal Commission concerning allegations of corruption that had been made against Ward. Ward was exonerated.

We now come to Kerr's 'desertion' of the Labor Party. At that time there was a tension developing within the Labor movement between its Left and Right wings. Communists had begun to infiltrate the trade unions and were attempting to take them over. Kerr, who described himself at that time as 'a fairly orthodox right of centre Labor lawyer, a social democrat', was recruited by Laurie Short to assist in pushing back against the communist tide. The anti-communist forces were known as the 'industrial groups', and Kerr acted for them in a number of legal actions. His earliest involvement was in an investigation into the 1949 elections in the Federated Ironworkers Association, which Short was convinced had been rigged to allow Ernest Thornton, a communist, to become National Secretary. In 1952 that investigation culminated in a declaration that the ballot had indeed been rigged.

Kerr, as a committed anti-Stalinist, was more than willing to help and accepted many industrial group briefs. Since the Labor Party is the political arm of the trade union movement, the fear was that it too would come under the influence of communists and drift further to the Left than was compatible with its underlying principles and, I suppose more pragmatically, its electoral prospects.

Kerr took the view that the Party leadership itself was not doing enough to curb the growing influence of the communists. According to Kerr, Evatt, who was then Leader of the Opposition, was ambivalent about the struggle but he enlisted Kerr's aid to help him win the support of the industrial groups as part of his strategy to win the 1954 election against Robert Menzies. In the event, he lost that election. Evatt claimed that this loss was, at least partly, attributable to the scandal surrounding the very public defection of Soviet diplomat and spy Vladimir Petrov and his wife Evdokia. In fact, the defection played little part in the campaign. However, Evatt also blamed the right wing, now known as the Movement, for not having kept their side of the bargain. He mounted an attack on the right wing, dominated by Catholics, claiming that they themselves were trying to take over the Party for their own ends. He campaigned to have them purged from the Party.

As a result, the Movement mobilised and formed a new party, the Democratic Labor Party, under the leadership of Jack Kane. This was the great Labor split of 1954-55, which ensured the survival of the Liberal/Country government of Robert Menzies and his successors until 1972.

Kerr was invited to join the DLP but, since he regarded it as essentially a Catholic party which was at odds with his secular outlook, he declined. He also decided that, under the dominant influence of its Left wing, the Labor Party was no longer in tune with his own way of thinking and that it would remain in electoral wilderness for many years. As we now know he was quite correct in this assessment. So, he left the Labor Party, stating that this had been a liberating experience, I assume, in the sense that it resolved the increasing tension between his own emerging political outlook and his old loyalties.

But was this really a 'desertion' as Kelly and Bramston so cynically describe it? A deserter is generally regarded as someone who abandons an organization to whom he owes some particular duty. Kerr owed nothing to the Labor Party. He was not a Member of Parliament or even a party office holder. Even Labor did not regard him as a deserter. If they had, he would have been labelled a 'rat', the standard soubriquet applied to ALP deserters, and he would never have been invited to become Governor-General.

The worst that could be said about Kerr in this instance is that he preferred not running with a losing team.

Following that momentous event, Kerr devoted himself to developing his practice, accepting briefs from both sides of politics based on the degree to which they attracted him as legal questions. But he also acquired other interests. In 1960 he was elected to the Bar Council, upon which he served until his elevation to the Bench in 1966. He was involved in the Council on New Guinea Affairs, the Industrial Relations Society, the Association for Cultural Freedom, the NSW

Marriage Guidance Council and the NSW Medical Board. He helped establish the Australian Bar Association and became Vice-President of the Law Council of Australia. He was also instrumental in establishing the Law Association for Asia and the Western Pacific and became its first president. During this period he flirted with the idea of standing for Parliament, in the Liberal interest. But he never did.

In 1965, his first wife suffered a sub-arachnoid haemorrhage and was severely disabled for a number of years. Kerr then resolved to accept the next offer of a judgeship that might come his way. This happened in 1966 when Liberal Attorney General Billy Snedden, appointed him to the Commonwealth Industrial Court and the ACT Supreme Court.

At this time, he also finally accepted that the possibility of a career in politics was now over.

In 1972 he was offered, and accepted, the position of Chief Justice of the Supreme Court of New South Wales, where he remained until he became Governor-General in 1974.

So, this is a man – accomplished, industrious, highly successful and comfortable with people on both sides of the political spectrum – of whom, possibly, the worst that could be said is that he enjoyed a drink. It is hard to reconcile this figure with the duplicitous, obsequious, pompous, self-seeking, disloyal buffoon with an incongruously high-pitched voice presented to us in *The Dismissal*.

They also go into a fair amount of detail on Kerr's political aspirations. It is true that Kerr did imagine a life in politics and it's probably true that his aspirations centred on the top job. This would not be unusual among successful men. He was courted by the Liberals on a number of occasions but was not interested in State politics or the Senate, only a seat in the House of Representatives. In the end he did not make the leap. As Kelly and Bramston put it:

> In these Liberal approaches to Kerr there was a consistent pattern: proposal, dalliance and rejection. Kerr wanted to leap yet realized

it would be unwise. He had the brains but not the toughness for political life. It became the fantasy life he would never have. But the fantasy was elaborate.

'I think I could have made a good job of leadership in the sense of taking people along behind me', Kerr said. Conceding he had 'been through this many times in my own mind', Kerr identified his core defect: 'not ruthless enough'.[8]

What was the 'elaborate' fantasy life to which they refer? Did he, cigar in hand, declaim Churchillian parliamentary speeches in front of his bedroom mirror? Unfortunately, they do not elaborate other than to say that Kerr believed he would have made a good leader. I'm guessing he meant during good times, but he was realistic enough to realise he would not be able to handle the tough times, as he, in fact, conceded.

They go on to say:

> When Kerr was governor-general, Whitlam teased him, saying: 'Everyone tells me that if things had worked out right, you'd be in my job.' Kerr passed it off but then Whitlam got serious: he told Kerr he didn't have the ruthlessness for politics. It was true, yet it was a misleading truth. Whitlam never grasped that Kerr was capable of a single act of pure ruthlessness.[9]

It seems we can now add 'very occasionally ruthless' to the catalogue of Kerr's shortcomings listed above.

So according to Whitlam, ruthlessness is a necessary, even desirable, attribute in a politician. The Merriam-Webster definition of ruthless as 'having no pity, merciless or cruel'. I suspect that this is not quite what Kelly and Bramston intend to convey. What they describe as Kerr's single act of pure ruthlessness is probably best imagined as an example of 'the ends justifying the means' action. The implication is that Kerr used dishonourable tactics in achieving his end. This logic does not mandate that the end itself must be dishonourable but, to resolve that question, we need to know what Kerr's 'end' was.

---

[8] Kelly and Bramston, op.cit., p. 61.
[9] Ibid., p. 61.

Throughout *The Dismissal*, its authors consistently promote the idea that Kerr's 'end' was the dismissal of Gough Whitlam as Prime Minister. That would, of itself, be a dishonourable end. But that was not what Kerr was working towards. His 'end' was a guarantee of supply to the government before the money ran out. That was not a dishonourable end. Indeed, it was Kerr's duty to facilitate this outcome.

His means, used as a last resort, was to withdraw Whitlam's commission and to appoint Fraser as caretaker Prime Minister on the basis that he could guarantee supply. Since the probity of Kerr's actions in this respect are essentially the main topic of *The Dismissal*, aspects of this question have already been covered earlier and will also be covered in later sections of this book. I will merely, at this point, note that the withdrawal of Whitlam's commission was neither illegal nor unconstitutional.

Kelly and Bramston then recount a memory of Kerr's second wife:

> Kerr's second wife, Anne Robson had this core insight into him ... Interviewed by Paul Kelly, Robson retold a conversation she had with Kerr after World War Two: 'John said very intensely, "there is something in me that has got to come out in this country."' Robson remembered this line forty years later. But ambition and pretension would constitute a fatal chemistry in Kerr's character.[10]

We do not know the context in which Lady Kerr made her remark, because we do not have access to the source material, but I think we can assume it was not made with a derogatory intent. It seems like a perfectly unexceptional example of a young man (Kerr would have been in his early to mid-thirties) expressing his belief in his own destiny. And it is a very tenuous *segue* to the observation that 'ambition and pretension would constitute a *fatal chemistry* in Kerr's character'. What were Kerr's pretensions? What is meant by this glib, and dare I say it, pretentious psychobabble? What is a fatal chemistry in psychological terms? Are they suggesting that, having achieved the highest non-elected office in the land and finding that his

---

[10] Ibid., pp. 61-62.

ambition remained unrequited, he decided to go out in a blaze of publicity and take Whitlam with him? Mozart could have set this to music – *Don Giovanni Down Under* perhaps. Again, this is just the sort of gratuitous innuendo that permeates the whole of the book.

This theme continues:

> Kerr's true character now emerged. Faced with two opposing Labor parties he found them both repugnant. As a non-Catholic he saw the DLP as a sectarian party with an ideological obsession. As a pragmatist he had no interest in attaching himself to a minority party and cause that would doom his future career, social standing and political options. Kerr was not a man to make such a sacrifice. He wanted to be with winners. His friends had misjudged him.[11]

Being a pragmatist is not a bad thing in itself. As a pragmatist, Kerr did not abandon any principle when he left the Labor Party, since he believed they were going in the wrong direction – a direction that was ideologically an anathema to him. That is, in no way, an adverse reflection on his character. And it is hard to see how an association with the Labor Party would harm his social standing. And in what sense had he misled his friends? They continue:

> The nakedness of his turn against Labor was startling.[12]

'The nakedness of his turn'? Do they mean he didn't bother to hide that he had left Labor? Would not any other approach leave him exposed, in the hands of this pair, to a charge of being two-faced? Do they mean he then became openly and vehemently critical of Labor? Where is their evidence of that? And who was startled by this turn of events? Kerr did not 'turn against Labor'. He drifted apart from it. However:

> Kerr grasped that under Evatt the ALP had made a catastrophic blunder.[13]

So, Kerr's pragmatism was justified. Let me re-iterate that up

---

[11] Ibid., pp. 65-66.
[12] Ibid., p. 66.
[13] Ibid.

to this point Kerr had never been a candidate for election under Labor nor even a party office holder. He owed Labor nothing.

In summary:

> His rejection of the ALP was comprehensive: intellectual, self-interested and visceral.[14]

His rejection of Labor was certainly intellectual. But visceral? Merriam-Webster defines visceral as 'not intellectual, instinctive, unreasoning, dealing with crude or elemental emotions'. So, it could hardly be both intellectual *and* visceral. What Kelly and Bramston really want to convey here is that Kerr entertained a strong antipathy, even hatred, towards the Labor Party. That is one of the main planks of their case against him – that he acted not out of principle but out of animosity. There is no evidence in Kerr's history that he entertained such animosity. He maintained cordial relations with many of his erstwhile Labor associates and continued to accept briefs from Labor.

In fact, Kelly and Bramston themselves report:

> Kerr said he felt comfortable with the Liberals but could not give them his political soul. 'I would in my own heart have felt it was a kind of act of apostasy,' he said. He felt Liberal endorsement would have been 'a kind of final, definitive, irreversible abandonment' of the last vestiges of his youth ... 'I always had some reason for not doing it,' he said of the Liberal career. The 'eternal question' in the family discussions was 'whether I would or wouldn't go into politics'. But Kerr knew professional politics was not his life.[15]

Well, he certainly knew politics was not his life when he accepted elevation to the Bench. And this extract certainly gives the lie to the assertion that he harboured a 'visceral' antipathy to the ALP.

And now we come to the contribution of Sir Roden Cutler – his damning assessment that Kerr's understanding of politics was weak and that he (Cutler) often found Kerr's judgement to be

---

[14] Ibid., p. 67.
[15] Ibid., p. 68.

wrong. To fully quote Kelly and Bramston:

> As Chief Justice he would serve as lieutenant-governor during the governor's absence. But the experienced NSW governor, Sir Roden Cutler was unimpressed, saying 'to be frank, I thought his understanding of politics was weak ... I often found that his judgement was wrong.'[16]

This was in the context of Kerr being appointed Chief Justice of NSW in May 1972. In this role he would also carry out the function of Lieutenant-Governor. As Kerr put it:

> The Chief Justice is almost invariably also the Lieutenant-Governor: in the absence of the Governor it is he who replaces him and who administers the State. I became Lieutenant-Governor when Sir Leslie Herron died, and this happened at a time when the Governor was overseas. Sir Leslie had been administering the State at the time of his death and I at once took over, carrying on for a month or more until the Governor arrived back. On one or two other occasions I administered the State in the Governor's absence.[17]

Sir Leslie Herron preceded Kerr as Chief Justice but remained on as Lieutenant-Governor until his death in May 1973. So, Kerr, who resigned as Chief Justice on 27 June 1974, served in the role of Lieutenant-Governor for just over one year. In this time, he acted in Cutler's absence for a month or two initially and then 'on one or two other occasions'. This raises two questions. Was Cutler's assessment of Kerr's understanding of politics and his judgement confined to those occasions when he acted as Governor? If so, how many times, in a period of one year, would Kerr have been called upon to draw upon his understanding of politics or to exercise his judgement, in a role that was largely ceremonial? Could he really *often* have made wrong judgements? Was he really that inept? Or, alternatively, does Cutler's assessment of Kerr's shortcomings refer to his wider commitments – as Chief Justice and or Governor-General? The context of the quote above from *The Dismissal* suggests not – that Cutler's assessment was restricted to Kerr's performance in the role of Lieutenant-Governor. There were

---
[16] Ibid., p. 69.
[17] Kerr, op.cit., p. 203.

not a lot of opportunities in that role for Kerr to demonstrate his lack of political nous or judgement.

This Cutler reference is sourced, via footnote, to 'Roden Cutler, Interview with Paul Kelly, August 1995'. The use of footnotes allows a writer to provide a reference to his source material that would allow the reader to check the accuracy and/or the *bona fides* of author's claims. In this case, the source material is not readily available. Kelly is its gatekeeper and therefore the provenance of his claims is questionable.

He could have written *'Sir Roden Cutler told Paul Kelly in 1995 that he was unimpressed, saying 'to be frank, I thought his understanding of politics was weak ... I often found that his judgement was wrong'*. But that would have alerted the reader immediately that this was little more than hearsay.

In fact, there is a total of 156 such references (i.e., to personal interviews) throughout the book. But getting back to Cutler, Kelly and Bramston refer to Kelly's 1995 interview on two other occasions. Firstly, on the matter of Kerr's fear that Whitlam may dismiss him and secondly on Cutler's reaction to a Coalition proposal to advise Liberal State premiers to refuse to issue writs for any half-Senate election called by Whitlam.

But remember, Cutler was Governor of NSW, the very same position held by Sir Philip Game when he dismissed Premier Jack Lang only some forty odd years earlier. It is inconceivable that Kelly did not ask Cutler his views on the substantive issue – the actual dismissal of Whitlam. As senior State Governor, Cutler was the immediate stand-in for Kerr if he were ill or out of the country. In fact, Kerr had planned an overseas trip, which he subsequently cancelled, for the time the crisis broke. It is inconceivable that Kelly did not ask Cutler what he would have done had he been in the chair at the time. So, what might his answer have been? If Cutler had been condemnatory of Kerr, you can be sure we would have heard about it in *The Dismissal*. Even if he had been diplomatic and refused to comment, I imagine a writer as adroit as Kelly could have essayed this into appearing as implicit criticism. That suggests that Cutler might have been supportive of Kerr on this question. We just don't know. The claim that Sir Laurence Street said that 'Kerr was a vain man ... I think he wanted to go down in history as a man who made a decisive action' is another example of the same technique. The full context of the quote is unavailable, and its provenance is, therefore, questionable.

Kelly and Bramston then cover the events surrounding Kerr's appointment as Governor-General. Kerr was Whitlam's third choice. His preferred option was for Sir Paul Hasluck to remain in the position, but the poor health of Hasluck's wife prevented that. His second choice, businessman Ken Myer declined the offer.

Kerr took some time to accept, as he was still a relatively young man and in no position to retire. He extracted from Whitlam an agreement that he could serve for ten years and that he would be granted a pension. That's obviously self-interested Kerr at work here.

The authors report that Whitlam and Kerr shared a mutual regard but recount one incident that they see as significant:

> Whitlam was a guest of honour at a NSW Bench and Bar dinner with Kerr attending as lieutenant-governor. Whitlam began his speech with a joke: with Kerr sitting to Whitlam's right, the prime minister said he had observed the chief justice moving further to his right for the last twenty years. Everybody laughed, including Kerr. But Whitlam would later make too many jokes at Kerr's expense.[18]

This is another of those examples of gratuitous innuendo. The whole purpose of recounting this anecdote is to *segue* into the claim that Whitlam later made too many jokes at Kerr's expense, the implication here being that Kerr's action was, at least in part, motivated by resentment of Whitlam's jibes.

That is an unworthy implication for which there is no evidence. However, I suspect this refers to Whitlam, on a couple of occasions in the months leading up to the crisis, suggesting

---

[18] Kelly and Bramston, op.cit., p. 70.

to Kerr that the resolution could come down to a race to the Palace to see which of them would be dismissed. Whitlam later claimed he was joking, and Kerr claimed he was not. Since this is the subject of another chapter, I will deal no more with it here except to note that the clarification I have offered here would not be obvious to the general reader, who would naturally assume the interpretation that a thin-skinned Kerr was offended and motivated, at least in part, by his resentment at otherwise harmless jokes.

The chapter concludes:

> Unbeknown to Whitlam, Kerr was searching for a legacy. Given a chance he would leave his mark. That is what his second wife Anne felt. And McAuley [Kerr's long-time friend], writing after the dismissal, felt 'Kerr would enjoy the opportunity for a dramatic moment'.[19]

This goes to a strong sub-text that runs through the book, namely that Kerr was planning to politically execute Whitlam from the time he assumed the position of Governor-General, either to make his mark in history or to maliciously deprive Whitlam of the prize that Kerr himself could never win. It is never explicitly stated, because it is such a long bow, but it lurks between almost every line where it can easily be spotted by the gullible reader.

And, seeing that Kelly and Bramston chose to conclude their chapter with Professor James McAuley, and just to make my point about context, I conclude my own chapter with the same gentleman. Here is the full quote from James McAuley, included in Kerr's own book:

> I concluded that John Kerr probably would act in the way he soon after did. He would enjoy the opportunity for a grand dramatic moment; he would appreciate the opportunity, such as few Governors-General are given, to enter the history books. But he would not make his decision for these reasons, nor for any partisan reason, nor in any callous disregard of the effect his decision may have on

---

[19] Ibid., p. 73.

individuals. He would have genuinely sought to discharge the duty of his office in the light of the law and good sense.[20]

To omit the last part of that quote is unforunate to say the least.

---

[20] Kerr, op.cit., p. 153.

6

The Guiding Stars: Evatt and Barwick

Chapter Six of *The Dismissal* examines the influence of Dr H.V. Evatt and Sir Garfield Barwick on Sir John Kerr's actions in November 1975 and, in particular, his thinking regarding the reserve powers of the Governor-General.

Never ones to miss an opportunity, the authors begin the chapter with the now familiar belittling reference to Sir John:

> In John Kerr's real life as a lawyer and his fantasy life as a politician, there were two towering role models who shaped his aspirations – HV (Doc) Evatt and Sir Garfield Barwick.[1]

We have established that Kerr flirted, over a long period of time, with the idea of a political career but eventually realised he did not have the stomach for it. No doubt, from time to time, he imagined what he could achieve as Prime Minister, but it seems a long stretch to suggest he lived a *fantasy* life around this unfulfilled ambition. That suggestion is designed simply to give the impression that Kerr was so obsessed with the idea that, to some extent at least, it distorted his perception of reality. It is designed to suggest that Kerr saw his role as Governor-General as fulfillment of his political aspirations and that he brought a political dimension into his conduct of that role.

---

[1] Kelly and Bramston, *The Dismissal*, p. 74.

They tell us:

> Evatt and Barwick were ideological opposites and political rivals. Yet they had a fundamental agreement on the central issue of the 1975 crisis: they believed in the dismissal power that Kerr exercised. Both men influenced Kerr's decision – Evatt from the grave and Barwick from the High Court.[2]

That is misleading. It suggests that Kerr was not able to reach his own conclusions without 'influence'. In other words, in the absence of Evatt and Barwick he may not have made the decision he did. To begin with, Kerr's views were informed by a work that Evatt had penned some forty years earlier. At that time, he was a young lawyer and protégé of Evatt. He was in the learning phase of his career. Nonetheless, he had the intellect to evaluate Evatt's thoughts and form his own opinion, which had developed years before 1975. He did not discover his belief in the dismissal power on taking office as Governor-General.

As to Barwick influencing his decision, this is just nonsense. As I note above, Kerr's opinion was well entrenched before he had occasion to collaborate with Barwick. No doubt he believed that Barwick shared his view, but Barwick's role, as far as Kerr was concerned, was simply to provide learned support after the event. In any case, if, as suggested by Kelly and Bramston, Kerr was just itching to deploy the reserve powers, he would not have needed to be influenced by Barwick. Indeed, they later observe in this chapter:

> He had drawn the High Court into his net. It was Kerr who took the initiative, not Barwick. It was Kerr who expressed concern about the situation, not Barwick. It was Kerr who said he wanted to get Barwick's advice rather than Barwick volunteering his own advice. After the dismissal, Whitlam was obsessed with the idea that Barwick had put the steel into Kerr. But this view doesn't fit the evidence.[3]

The above passage refers to a conversation between Kerr and Barwick at a dinner in September 1975, some weeks before the

---

[2] Ibid.
[3] Ibid., p. 84.

Senate actually denied supply, but when it was clear a crisis could develop. Kerr asked Barwick if he would be prepared to advise him should the need arise. Barwick temporised, replying that it would depend on what was asked and the circumstances applying at the time. He left the door open for Kerr to consult him. This will be covered in more detail later but for now it suffices to prove that not even Kelly and Bramston really believe Kerr was 'influenced' by Barwick.

We are then told that:

> In retrospect, Whitlam's effort in 1975 to persuade Kerr that the reserve powers of the Crown were obsolete was a doomed project. How could Whitlam compete against the combined forces of Evatt and Barwick who had dominated Kerr's life ... Kerr knew the reserve powers existed and he was as certain about this as anything in his legal life.[4]

This suggests that a dogmatic Kerr was impervious to any arguments from Whitlam against the existence of the reserve powers. But, in fact, Whitlam never engaged Kerr personally on this topic. In a later chapter, titled 'Whitlam's Blunders', Kelly and Bramston make it clear that Whitlam's only attempt at persuasion was to insist publicly on a number of occasions that the Governor-General *must* act upon his advice. In an interview with Sir Paul Hasluck in 1985, former Whitlam Minister, Clyde Cameron, recounted an incident at an Executive Council meeting in 1974, in which Kerr broached the subject of the reserve powers in connection with a double dissolution. According to Cameron, Whitlam rebuffed Kerr and thereafter refused to countenance any discussion on this topic:

> John Kerr raised this with Gough at an executive council meeting when I was appointed as Minister for Science. But Gough didn't want to hear about it. But it seemed to me that Kerr wanted to discuss with Gough the whole question of the relationship between the Governor-General and the Prime Minister on the subject of double dissolution. Because, at that time, Withers and others were already threatening to refuse supply. And Gough, foolishly, in my

---

[4] Ibid., p. 75.

opinion, rejected, or turned away from the opportunity which was being offered to him to discuss the matter with Kerr. And, it seemed as though Gough never wanted to discuss anything that might be unpalatable to him. He liked to only talk about the things that he believed were nice to talk about. He didn't want to face reality if it was unpleasant.[5]

Throughout *The Dismissal*, the authors hammer the point that Kerr failed to consult with Whitlam. This may be the reason. Whitlam had made it quite clear, very early in the piece, that he would be impervious to Kerr's approaches.

Later they note that Evatt and Barwick, on opposite sides of the political fence had been combatants in the great ideological struggles of the 1950s and:

> By contrast, the reserve powers seemed an abstract, even arcane, issue. They transcended contemporary debates and were irrelevant to the raging ideological conflicts of the age.
>
> The reserve powers derive from the medieval Crown and are deemed to be those discretions that still reside with the Crown after the transfer of its powers to the parliament, executive and judiciary within a system of democratic constitutional monarchy.[6]

This might be an appropriate point to diverge from the discourse in *The Dismissal* and examine the reserve powers. As I outlined in my Introduction, the reserve powers are:

> The power to dissolve (or refuse to dissolve) the House of Representatives (section 5)
>
> The power to dissolve Parliament on the occasion of a deadlock (section 57)
>
> The power to withhold assent to bills (section 58)
>
> The power to appoint (or dismiss) ministers (section 64)

---

[5] 'Reminiscential Conversations between Rt Hon Sir Paul Hasluck and the Hon Clyde Cameron', 1985, https://nla.gov.au/nla.obj-215705852/listen/7-2551~7-2607
[6] Kelly and Bramston, op.cit., p. 76.

The power to dismiss, or as I prefer to term it 'withdraw the commission of', a Prime Minister is implicit in the wording of Section 64 which states:

> The Governor-General may appoint officers to administer such departments of State of the Commonwealth as the Governor-General in Council may establish.
>
> *Such officers shall hold office at the pleasure of the Governor-General.* (emphasis added)

Since these reserve powers are specified in the Constitution, their existence can hardly be doubted. What is at issue is if, and when, they should be invoked.

The first point to make here is that they do not derive from the medieval Crown. Kelly and Bramston make that claim to bolster their suggestion that the powers are arcane (secret) and, flowing from that, therefore their use is somehow undemocratic. But as can be seen from the above, the first two are uncontroversial and are employed regularly. Although they refer repeatedly to the reserve powers, since they are at the heart of the matter, Kelly and Bramston never define what they are, as I have done above. I believe this omission was deliberate, aimed at fostering the impression in the mind of the unschooled reader that the reserve powers consist of the power dismiss a popularly elected government and some other equally undemocratic and archaic relics of the distant past.

In fact, the powers derive, not from the medieval Crown, but from the Glorious Revolution of 1688, which finally established the supremacy of Parliament. This was a step-change, a watershed moment in which Parliament rewrote the relationship between itself and the Crown in the 1689 Bill of Rights, which removed specific powers from the Crown acting alone and established the doctrine of Parliamentary Supremacy. On that basis Parliament offered the throne to William and Mary of Orange, to rule jointly. Over the subsequent years the power of the monarch was further curtailed by Acts of Parliament, but what we now know as the reserve powers were never abolished by legislation in the United Kingdom, as they could have been at any time. In 1901 they were explicitly written into our Constitution. This could hardly have been done with the proviso that they never be used.

Of interest is the power to withhold assent from a bill. I believe this is regarded by some authorities as defunct, since the last time it was used in Britain was in 1708 when Queen Anne refused assent to the Scottish Militia Bill. But this was done on the advice of her Ministers. It could therefore be argued that this power is subject to the convention that the Crown always acts on the advice of its Ministers. Professor Greg Taylor, writing in the Australian Law Review in 2007, observed:

> It seems clear that the Queen would now be breaching a convention of the British Constitution if she did so at least without, or contrary to, ministerial advice, always assuming that there were no highly exceptional circumstances involving threats to democracy itself which were not susceptible of correction at a later election.
> In modern times, there is 'nothing to be said for a power to refuse assent to a Bill because the [Crown] thinks it wrong' (quote from Sir Ivor Jennings).[7]

I believe this is an important power and should be unconstrained by a convention that the Crown must act on the advice of its Ministers. In fact, what would be the point of having reserve powers if they were to be so constrained? And why would such a power be *written* into our Constitution without specifying such a restriction unless it were intended that the Governor-General had some discretion in the decision? In fact, that is exactly what the Constitution says:

> When a proposed law passed by both Houses of the Parliament is presented to the Governor General for the Queen's assent, he shall declare, *according to his discretion*, but subject to this Constitution, that he assents in the Queen's name, or that he withholds assent, or that he reserves the law for the Queen's pleasure. (emphasis added)

To add weight to my contention, Section 59 of the Constitution states:

---

[7] G. Taylor, 'Two Refusals of Royal Assent in Victoria', *Sydney Law Review*, 2007, p. 1.

> The Queen may disallow any law within one year from the Governor-General's assent, and such disallowance on being made known by the Governor-General by speech or message to each of the Houses of Parliament, or by proclamation, shall annul the law from the day when the disallowance is so made known.

That clearly countenances the idea that the Crown may, effectively, refuse assent contrary to the advice of the Ministers. And this discretion (to act against the advice of Ministers) in the case of this particular power, must clearly extend to that of appointing and removing Ministers.

Actually, I believe Section 59 no longer has a place in our Constitution and it amazes me that it has not already been removed.

Professor Taylor concedes that the assent power can be used, without Ministerial advice, in highly exceptional circumstances. But Sir Ivor Jennings' caveat, written in 1959, that 'modern times' would render its use invalid, might have been overtaken by events since modern times now are very fraught with threats to democracy. Governments, which are comprised of political parties, are now very susceptible to shallow and specious concepts stridently promoted by well-funded activists on social media and to rent-seeking multi-national corporations. I can easily envisage a bill that might make it through both Houses and be accepted in the short term by a gullible or supine public yet be anathema to the basic principles that underpin our democracy. Let me give one example. It has recently been suggested that the law in criminal sexual assault cases be amended to lower the burden of proof to that of civil matters i.e., balance of probabilities. This is because it is so difficult to establish guilt in such cases. The problem with this proposal, is that by the same token, it is easy to manufacture a spurious case. This would undermine one of the central tenets of our criminal justice system and, indeed, our democracy – equality before the law. I would like to think that should such a bill come before the Governor-General, he would have the courage to refuse assent. Another example, of course, is the constant attacks on free speech that 'modern times' have delivered us. Current British laws and police practice on 'hate speech' are an alarming pointer. And closer to home, the possibility that a government might seek to legislate to extend its term of office or indefinitely suspend civil liberties in response to, say, a pandemic, cannot be dismissed out of hand. Of course, my hypothetical Governor-General who took such action would run the risk of being recalled. However, he would have made a stand on principle and that alone may give a government pause.

I have digressed somewhat, but the point of the above diversion is that, given the opprobrium heaped upon Sir John Kerr, not least by Kelly and Bramston, it is highly unlikely that any Governor-General will feel either entitled or courageous enough to exercise the discretion that he/she undoubtedly has. I would like to help correct that situation.

Kelly and Bramston note that Evatt 'concluded that the powers, including the dismissal power, did exist' and:

> This position was contrary to that adopted by Whitlam and Attorney-General Kep Enderby during the crisis. Their view reflected that of British Prime Minister Herbert Asquith during the 1909-11 crisis, when Asquith, in Evatt's words, 'subscribed to the Whig view of the Constitution'. Asked by Paul Kelly in 1995, twenty years after the dismissal, whether he believed in the reserve powers an unforgiving Whitlam gave an emphatic answer: 'No'.[8]

Well, he would say that, wouldn't he? Two points here. Firstly, the 1909-11 crisis occurred in Britain and the Constitution referred to is the British Constitution. It is different to ours, which leads into the second point that, despite Whitlam's emphatic answer, he was quite wrong, as I have shown above. They continue:

> In his memoir of the crisis, Whitlam elaborated: 'It is absurd to suggest that the Governor-General is exercising in the Queen's name powers which she does not possess and would not presume to invoke'. This was an intellectual and power contest that Whitlam lost.[9]

---

[8] Kelly and Bramston, op.cit., p. 77.
[9] Ibid.

Time for another digression. To set the scene let me observe that the Queen of England and the Queen of Australia are the same person, but they are not the same political entity. As we have seen, the powers do exist. But it *is* true to say that the Queen would not invoke them. In theory, the Queen of Australia does have power, by virtue of our Constitution, that the Queen of England may not have (or may be constrained by convention from exercising) and it is simplistic to imagine she would necessarily act the same way in Australia as she would in England. Conventions are always trumped by statute law and in Australia the reserve powers are legislated. In Australia, the Queen is one half of a symbiotic pair, analogous to the Holy Trinity. Together, she and the Governor-General comprise an entity that we might think of as the Crown. The Governor-General does the hands-on work, while the Monarch is the continuing link to the history, customs and principles that underpin our democracy – a heritage that belongs not just to Great Britain but to all of us who live under a Westminster system. In her role as Queen of Australia, Her Majesty is not so much a ruler as a custodian of that heritage. You might think of her as the constitutional conscience of the Governor-General. It is the Crown that has the power, and it is exercised by the Governor-General.

As an aside, may I venture into the vexed question of the so-called Australian Republic. Much of the debate surrounding this question centres on who is our Head of State. The Australian Republican Movement says it is the Queen. Australians for a Constitutional Monarchy says it is the Governor-General. Both are partly right but it is a pointless argument. In my view, it is that entity I have described above – the Crown – that is our Head of State. On some occasions, the Head of State manifests itself in the person of the Queen. On others, it's the Governor-General.

Essentially, what the ARM wants is the removal of the Monarch as the symbolic element of this entity. Their argument is that it is inappropriate for us to swear allegiance to a foreign citizen. That is not an unreasonable proposition – many people will agree with it. I did myself, at one stage. But the ARM does itself no favours with its rhetorical over-reach and the absurdly complicated model it has devised to bring about what is, or should be, an essentially cosmetic change – akin to removing the plush velvet drapes room the living room and leaving the windows unadorned.

Continuing, let me say, at this point, I don't blame Whitlam for being aggrieved. Having won a handsome victory in 1972 and been forced to the polls by the Senate in 1974, I can understand he would have been incensed to have to go through it all again in 1975. From my own perspective, I voted for Labor in 1974, not being impressed with Opposition Leader Billy Snedden, and believing that Whitlam had not been given a fair go. However, by 1975 I was appalled at the incompetence of the Whitlam government and applauded Sir John Kerr heartily when he gave us the chance to despatch that motley crew into political oblivion.

Evatt not only believed the reserve powers exist but also that they had value, as Kelly and Bramston observe:

> In his book Evatt said: 'What may fairly be called the Whig view of the Monarchy, whatever validity it is thought to have in point of theory, is not true in point of fact.' Evatt attacked the theory in saying that it sought 'to reduce the power of the Monarch to a nullity in those very times of great crisis when his intervention alone might save the country from disaster'. Evatt said the historical experience revealed 'an immense amount of sheer uncertainty and confusion' surrounding the powers and, as a consequence, he proposed their codification in the form of rules of law.[10]

Whether Evatt would have thought his former protégé had used the powers appropriately, or that this was a great crisis, is a matter of conjecture. Possibly not, but the point is, he believed they existed, they should be used when necessary and that the Governor-General has his own discretion in exercising them.

Earlier, Kelly and Bramston assert:

---

[10] Ibid.

> Evatt wrote as a constitutional scholar and a social democrat worried about the implications for reforming Labor governments.[11]

That assertion gives the impression that Evatt foresaw, and would have deplored, what might happen in 1975. That he was worried about the possibility of an unscrupulous Governor-General frustrating the will of the people for political reasons. If true, it would undermine the reliance that Kerr put in Evatt's work in justifying his decision. But is it true? Was Evatt worried specifically about the implications for 'reforming Labor governments'?

If Evatt expressed such concern, we would expect to find it in Chapter One of *The King and His Dominion Governors* – 'The General Problem with the Reserve Powers of the Crown'. It seems clear from the thrust of this chapter that Evatt's sole concern, and the whole point of his book, is that the uncertain nature of the reserve powers renders their use problematical and inevitably subject to controversy and bitterness. He did not wish to see them eliminated but codified.

In this chapter he does advert to the controversial commissioning in 1931, by King George V, of Ramsay McDonald as Prime Minister despite him having lost the confidence of his Parliamentary party. In this case, McDonald, one of the founders of the Labour Party, headed a minority government with the support of Lloyd George's Liberals. After an internal falling out with some of his senior Cabinet colleagues over proposed drastic public spending cuts, McDonald submitted his resignation but was persuaded by the King to form a coalition government with the Conservatives and the Liberals. Presumably, the King regarded the Great Depression as an 'extraordinary circumstance' which required a 'government of national unity'. And indeed, it was called the National Government. McDonald was expelled from the Labour Party as a result. I have cited this case at some length because Evatt's coverage of it attests to the fact that he was writing as a constitutional scholar, *not* a partisan political player:

---

[11] Ibid., p. 76.

According to Laski, the action taken was made possible through the fact that the commission to form a Ministry proceeded from the King to his Prime Minister, and the result was to nullify the wishes of the great majority of the Cabinet, of the Parliamentary party behind the Cabinet and of the party supporters in the electorate. The point which is noteworthy at present is not at all the particular action taken, but the fact that the undefined content of the conventions of the Constitution rendered it possible. Mr McDonald, according to Laski, became the King's personal nominee for the role of Prime Minister, and the precedent was regarded by Mr Leonard Woolf as one which: 'might be developed so that the Crown could be used to break down the democratic system of party government, and to introduce ... a system not materially different from that of a dictatorship.'

That observers so acute as Laski and Woolf, albeit opponents of Mr McDonald, consider it not impossible that 'theories of constitutional form will be adjusted overnight to suit the interests of conservatism', seems to show that, in the interest both of the Monarch and his people, the correct relationship between the Crown and its Ministers should be determined by definite rules which will make it impossible to impute the slightest unfairness or favouritism to the exercise of any legal prerogative.[12]

The import of the italicised text i.e., that Evatt was not concerned with political implications, is strengthened by the fact that he did not include detailed coverage of this incident in the body of his book.

As an aside, it seems to me that codification of the reserve powers is likely to emasculate them. They are designed to cover unforeseen eventualities – those which, by their very nature, are not able to be covered in the Constitution itself. Much of the 'sound and fury' generated in the 1975 crisis came from what was claimed, on both sides, to be breaches of convention. Since conventions arise informally over a period of time, and are generally intended to manage unforeseen constitutional anomalies, the way in which the reserve powers should deal

---

[12] H. V. Evatt, (1967). *The king and his dominion governors: a study of the reserve powers of the Crown in Great Britain and the dominions;.* London : Cass, p. 11.

with breaches of them cannot be anticipated.

Kelly and Bramston continue:

> [Kerr] saw the practical use of the dismissal power, recognised it could protect institutions and realised its application would always be contentious.[13]

The above extract is significant in two ways. Firstly, the authors implicitly recognise that the 'dismissal' power does exist and that it can be used when necessary. Secondly it makes clear that Kerr knew there would be adverse consequences for him if he exercised that option. It calls into question the assertion, repeated throughout the book, that Kerr acted out of self-interest.

Hopefully, the above examination puts to bed the notion that a) the reserve powers do not exist and that b) in any case, they should never be used. If that is accepted, then the only accusation that Kerr need answer is whether he exercised the powers appropriately in the particular circumstances pertaining at the time. Or, more precisely, given that there is an element of judgement involved, did he act in good faith? Kelly and Bramston say not and have gone out of their way to amass a mountain of circumstantial evidence against Kerr, much of which I have already exposed.

But moving on:

> In an extraordinary revelation, Kerr's friend Sir Anthony Mason said that during their discussions about the offer of appointment, Kerr 'thought there would be opportunities to contribute to policy issues and he referred to the Reserve Powers and the possibility that an occasion could arise for their exercise'. Mason said he didn't interpret Kerr's remark as a 'prediction' but more of 'an argument that I was underestimating the importance of the office of Governor-General'.[14]

It is good that they included Mason's caveat that he did not believe that Kerr was actually planning on using the reserve

---

[13] Kelly and Bramston, op.cit., p. 77.
[14] Ibid., p. 78.

powers before he even took up the appointment. But clearly, they don't buy it, since, as I have already pointed out it is a major theme of the early chapters of *The Dismissal*. Mason's point seems perfectly valid to me.

They continue:

> It was a remarkable situation. Not only was Kerr convinced the reserve powers were real, but he was updating himself on their application before taking office and telling his intimate Mason the possibility of their use could not be ruled out. Whitlam would have been astonished had he known. In truth, given Kerr's history, he was about the last person in Australia likely to be persuaded by a headstrong prime minister that the reserve powers no longer existed.[15]

Why was it a remarkable situation? The reserve powers do exist, and their use cannot be ruled out. Keep in mind here that the reserve powers are not just the power to dismiss a Prime Minister, but they include provisions to dissolve Parliament that are regularly employed. But the circumstances surrounding their use vary and the Governor-General has the power to, for example, refuse advice for a dissolution. Would it be remarkable that an incoming Governor-General, even one as well versed in the reserve powers as Kerr, might want to canvass with a friend the use of these powers, given that the political circumstances of the time made their use a distinct possibility? To suggest that because Kerr 'could not rule out the possibility' of the use of the reserve powers, he was already planning to dismiss Whitlam, is a drawing very long bow indeed.

Further on this theme:

> Whitlam had never foreseen the problem. Why would he? For Whitlam, if the thought had ever crossed his mind, the notion that he should assess the new governor-general's attitude towards the reserve powers would have been fantastic nonsense. Whitlam did not think about the reserve powers because he assumed, like many Labor lawyers, politicians and journalists, that they were anachronisms, not just outdated but probably extinguished in the same way that property franchise or denial of female suffrage had been

---
[15] Ibid.

extinguished.[16]

As an example of the authors sophistry, that takes some beating. If the reserve powers had been extinguished *in the same way that* property franchise or denial of female suffrage had, then Whitlam, many Labor lawyers, politicians and journalists would not need to assume as much. They could simply cite the relevant legislation – of which there is none. If Kelly and Bramston really mean that Whitlam only regarded the dismissal power as anachronistic, and probably extinguished, then he would have been a particularly obtuse political operative, since, as we know the power had been last used, by Governor Philip Game, within Whitlam's lifetime. It is absurd to suggest a power – one that was only intended to be used in rare circumstances – would become moribund because it had not been invoked for a mere forty years.

Kelly and Bramston then nail their reserve power denialism to the mast:

> Kerr, in fact, was an unfortunate choice for Whitlam in Yarralumla. A military man, with a sense of hierarchy, uninterested in second-guessing government legal advice would have been ideal.[17]

A cipher, in other words. Precisely what Kerr saw himself not to be. If the reserve powers are to serve their purpose (to protect the Constitution), then the ideal Governor-General is one who thoroughly understand them and is prepared to invoke them when necessary. It is not the Governor-General's role to mould himself to the ideology and beliefs of the Prime Minister.

We next hear how after Kerr had become estranged from Evatt, he turned to Barwick as his new 'guiding star'. Barwick was a legal powerhouse, who had built a substantial reputation as a barrister, a career which ended when he ran successfully for the Liberal Party in the seat of Parramatta. He quickly became Attorney-General and then Minister for External Relations. Following the 1964 retirement, as Chief Justice of the High

---

[16] Ibid., pp. 78-79.
[17] Ibid., p. 79.

Court, of Sir Owen Dixon, Barwick was appointed to replace him. Kelly and Bramston's characterisation of Barwick as Kerr's 'guiding star' is a bit of an overreach as this passage, quoting Kerr, makes clear:

> In the end Kerr was explicit: Barwick was the man he wanted to follow. Kerr had worked with Barwick as attorney-general and had been briefed by him. After Barwick went to the High Court, Kerr said, 'I continued my association with him.' These were different men with different personalities. 'His style had, from the beginning, not been mine,' Kerr said. But over time he viewed Barwick 'more sympathetically' and 'occasionally' they would visit one another. 'I enjoyed his company, anyway,' Kerr said. 'I always held him in high esteem,' Kerr said that 'in a very real sense when I lost Evatt as a person whose path to follow ... in many ways I adopted Barwick as a kind of pattern. Everything that he did I, in due course, did.' Barwick was the model.[18]

The sense I get from this is that Kerr admired Barwick but was in no way in awe of him nor consider himself to be an acolyte. He was not operating under any undue influence from Barwick.

And here is a bit more over-reach:

> As governor-general, Kerr enjoyed a bonus: Barwick as Chief Justice. In any crisis his instinct was to mobilise Barwick on his behalf. Kerr knew it would be a mistake to leave Barwick alone. He was too dangerous to be ignored. Kerr instinctively grasped he needed Barwick with him. And if he had Barwick in any crisis, he had the prestige of the High Court.[19]

We don't know what Barwick's predecessor as Chief Justice, Sir Owen Dixon, would have thought about the events of 1975, since he died in 1972. But we do know that Barwick's successor, Sir Harry Gibbs, agreed with Kerr's actions, as did Gibbs' successor Sir Anthony Mason. So perhaps Barwick was not an especially fortuitous 'bonus'. And Barwick 'was too dangerous to be ignored'? What are they suggesting a malevolent Barwick might have done had he not been consulted by Kerr? I have

---

[18] Ibid., p. 81.
[19] Ibid.

covered the propriety of Kerr's action in seeking advice from Barwick in Chapter Four. But this seems to go further than that. It suggests that Kerr and Barwick formed some sort of cabal to remove Whitlam. And that, had Kerr proposed some other resolution, Barwick might have acted in some way against him. That is a monstrous suggestion and unsupported by any evidence.

As part of their subliminal message that Kerr was planning on dismissing Whitlam right from the time he took office, Kelly and Bramston find another piece of vital evidence:

> Once in office, Kerr's fascination with the reserve powers was further revealed when he took the initiative for the Australian National University to conduct a seminar on the subject. In March 1975, long before there was a crisis, Kerr approached the acting vice-chancellor, Noel Dunbar, with an unusual request. He wanted 'a group organised within the university' to meet with him to 'discuss the constitutional position and powers of the Governor-General'.
>
> Mason, pro-chancellor of the ANU, played a key role in organising this group. He identified participants to Kerr after consulting with professors Geoffrey Sawyer and Leslie Zines. Mason told Kerr that, as discussions could involve 'important questions which may sooner or later come before the High Court for decision' he would limit his attendance to just the initial meeting. But Mason wasn't going to miss out. 'On the other hand, as Pro-Chancellor I am anxious to ensure that the university makes a comprehensive contribution to the discussions which you have initiated,' he wrote Kerr.[20]

'Fascination' might be putting it rather too strongly. Since the reserve powers are a fundamental tool of the Governor-General – the source of any independent action he may take in the role – it would seem natural that, despite his own extensive knowledge of them, he would want to explore a range of opinion. After all, his consideration of the reserve powers to this date had been academic only. That would seem to me to be the action of a conscientious man embarking upon a new endeavour. And it is not clear to me why this request would be 'unusual', other

---

[20] Ibid., p. 82.

than by virtue of the fact that it may not have happened before. I suspect that Kelly and Bramston's gratuitous use of the word 'unusual' is meant to convey 'suspicious' or 'sinister'.

The first two meetings were held on 2 and 10 September but after that, as Kelly and Bramston report: 'The university became uneasy about the talks. "It soon became evident that the course of politics was moving in the direction of crisis," Sawyer wrote in a note. "Sir John Kerr gracefully agreed to ceasing our tutorials".'[21]

It seems that views of the participants in that group, on the existence and extent of the reserve powers, varied.

Kelly and Bramston quote the thoughts of one observer who was not a participant, now Professor Geoffrey Lindell of Adelaide University Law School, but then a senior lecturer at ANU:

> Geoffrey Lindell, then a senior lecturer, was aware of the meetings. He recalled, 'I was mildly surprised that so early in his term Sir John sought guidance on the powers of the Governor-General given that the office was largely ceremonial subject to the existence of the reserve powers which could and should only be used in exceptional circumstance.'[22]

Here Lindell at least acknowledges that the powers exist and can and should be used, albeit in exceptional circumstances. But why would he be surprised that Kerr would seek to inform himself 'so early in his term'? Would it have been better for Kerr to wait until a crisis developed before he bothered to update himself? In fact, given the political circumstances – a headstrong government re-elected after a double dissolution with a reduced majority and a failure to gain control of the Senate – it would take a particularly incurious Governor-General not to recognise the potential for a political crisis to arise.

Despite claims that Kerr was 'fascinated' and 'obsessed' with the reserve powers (of which they provide no evidence) it is

---

[21] Ibid., p. 83.
[22] Ibid., p. 81.

likely that Kerr didn't think much about them at all since his younger days. In what context did he develop this 'obsession'? During his war years? In conducting his busy practice – in equity, not constitutional law? In legal seminars? As a judge on first the Federal Industrial Court and then as Chief Justice of the NSW Supreme Court? Kerr had a long-time interest and active involvement in the emergence of post-colonial Pacific nations. He certainly revisited the subject of reserve powers in the context of his contribution towards the development of a constitution for Papua/New Guinea. That hardly qualifies as obsessive.

But, given that he did have a degree of knowledge that most occupants of the office would not have had, it would seem natural that he would want to brush up his understanding, with the assistance of a coterie of current legal scholars. It is certainly true that he anticipated the possibility that he might have to employ the powers. And the seminar was not just about dismissal, but all the powers. One of them is the power to refuse a dissolution. And that is one, the use of which could be quite likely.

Kelly and Bramston provide evidence of this:

> [Dennis] Pearce, who recalls attending at least one meeting, describes what took place. 'We chatted informally about John Kerr's powers as Governor-General. He was very interested to know what we all thought. He gave no indication of what he was thinking. He mainly listened.' Pearce says it is likely the issue of dismissal was discussed. 'He wanted to canvass the extent and scope of the reserve powers. I am sure Jack Lang's dismissal would have come up, as it inevitably did in discussions about the reserve powers. I don't think any of us were even considering the possibility of dismissal of Whitlam at that time.'[23]

The emphasis, in recounting this incident, on the dismissal power, is simply *post hoc* cognitive bias. Pearce said it was only likely that dismissal came up. So, it can hardly have been a dominant theme. And the fact that Kerr mainly only listened,

---
[23] Ibid., pp. 82-83.

suggests he was not there to drum up support for his own preordained views on the powers.

We now return to the conversation, adverted to earlier in this chapter, in which Kerr sounded Barwick out about his willingness to provide advice should the need arise. As we know, Barwick temporised and left the door open. They continue:

> The reality is that Kerr, given not just his belief but his obsession with the reserve powers – and that was a rare obsession in those days – was virtually the most unsuitable person in Australia to appoint as governor-general given Whitlam's viewpoint. It is tempting to see the dismissal as Kerr engaging in an act of intellectual homage to those patrons he honoured: Evatt and Barwick.[24]

There's that 'obsession' again. And this time 'rare'. Was Professor (later Sir) Zelman Cowan, Kerr's successor as Governor-General, also being obsessive when he wrote the foreword to the second edition of *The King and His Dominion Governors* in 1967, a mere eight years earlier? But other than that, this passage is breathtaking in its asininity. The reserve powers do not owe their existence to the viewpoint of any particular Prime Minister. Are they suggesting the choice of Governor-General, and the exercise of discretionary powers that he undoubtedly has, should be governed by the attitude of one particular person towards those powers? In hindsight, it may well have been in Whitlam's personal interest to have appointed someone who would act as a rubber stamp, but that would not have been in the interest of the nation as a whole. But that's not the worst of it. In this passage, Kelly and Bramston comes as close as they get to saying that Kerr engineered the whole thing. 'An act of intellectual homage' indeed. That is an outrageous suggestion and their use of the phrase 'tempting to see' implies that it is just a rhetorical device – that they themselves don't really believe it. But they are clearly inviting their reader to do so.

One final word about the reserve power to withdraw the

---

[24] Ibid., p. 84.

commission of a Prime Minister, or any Minister for that matter. It is without doubt that the power currently exists, because it was last exercised in 1975 and, since then, not one attempt has been made to amend the Constitution to eliminate this possibility. Not even in the sound and fury of the immediate aftermath of the crisis. And if it exists now, by a form of reverse logic, it must have existed when Kerr exercised it.

7

Fraser Strikes, Whitlam Resists

If there was a villain in the 1975 crisis, and setting aside political allegiances, it would have to be Malcolm Fraser.

So, after six chapters of *The Dismissal* devoted to demonizing Sir John Kerr, we finally get to Fraser. And to be fair, Kelly and Bramston don't spare Fraser his share of criticism. But they are also content to spread the blame around a little, noting that Fraser was bolstered by the opportunism of the Liberal and Country Party machines. They begin:

> It was Fraser who initiated the crisis by trying to force a late 1975 general election. In an act of self-righteousness and self-interest, Fraser convinced himself that the Whitlam government had forfeited its right to govern and had to be terminated ... The paradox of Fraser was his simultaneous dedication to high principle and predilection for political violence ... He decided his mission was to save the nation and that it must be saved at once. Only a ruthless leader of high-minded principle could justify the inflamed public mood, social divisions and throttling of the government institutions that Fraser triggered. The legacy became a permanent shadow on his prime ministership.[1]

All that is true, but the cosy juxtaposition of 'high-minded principle' and 'ruthlessness' jars somewhat. And it is at odds with Fraser's later conduct, which could hardly be described as principled.

---

[1] Kelly and Bramston, *The Dismissal*, p. 86.

They continue:

> Fraser's mechanism was to use the Senate's power to block bills appropriating funds for the ordinary services of government, thereby blackmailing Whitlam into an election. Such a method had not been implemented since Federation. Fraser used a constitutionally valid Senate power over money bills to smash an established convention, assert the Senate's right to declare no-confidence in a government, terminate the House of Representatives term and force an election at a time of his choosing.[2]

That is mostly true. Whether there was an 'established convention' that would prevent the Senate from blocking supply is arguable. The word convention has many meanings. In this context, the Merriam-Webster dictionary entry: 'a general agreement about basic principles or procedures', would seem to the most apt. Constitutionally, conventions are a very useful tool to facilitate government operations in situations where there is some statutory ambiguity. They are not engineered from scratch – they evolve as circumstances change and unforeseen ambiguities manifest themselves. The only conventions that would make sense in Australia would be those that evolved in Australia. Whatever conventions existed governing the power of an upper house over a lower house, *vis-a-vis* money bills, in any other Westminster system, were extinguished in Australia from the moment the Constitution, that came into force in 1901, specifically gave the Senate the power to reject money bills.

So, was there an *established* convention that the Senate never blocks supply? Sir John Kerr himself and most of the commentariat of the time thought so. But is that true? It seems to me that a convention doesn't exist merely because people claim or believe it does. For a convention to have any substance there would have to be at least one instance of that convention working. In this case, an occasion where an opposition deliberately declined to block supply when it had the opportunity and motivation to do so. From my reading, up until, 1975, there were only four occasions when the governing party,

---

[2] Ibid., p. 87.

and its allies, did not have control of the Senate. Two of these were during the early tumultuous years of the new Parliament (up to 1914), when the Senate was controlled by Protectionist Party of Alfred Deakin, who were allied with Labor against the Free Trade Party and Commonwealth Liberal Party. During this period, the Free Trade Party controlled the government benches for one single year term and the Commonwealth Liberals for two single year terms, in which they faced a hostile Senate. In 1914, the Labor majority in the Senate rejected a government bill such that it satisfied the provisions of Section 57 of the Constitution, and the Prime Minister, Joseph Cook, advised a double dissolution, which was granted and, as a result of which Labor gained control of both Houses. This was not a money bill. It is difficult to imagine that a meaningful convention regarding blocking of supply could have emerged in this confused period, so soon after Federation, and before the political landscape resolved itself into the two-party system that dominated until 1975.

So, let's look at the period between 1914 and 1975. During this period, only two governments faced a hostile Senate – the Scullin Labor government from October 1929 to October 1932, and the Menzies government elected in December 1949. Scullin's legislative agenda in response to the Great Depression, based on Keynesian stimulus spending, was defeated by the Opposition but there is no indication supply was ever threatened. But just because the Opposition did not choose to block supply in this situation, does not establish a convention. It is possible that the Opposition, at this stage of the Great Depression, decided the Opposition benches were more comfortable than the Treasury benches. They might have thought 'let's sit this one out'.

As to 1951, at this time Labor had control of the Senate and amended the Commonwealth Bank Bill introduced in March 1950 and passed by the House in May 1950. The government rejected the amendment and re-presented the original bill in the House where it again passed and was again sent to the Senate. The Senate then referred it to sub-committee in March 1951 upon which Prime Minister Menzies advised Governor-

General, Sir William McKell, to grant a double-dissolution. McKell agreed and at the subsequent election the government was returned with a majority in the Senate. In this instance the Opposition only had control of the Senate for one year. So, again it is difficult to see how a meaningful convention could have been established in this period.

There is no evidence that, in any of the situations listed above, the Opposition seriously contemplated blocking supply but then backed away as a matter of principle.

In any case, statute law must always trump convention, and it is statute law to which Sir John Kerr had to conform. Even if there had been a convention, Fraser's action was constitutionally valid.

Furthermore, what Kelly and Bramston don't tell you is that Labor itself did not believe such a convention existed. I quote from Kerr:

> I recall the well-known statements made in Parliament by Mr Whitlam and Senator Murphy, confirming the Senate's powers and referred to constantly during the October-November period.
>
> Mr Whitlam, in the House, on 12 June 1970 said:
>
>> 'Any government which is defeated by the Parliament on a major taxation Bill should resign ... This Bill will be defeated in another place [the Senate]. The Government should then resign.'
>
> Mr Whitlam, in relation to the 1970-71 Appropriation Bill, clearly indicated a view that the Senate could 'destroy' a budget and by this means 'destroy' a Government sponsoring such a Budget. He said:
>
>> 'Let me make it clear at the outset that our opposition to this Budget is no mere formality. We intend to press our opposition by all available means on all related measures in both Houses. If the motion is defeated we will vote against the Bills here and in the Senate. Our purpose is to destroy this Budget and to destroy the Government which has sponsored it.'

> The only way 'destroying' a Budget could produce destruction of
> the Government would be by forcing it to the people. This result,
> Mr Whitlam must have believed, had necessarily to follow from
> denial of supply by the Senate.[3]

Sir David Smith, Kerr's Official Secretary at the time, notes that the above occasion was the 170th attempt, since 1950, by Labor to block supply to the Coalition.[4]

I do not know whether Whitlam ever deigned to defend the contradiction in his position between 1970 and 1975. It is true that, in 1970, Labor never had the numbers in the Senate to achieve this aim – but they sought, unsuccessfully, to have the DLP Senators support them, as Sir David Smith also points out:

> As Jack Kane, one-time federal secretary of the Australian Democratic Labor Party and former DLP Senator for New South Wales, wrote in 1988:
>
>> There is no difference whatsoever between what Whitlam proposed in August 1970 and what Malcolm Fraser did in November 1975, except that Whitlam failed ... Senator Murphy, for Whitlam, sought the votes of the DLP Senators, unsuccessfully. That is the only reason why Whitlam did not defeat the 1970 budget in the Senate and thus fulfil his declared aim to destroy the Gorton government.[5]

Are we to believe that, had he in fact gained that support, he would not have used it?

Of course, there is an understanding that a popularly elected government should be allowed to govern unless extraordinary circumstances intervene. That understanding would be based as much on self-interest as chivalry. Under normal circumstances, an opposition that denied supply and forced a government to the people simply because it could, is likely to be severely punished electorally.

---

[3] Kerr, *Matters for Judgement*, pp. 320-321.
[4] David Smith, Peter & Yuwali Johnson. (2005). *Head of state: the governor-general, the monarchy, the republic and the dismissal.* Paddington, N.S.W: Macleay Press, p. 264.
[5] Ibid., p. 265.

They continue:

> Fraser's decision to block supply was neither inevitable nor essential. By late 1975, there was near universal agreement that Whitlam would be defeated at the next election whenever it was held. Announcing his decision, Fraser made the absurd claim, 'the Opposition now has no choice'. As a leader of immense authority, Fraser had every choice. He could allow the normal Parliamentary term to continue, or he could deploy the Senate to destroy the Whitlam government, which he denounced as the 'most incompetent and disastrous' since federation.[6]

Fraser's claim that the 'Opposition now has no choice', may have been absurd but it is standard political rhetoric. However, if Fraser genuinely believed that the government was the most incompetent and disastrous since Federation, did he not have a duty to do something about it? Fraser only persisted because he believed the electorate would support him, and it did.

Fraser had plenty to evidence to support his belief, as even Kelly and Bramston later concede:

> The Whitlam government had become discredited on multiple and lethal fronts. Its convoluted economic policies against a backdrop of global stagflation saw both unemployment and inflation surge to unacceptable highs. As a centralist Whitlam spread fear on the non-Labor side that he wanted a fundamental change to the Federal system, thereby alienating the Coalition parties at State level, in particular in New South Wales and also Queensland where Nationals premier Joh Bjelke-Petersen became a virulent enemy. Finally Whitlam created the impression he was unfit to govern because of a series of improprieties, the nadir being the Tirath Khemlani loans affair, which was financially unjustifiable, legally dubious and politically irresponsible, at which point much of the governing elite decided that extreme measures to remove Labor were legitimate.[7]

And if Fraser had the means at hand to remove this government, would he not be derelict, at least in his own mind, if he did not deploy them? Fraser's actions may have been ruthless, but Whitlam, having belittled Kerr's aspirations for a political

---
[6] Kelly and Bramston, op.cit., p. 87.
[7] Ibid., p. 89.

career because he was not ruthless enough, could hardly complain when he himself was out-ruthlessed.

And, at that time, the next election was not due for about eighteen months. It must be remembered that governments are made by the people electing them to office. If they fail to fulfil their obligation to govern well, why then should they be allowed to continue to wreak havoc for such a long period of time? There is only one answer to that question and the voters delivered it in December 1975. That result proved that Fraser's assessment of the 'exceptional circumstances' that prevailed in late 1975 was correct.

There follows a brief and uncritical examination of Fraser's background and rise to prominence ending with this:

> Fraser was the instrumental figure in the downfall of John Gorton as prime minister in 1971, in the overthrow of Billy Snedden as Liberal leader and finally in the destruction of Gough Whitlam.
>
> The method of Whitlam's defeat brought Fraser's ruthlessness to a new intensity: after blocking supply in the Senate, he pressured and persuaded Kerr to dismiss Whitlam and finally, he connived in the act.[8]

As far as Fraser's ruthlessness is concerned, this is essentially true. But as to Fraser pressuring and persuading Kerr and conniving in the act, this is a complete mischaracterisation of the relationship between the two men. I have examined this claim in Chapter Two and will return to it again later. If there was connivance, it was not in the act of dismissing Whitlam but rather in the tactics needed to ensure both the passage of supply and to secure an election, which was the whole point of Kerr's decision. Co-operation would be a better description. However, I also take issue with the suggestion that Fraser pressured and persuaded Kerr to sack Whitlam. Fraser certainly caused Kerr to *indirectly* come under pressure, firstly by virtue of initiating the crisis, and secondly, by the release of the Ellicott opinion, which argued Kerr should sack Whitlam and do it now. But

---

[8] Ibid., p. 88.

he never directly exerted pressure to which Kerr succumbed. And he never *persuaded* Kerr to sack Whitlam. This wording suggests that Fraser engaged in personal dialogue with Kerr to that effect and is designed to reinforce the claim that Kerr was his puppet and was a weak man. That is not true. What Fraser did do was persuade Kerr that he, Fraser, was firm in his resolve to block supply until an election was called. It was Fraser's 'crash through or crash' moment, a theme I will return to later. Kerr made his own decision based on that belief.

This may seem a trivial point, but by now I hope the reader has recognised that I include it, not out of a desire to be pedantic, but to highlight the cumulative stream of pinpricks with which Kelly and Bramston hope to fatally damage the reputation of Sir John Kerr.

The Dismissal now recounts the events that led up the double dissolution election of May 1974.

In 1972, when Whitlam won office, there was no contemporaneous half-Senate election as there would normally be, they having become unsynchronised in 1963. As a result, Whitlam inherited the old Coalition era Senate, which frustrated his legislative agenda:

> By April 1974, the legislative deadlock between the two houses was the greatest since federation. The Senate had twice rejected ten bills and another nine bills had also been rejected. Six of the rejected bills constituted grounds for double dissolution – they included bills to introduce Medibank and reform the electoral system on the principle of 'one vote, one value'.[9]

Incidentally, readers might wonder how our electoral system infringed the fundamental principle of 'one vote, one value' and, if it did, why would the Coalition not wish to see this problem redressed. This refers to the Commonwealth Electoral Bill 1973, which sought to make Commonwealth electorates more even in size by reducing the allowable quota variation from 20 per cent to 10 per cent. So, this was not a 'reform of

---

[9] Ibid., p. 90.

the electoral system', simply a provision designed to adjust an administrative parameter, as a result of which we still fell short of 'one vote, one value'.

Initially, Whitlam did not favour a double dissolution, the device having only previously been employed twice before in Australia – in which the government had been returned on one occasion and rejected on the other. There was a half-Senate election due by July 1974 and Whitlam conceived a plan to redress the Senate disparity by inducing DLP Senator Vince Gair to resign his seat (he was offered the Ambassadorship to Ireland) just prior to that election, which would result in the writs being issued for six seats rather than the five which would otherwise have been contested. Whitlam expected to win three of the six, rather than two of five. Along with the other seats he could normally expect to win, that would have given Whitlam a bare Senate majority. He made a similar offer to DLP leader Frank McManus, who refused.

In the event, Gair did resign and duly took up his position, but the strategy was overtaken by events. Journalist Laurie Oakes got wind of the Gair appointment and broke the news on 2 April. The Coalition was incensed and vowed to block supply.

That never happened because Whitlam took the initiative and advised Governor- General Sir Paul Hasluck to dissolve both Houses and issue writs for a general election. Whitlam won the May 1974 election with a reduced majority in the House of Representatives but failed to secure a majority in the Senate.

A joint sitting of both Houses, under the provisions of Section 57 of the Constitution, was held in August 1974 and all the six subject bills were passed.

The way in which the Coalition used its numbers in the Senate to frustrate the government so early in its term seems to be at odds with the general principle that a duly elected government should be permitted to govern.

And from this point, the Coalition tactics certainly become

somewhat more questionable. The situation after May 1974 was that:

> Labor had just failed to secure the Senate it needed. The new Senate was twenty-nine Labor, twenty-nine Coalition, one Liberal Movement (Steele Hall) and an independent who joined the Liberals post-election, taking their numbers to thirty. After the election, Snedden insisted that 'we were not defeated'. He denied Whitlam had any mandate and refused to concede Whitlam's right to a three-year Parliamentary term. This was important: it was a denial of Labor's election victory.[10]

Even for one, such as myself, who eventually supported the removal of the Whitlam government, Snedden's position, at that time, was untenable. Whitlam had taken the risk of going to the people early and his 1972 victory, although diminished, had been re-affirmed by the voters.

Kelly and Bramston continue:

> When Fraser became Liberal leader, the question of blocking supply was front and centre. He adopted a formula to turn the political heat back on Labor. Fraser said he wanted election talk 'out of the air' and announced that governments were entitled to their three-year term unless 'quite extraordinary events intervene'.[11]

So far, all according to Hoyle then.

Then Whitlam made a mistake. In February 1975, he appointed Attorney-General Lionel Murphy to the High Court. At that time there was a convention that 'casual vacancies' in the Senate would be filled by a member of the same party. Under this convention, Murphy should have been replaced by another Labor member. This appointment would be made by the relevant State Premier. In this case New South Wales Liberal Premier, Tom Lewis, broke with tradition and appointed an independent, Cleaver Bunton, the mayor of Albury. As Kelly and Bramston tell it:

> While this reduced Labor's numbers to twenty-eight it would not

---
[10] Ibid., p. 92.
[11] Ibid.

matter on the supply issue because Bunton voted with Labor. But the Senate casual vacancy convention had been breached.[12]

It seemed indefensible to me then, and it still does, that a *political* appointment, which Murphy's clearly was, could be regarded as a 'casual' vacancy. Murphy's ten-year legal career could hardly be described as stellar, although he did take silk in 1960, the year before he entered the Senate. Murphy proved himself to be a judicial activist, which could easily have been foreseen by Whitlam. In other words, he was not appointed because of his legal standing and what he could bring to the Court but because he could be relied upon to advance what we now call a 'progressive' agenda. In the House, even a genuinely 'casual' vacancy, such as a death, requires a by-election. So, I have no quarrel with Lewis's decision in this instance, but it did provide a precedent for Queensland Premier Joh Bjelke-Petersen to later commit a considerably more cynical and unjustified breach of the convention.

According to Kelly and Bramston:

> This breach of convention became pivotal when a Queensland ALP senator, Bert Milliner, died in June 1975. The power to determine the successor lay with Bjelke-Petersen via his control of the Queensland Parliament. This would become decisive in the subsequent crisis. Bjelke-Petersen now had his fun. He tortured and tormented the Labor Party. He rejected Labor's candidate, Mal Colston, and asked Labor to submit a panel of names from which he might pick a new Senator. The Queensland ALP, irrational with rage and standing upon its pride, refused. It was a serious blunder. They should have given Bjelke-Petersen the names and even tried to find some ALP candidates he might like. Only one thing mattered, sheer, raw Senate numbers.
>
> In the end Bjelke-Petersen repudiated Labor, smashed the convention and appointed a French (sic) polisher by trade, Albert (Pat) Field who had rung his office to offer his services. Having been given his background, Bjelke-Petersen said 'he sounds like a true-blue Labor man'. En route to Canberra, Field said in an interview,

---

[12] Ibid., p. 93.

he would never vote for Whitlam, attacked him for calling the premier a 'bible-bashing bastard' and backed an early election. He was sworn in amid a walkout of Labor Senators. Labor challenged Field's eligibility to sit, and he was given a month's leave. He never voted on supply but his appointment changed the numbers.[13]

It is arguable whether the actions of a maverick such as Bjelke-Petersen 'smashed' the convention. He simply ignored it. They continue:

> On the supply issue, the vote was now thirty to twenty-nine the Coalition's way, with Steele Hall voting with Labor. If Bjelke-Petersen had followed convention and appointed an ALP senator, the vote would have been thirty all. Bjelke-Petersen had delivered a majority Senate vote to Fraser and Withers. It was this majority that enabled them to defer supply. A split vote can block a bill or resolution but a majority vote is needed to carry a bill or resolution and Fraser need that majority for his deferral motion.[14]

This is significant because it was essential to Fraser's game plan that he not reject supply outright but defer it, as will become clear later.

And:

> The Liberals professed to be dismayed at the smashing of the Senate's casual vacancy convention. Yet their hypocrisy was undisguised. They were so dismayed they relied upon the majority gifted in a moral and political atrocity by the Queensland Parliament. As Whitlam often said, the Senate that denied the 1975 budget was 'corrupted' and tainted. It was not the Senate as elected by the people. The vote that forced the crisis was secured by a negation of democracy.[15]

It's hard to argue with most of that, except to note that the Senate would also not have been the one 'elected by the people' if Whitlam's Gair and McManus ploys had come to fruition, and consequent to his appointment of Murphy to the High Court. It was Whitlam who started playing games with Senate

---

[13] Ibid.
[14] Ibid., p. 94.
[15] Ibid.

numbers, so his hypocrisy in this respect might be thought to be only marginally less than that of the Coalition.

And:

> Fraser could have instructed a Coalition Senator to abstain. But morality was not allowed to interfere with self-interest ... It is true that Fraser, as prime minister, later sponsored a 1977 referendum to write the convention into the Constitution, preserving it forever. It was a worthy reform that ensured the Senate abuse of power Fraser deployed to take office could not be repeated.[16]

To which might be added '... and laid bare, forever, Fraser's shameless hypocrisy'. As an aside and further to my earlier point, it seems strange to me that the constitutional amendment did not include a definition of 'casual' to exclude political opportunism or even 'spending more time with one's family'. One way to handle this would be to fill such a 'non-casual' vacancy with the first failed candidate on the State ballot at which the departing Senator was elected. And the same consideration could apply for House of Representatives seats. Sir Garfield Barwick's appointment could also be considered political. Admittedly, it resulted in a by-election, but this posed no risk for the Government because Barwick held a safe Lower House seat.

To paraphrase Kelly and Bramston, by October 1975 the momentum for denial of supply was growing. On 10 October the High Court ruled that each of the Australian Capital Territory and the Northern Territory were entitled to two senators each. I won't go into details of this, but the thrust of the author's argument is that the Coalition feared that, if Whitlam called a half-Senate election before mid-1976, there was a possibility he could gain control of the Senate. This was because the new Senators from the Territories would take their place immediately (rather than on 1 July 1976 when the new Senate was due to be sworn in), as would the two Senators elected in place of the two 'casual vacancy' Senators, Bunton and Field, who were almost certain to not be returned.

---

[16] Ibid.

This might have been of concern to the Coalition but would not constitute the kind of extraordinary event that Fraser had stipulated would be needed to trigger a denial of supply. The way they proposed to circumvent this possibility was, in the event of Whitlam calling a half-Senate election, to invite the Premiers of Coalition held States (Victoria, NSW and Queensland) to instruct their Governors not to issue writs. The process for issuing writs for an election is that the Governor-General, having accepted the advice of the Prime Minister, himself issues writs for the House of Representatives. In the case of the Senate, the Governor-General will write to each State Governor, inviting them to issue writs for a Senate election on the proposed date. State Governors are provided advice, through their own Executive Councils comprised of the Premier and Ministers, that the suggested date is acceptable, and upon that advice, the Governor signs the writ.

For a Premier to advise a State Governor not to issue the writs, would mean advising their own Governors to defy the Governor-General. That would effectively pit the Crown in a State against the Crown in the Commonwealth.

To me, that seems a grotesque and constitutionally unsustainable position and would have been grossly irresponsible. But fortunately, it never came to pass. That it was even canvassed does suggest a degree of arrogance and desperation on the part of the Coalition forces.

Be that as it may, the real trigger for Fraser to block supply was the forced resignation of Senator Rex Connor, architect of the Loans Affair disaster (detailed in my Introduction). As Kelly and Bramston note, Whitlam forced Connor's resignation on the grounds that he had misled Parliament in denying his ongoing contact with Khemlani:

> The affair revealed the Whitlam government stayed true to its character: proving its impropriety at a moment of maximum danger. In political terms, this closed the debate about whether or not Fraser would deny the budget. Fraser was handed an embarrassment of political weapons. It became easy for him to justify blocking the

budget and hard to reject this option. Connor's enforced resignation satisfied the test Fraser had required: that he would need 'extraordinary' or 'reprehensible' events to force an election through the Senate. Those events were now a stage-and-screen spectacular. It was as though the Greek gods had conspired to doom Whitlam in a performance of tragedy, farce and incompetence.[17]

This is a telling passage. Despite deploring Fraser's tactics in getting to this point, it is clear that Kelly and Bramston are prepared to forgive, or at least accept, Fraser's subsequent conduct. They are virtually saying he had no choice but to press ahead and it was, effectively, Whitlam who put him in that position. That would explain why, despite heaping opprobrium upon Sir John Kerr throughout their book, Fraser gets off with not much more than a slap on the wrist. He is indicted on charges of ruthlessness and hypocrisy, pretty much standard fare for politicians. Not for him any of the more egregious crimes such as 'being in possession of an incongruously high-pitched voice' or 'being a beneficiary of patrons'.

We now turn to Whitlam's response:

> A month earlier, on 12 September, Whitlam had delivered a speech in Goulburn that foreshadowed his tactics. They were the reverse of autumn 1974, the reason being that Whitlam, like Fraser, knew Labor would now lose any election. His plan therefore was to resist the election. He wanted to buy time till the government, with Bill Hayden as treasurer and Jim McClelland as labour minister, recovered in the polls. But Whitlam was also planning his greatest audacity.
> ... As prime minister he now found his life's work threatened by a Senate, elected on a State based, undemocratic franchise, purporting to turn its constitutional powers into a weapon to terminate the term of the House of Representatives that he controlled. It was a negation of everything he had striven to achieve, of everything he believed.[18]

I interrupt at this point to remind readers that, in 1970, Whitlam had been rather less outraged at the notion that the Senate might

---

[17] Ibid., p. 96.
[18] Ibid., p. 98.

use its powers to 'destroy' a budget and the government that sponsored it. The authors continue:

> ... A wilful personality with a sense of destiny and a leader alert to constitutional powers, Whitlam embarked on the grandest application of 'crash through or crash' in his career.
>
> He said: 'There are no laws applying to a situation where supply is refused by an Upper House, no laws at all. There is no precedent in the Federal Parliament ... and there is, in fact, no convention because people never used to think it could happen, so it's never been discussed. And accordingly, one can only say that there is no obligation by law, by rule, by precedent or by convention for a Prime Minister in those circumstances which are threatened to dissolve the House of Representatives and have an election for it.'[19]

Firstly, let me observe that if Whitlam was alert to constitutional powers, why was he, as he later claimed, completely in the dark as to the possibility that they might be used against him by the Governor-General?

Be that as it may, the above passage is significant in that Whitlam denies the existence of a convention that the Prime Minister denied supply must advise an election. He bases this claim, essentially, on the fact that there was no precedent, and since I have used the same argument to argue that there was no convention that prevented the Senate from blocking supply, I can, to some extent, see his point of view. However, there may not have been a precedent in Australia, but this would be a case where the convention would have been carried over from the United Kingdom, because the Constitution did not specifically rule it out. Part of Sir John Kerr's deliberations were based on the existence of such a convention. But even if there were no obligation to advise an election, there certainly was an obligation on Whitlam to find some other way to secure supply, without which he could not govern. And again, as we shall see, this was the essential issue that Sir John Kerr had to wrestle with. Whitlam had to convince Kerr he had another way. The following extract goes to this point:

---
[19] Ibid.

> This was a declaration that he would not be intimidated. The Senate might pass its motions but Whitlam would ignore them. He asserted his right as prime minister to defy them. Whitlam had two motives. The first was to persuade Fraser against blocking supply, a ploy which failed. The second was to equip his campaign to break Fraser and his Senators with a constitutional legitimacy and popular appeal. Whitlam was going to tough it out. He judged that if such brinkmanship forced Fraser's retreat, then his leadership would never recover and Labor would enjoy a transformation of its fortunes.
>
> Whitlam intended to teach Fraser that using the Senate to break convention was not cost-free. His plan was to transform the issue from Labor's unpopularity to the integrity of Australia's democracy.[20]

Sir John Kerr comes in for strong criticism, from a number of quarters, that he should have stayed out of the contest and let the political leaders sort it out. The above passage suggests that Kelly and Bramston perceived an intransigence on the part of both leaders – high minded principle on Whitlam's part and political survival for Fraser – which would negate the possibility that these two could come to any kind of political compromise that would absolve the Governor-General of any role in the resolution of the crisis.

They continue:

> [Whitlam] took his stand on the principle of responsible government implicit in the constitution: a prime minister was commissioned because he commanded a majority in the House of Representatives.[21]

No. There is nothing in the Constitution to this effect. A prime minister is commissioned because the Governor-General believes he has the means to guarantee effective government. *Under most circumstances*, that would be because he commands a majority in the House of Representatives.

> The government was made and unmade by its confidence in the

---

[20] Ibid., pp. 98-99.
[21] Ibid., p. 99.

lower house, 'the People's House'. Whitlam said while he had the confidence of the House, he was entitled to govern.[22]

Whitlam may have been 'entitled' to govern, but, at that point, he lacked the means to do so.

Kelly and Bramston also qualify Whitlam's entitlement:

> However, this view was qualified by the federalism principle. The founding fathers created the Senate as a state's house with virtually equal powers with the House of Representatives. This was a political bargain that made possible the creation of the nation. The Senate was given such powers to protect the states and preserve the federal nature of the Constitution. In practice, however, the Senate operated as a chamber governed by party and party interests.
>
> The architects of the Constitution knew they had implanted a contradiction at its heart. The conflict between responsible government and the Senate's powers in the name of federalism was a political time bomb. In an immortal passage, those great scholars of the Constitution John Quick and Robert Garran wrote: In the end it is predicted that either Responsible Government will kill the Federation and change it into a unified State or the Federation will kill Responsible Government and change it into a new form of Executive more compatible with the Federal theory.
>
> Whitlam now became a killing agent in the cause of responsible government. He was asking the people to resolve the contradiction by repudiating Fraser's use of the Senate to force the House to submit. This was the epic nature of the 1975 crisis. Whitlam's aim was to break Fraser, break the Senate's position and, beyond that, resolve the constitutional contradiction in favour of the House of Representatives.
>
> As their titanic battle was joined, Fraser and Whitlam had a shared view – Sir John Kerr would be pivotal in deciding the outcome.[23]

The argument regarding the contradiction between the doctrine of responsible government and the power of the Senate is a valid one – although it is by no means as black and white as

---

[22] Ibid.
[23] Ibid., pp. 99-100.

Kelly and Bramston would have you believe – but as far as the events of 1975 are concerned it is purely academic. For good or ill, that is the situation that pertained at the time. However, in the interests of accuracy, I cannot let the reference to Quick and Garran go unchallenged. They did not say the words attributed to them. These were actually the words, *quoted* by Quick and Garran, of Sir Samuel Griffith, Sir Richard C. Baker, Sir John Cockburn, Mr. Justice Inglis-Clark, and Mr. G. W. Hackett, 'who have taken the view that the Cabinet system of Executive is incompatible with a true Federation'. Those gentlemen then proposed some amendments to the draft Constitution to take account of this conflict. What Quick and Garran themselves said was:

> It is not our province to comment on the opinions and contentions of these eminent federalists. Their views have not been accepted; and, for better or for worse, the system of Responsible Government as known to the British Constitution has been practically embedded in the Federal Constitution, in such a manner that it cannot be disturbed without an amendment of the instrument. There can be no doubt that it will tend in the direction of the nationalization of the people of the Commonwealth, and will promote the concentration of Executive control in the House of Representatives. At the same time it ought not to impair the equal and co-ordinate authority of the Senate in all matters of legislation, except the origination and amendment of Bills imposing taxation and Bills appropriating revenue or money for the ordinary annual services of the Government.[24]

So Quick and Garran, 'those great scholars of the Constitution', were rather more sanguine about the Constitutional arrangements in this respect than Kelly and Bramston would have you believe. And in fact, events have proved them right. The nation has trended towards nationalization in an evolutionary manner and the Senate has exerted its muscle *vis-à-vis* blocking supply on only one occasion – 1975. And this was in response, as Kelly and Bramston have conceded, to extraordinary circumstances. So perhaps the contradiction is not quite so problematical as they fear. And, as I noted earlier, political self-interest is likely

---

[24] John Quick & Robert Garran. (1901). *The annotated constitution of the Australian Commonwealth*. Sydney: Angus & Robertson, pp. 706-707.

to inhibit the Senate from blocking supply – on those occasions when it has the capacity to do so – more often than not.

The claim that Whitlam now made it his mission to correct this anomaly sounds noble but rather fanciful. He may have dressed up his rhetoric in this way, but it is much more likely he was simply acting in his own self-interest – a charge that Kelly and Bramston both freely level against Fraser and Kerr. The statement that 'he was asking the people to resolve the contradiction by repudiating Fraser's use of the Senate to force the House to submit', does not hold water. The only way the people could resolve the issue would have been by means of a House of Representatives election – which Whitlam refused to countenance. And in the event, they did not subscribe to the view that breaking the power of the Senate was worth the price of re-installing a massively incompetent government. And, in fact, they had delivered this message in May 1974 when they returned Whitlam with a reduced majority. As is often said, 'politics is the art of the possible'. Whitlam ignored this reality at his cost.

As I have said earlier, while I deplored the Whitlam government, I have genuine sympathy for the man himself, to the extent that he found himself stymied by a ruthless opponent employing, at times, questionable tactics. But what I am concerned with in this book is not so much the actions of either Whitlam or Fraser, but how those actions impacted the role of the Governor-General. Sir John Kerr had to play the hand he was dealt by these two. It was not his role to punish Fraser for being ruthless and opportunistic nor to protect Whitlam because he was a victim. His job was to uphold the Constitution.

8

Kerr Turns Against Whitlam

Having dealt with Fraser in just one chapter, Kelly and Bramston now turn the blowtorch back on Kerr:

> Even before supply was blocked Gough Whitlam had lost the trust of John Kerr, who had become wary and resentful of the prime minister. Kerr had reached a fatal conclusion: there was no point in him speaking honestly to Whitlam. He decided not to try. The trust between the Queen's representative and her chief adviser was broken. Incredibly, Whitlam knew nothing of this, nor that the problem originated in Kerr's early days in office.[1]

This is overstating the case. Certainly, Kerr became wary, but this was directed not specifically at Whitlam but at his whole Cabinet and the quality of advice they gave him. And there is no evidence that he ever became resentful of Whitlam personally, at least not prior to the aftermath of 11 November.

The essence of this chapter of *The Dismissal*, is that Kerr repeatedly failed in his duty to 'warn and advise'.

The claim that this wariness went all the way back to Kerr's early days in office is misleading. What is true is that his attitude and perception of Whitlam's intransigence had its genesis in two incidents that occurred relatively early. The impression that Kerr harboured a secret grudge almost from day one is false, as Kelly and Bramston go on to demonstrate:

> Kerr stayed friendly and jovial with Whitlam but kept secret his heart and calculations. The authority for this is Kerr himself: he said

---

[1] Kelly and Bramston, *The Dismissal*, p. 101.

by 14 October, on the eve of the Senate's action, he felt Whitlam was beyond reason. 'From that time forward my opinion was that he was beyond the reach of any argument of mine or even discussion,' Kerr said. 'Everything he said publicly, or privately to me, thereafter strengthened me in that view.'[2]

So, what the above passage conveys is that Kerr's attitude towards Whitlam had hardened *only one month* before the fateful day, not from his early days in office. They continue:

Whitlam had lost Kerr. He had not necessarily lost the coming struggle. But his assumption that 'Kerr would do the right thing' was false. The story of how Kerr's early worries grew into distrust is riddled with vanity, complacency and deception.[3]

Oh dear, here we go again. 'Vanity, complacency and deception'. It seems pejorative references to Kerr's character must always come in threes. He was an 'adroit opportunist, beneficiary of patrons and liked running with the winning team'. His abandonment of Labor was 'intellectual, self-interested and visceral'. His 'opportunism, his ambition to make his mark and being on the winning side was a consistent theme in his career'. It seems these verbal portraits of Kerr are always in triptych form. If they were on canvas there would be enough material to occupy their own wing in the National Portrait Gallery.

Kelly and Bramston cite two incidents that led to Kerr's mistrust of the Whitlam Ministry.

The first related to issuing the Proclamation for the Joint Sitting of both Houses of Parliament in consequence of the 1974 double dissolution. This was the session in which six bills that had been blocked by the Senate, and were listed as the justification for that dissolution, were now to be voted upon. Kerr found that the six bills included one, the Petroleum and Minerals Authority (PMA) bill, which did not meet the criteria for triggering a double dissolution. The Proclamation of the double dissolution itself had been issued by Kerr's predecessor, Sir Paul Hasluck.

---

[2] Ibid.
[3] Ibid.

Kerr, in his autobiography, disposes of this incident in a single paragraph:

> Sir Paul Hasluck had accepted legal advice to the contrary and had included a reference to the Petroleum and Minerals Authority Bill in his double dissolution Proclamation. I was advised to include it with the other five proposed laws in my joint sitting Proclamation. I sought legal advice, through the Prime Minister, as to whether I was bound to do this. I received advice that I was. Ultimately, I decided that I should act upon the overall legal and political advice tendered to me and include the Bill in the list of proposed laws which the joint sitting might deal with and vote on, although my own view was that any resulting Act would be invalid. It was later held by the High Court that the Petroleum and Minerals Authority Act passed by the joint sitting of 1974 was invalid because the provisions of Section 57 had not been complied with in its case. The Court also held that there was no need to list any of the six bills in the Proclamation, but that doing so was surplusage and did not invalidate the Proclamation.[4]

Kerr wrote about this incident, not as an example of the doubtful quality of the advice he received, but to illustrate the point that, where a questionable issue is justiciable, the Governor-General 'acts on advice'. No doubt he was unimpressed with the advice in this case, but it is a long stretch to suggest this was the beginning of a disenchantment with, or distrust of, Whitlam personally.

Kelly and Bramston note:

> In a note on this issue left in his personal papers, Kerr said the law officers advised that 'I was bound' by Hasluck's decision and 'could not act inconsistently with the way in which he had acted'. Given an election had been held on the issue, the advice seems sensible ...
>
> Kerr said with disdain this was his first exposure to the way Attorney-General Lionel Murphy gave advice and that he was 'surprised' that Maurice Byers, as solicitor-general, failed to express a view on the issue of substance of the PMA ...

---

[4] Kerr, op.cit., pp. 238-239.

> The point is that both Hasluck and Kerr did the right thing. They acted on advice and left the High Court to pass judgement on the act's validity.[5]

It is not stated what Hasluck's reaction to the inclusion of an invalid bill in his Proclamation of the election was. Did he 'advise and warn'? Clearly, in this case, Kerr, by virtue of his questioning its inclusion, did effectively 'advise and warn'.

The major topic of this chapter is the Loans Affair. In the words of Kelly and Bramston:

> Far more significant, however, were the events of 'Black Friday' the night of 13 December 1974 at the Lodge, when one of the most infamous events in Australian political history occurred. Senior ministers gathered in secret to authorize the raising of a US$4 billion loan for natural-resource projects through a highly dubious middle-man, Tirath Khemlani, bypassing the Treasury's orthodox financial channels. Veteran correspondent Alan Reid called this event the 'death warrant' of the Whitlam government. Authorization took the form of an Executive Council minute that required the governor-general's signature. The Whitlam-Kerr relationship never recovered from this night.[6]

The 'death warrant' of the Whitlam government. It was indeed, and it was all the work of Whitlam and his Cabinet. It is doubtful, however, that the Whitlam-Kerr relationship broke down as a result of this incident, although Kerr certainly became more wary. Further from Kelly and Bramston:

> During the afternoon and evening of 14 (sic) December, the four most senior ministers were at the Lodge. Whitlam, Murphy, Treasurer Dr Jim Cairns, and the architect of the scheme, Minerals and Energy Minister Rex Connor. In frantic events over the previous days, the Attorney-General's Department had expressed grave misgivings about the legal basis of the plan. The Treasury, led by Sir Frederick Wheeler and John Stone, was alarmed and tried to scuttle the project. On the night, Wheeler advised Cairns not to sign the minute, advice he ignored.[7]

---

5   Kelly and Bramston, op.cit., pp. 102-103.
6   Ibid., p. 103.
7   Ibid., p. 104.

Here is evidence that Whitlam and his Ministers ignored the most authoritative advice they could be given – that of their own senior departmental officials – and yet the chapter of *The Dismissal* that deals with the Loans Affair focusses almost entirely on Kerr's putative dereliction of duty in not using his prerogative 'to advise and warn'. They continue:

> Each man made grievous mistakes in dealing with the other: Whitlam treated Kerr with complacency that assumed he was a cipher and Kerr failed to raise the necessary questions with Whitlam that would be expected from a competent governor-general.[8]

Kelly and Bramston never specify what these necessary questions might have been.

Kerr devotes virtually a whole chapter to this incident. There were two issues that concerned him. The first was the legality of the proposed loan. And the second was the unorthodox manner in which the Executive Council meeting had been called. It is this latter that Kelly and Bramston refer to when they cite Whitlam's complacency in treating Kerr as a rubber-stamp. And yes, it was in this incident that Kerr's wariness had its genesis.

Kerr gives a good explanation of the Executive Council:

> The Federal Executive Council is established by section 62 of the Constitution to advise the Governor-General in the government of the Commonwealth. But executive decisions are in practice made by the Cabinet or by individual Ministers and come, when necessary, to the Governor-General in Executive Council for final approval. This is given at meetings called as and when required and attended usually by the Governor-General and only two or three of the Ministers, all of whom are members of the Executive Council.[9]

Meetings are requested by the relevant Ministers and are approved by either the Governor-General or the Vice-President of the Executive Council, who at that time was Labor Minister, Frank Stewart.

---

[8] Ibid., p. 103.
[9] Kerr, op.cit., p. 224.

On 13 December 1974, Sir John Kerr and his Private Secretary, David Smith, attended an official function at the Sydney Opera House. At 7pm that evening, Whitlam instigated an Executive Council meeting. This was necessary because the Ministers involved in masterminding the loan proposal – Whitlam himself, Attorney-General Lionel Murphy, Treasurer Dr Jim Cairns and Energy Minister Rex Connor – decided that they needed to get Executive Council approval urgently, as they were all dispersing for Christmas and Whitlam was going overseas the next day. They tried to contact Kerr to get approval for the meeting but, as he had already left for the opera, they left a message at Admiralty House, which David Smith only received upon his return. In the event he was able to contact the relevant official at about 2am. As Kelly and Bramston put it:

> When an official finally reached David Smith at 2 a.m., he was incredulous, saying: 'There couldn't be an ExCo meeting unless the Governor-General was informed.' Standard procedure for ExCo meetings is that while the governor-general is not required to attend every meeting his approval is obtained before a meeting occurs and he signs the relevant documents after any meeting.
>
> In the morning Smith briefed a disturbed Kerr at about 8 a.m. A short time later, Whitlam rang Kerr at Admiralty House in Sydney. Whitlam said that because of exceptional circumstances it had been necessary to hold an urgent ExCo meeting. Kerr said Whitlam told him because of the hour it was decided not to wake the governor-general but seek his approval after the event. Whitlam said the four ministers agreed on the decision and its urgency. They had all signed the ExCo minute. Whitlam, according to Kerr, said that 'if I would have been prepared to give approval in advance, I could do so afterwards though it certainly was unusual to ask for it'. He explained the purposes and reasons for the loan. According to Kerr, Whitlam said the attorney-general's advice was that the loan could be regarded for temporary purposes. He said a special messenger was en route to Sydney with the documents and would arrive soon. Whitlam advised Kerr to approve the meeting and sign the minute.[10]

There is one mystery in this account and that is that the Vice-

---

[10] Kelly and Bramston, op.cit., p. 105.

President of the Executive Council also has the authority to approve a meeting. It is not clear why approval for the meeting was not sought from Minister Stewart, which would have eliminated any doubts (which emerged later) about the validity of the meeting.

Kelly and Bramston continue:

> In a lengthy nine-page note written in July 1975 about these events, Kerr said that after the minute arrived he examined it 'and came to the conclusion that the Attorney's legal advice was by no means certainly correct and was probably wrong'. Kerr spoke several times that morning to the secretary of the ExCo. He established that various Crown law officers had been at the Lodge meetings. He tried to speak to Harders (Secretary of the Attorney-General's Department) but he was unavailable. Kerr reached Byers [the Solicitor-General – a public servant] to clarify what had happened, and Byers told him that Murphy's advice was 'arguable'.
>
> Kerr concluded the legality had been 'clearly canvassed at the official's level and the Attorney-General's opinion had prevailed'. He said: 'The point here was that the act proposed was not plainly illegal and the point of law was not plainly unarguable on the facts known to me.' His view was that future legality could be tested in the courts. It was not his job 'to usurp the role of the High Court in constitutional matters'. He concluded that if the loan was raised the 'legal error' would be addressed in the courts.
>
> In deciding what to do, Kerr asked himself two questions: if awakened in the night would he have authorised the meeting, and if he had attended the meeting would he have accepted the advice of the ministers and signed the minute? He decided the answer to both questions was yes. Kerr said he was 'confronted by a solid political and formal decision made unanimously'. He decided it would be 'absurd' to insist upon another ExCo meeting. Kerr said his signature did not constitute 'personal approval' but reflected the convention of acting upon ministerial advice. He decided therefore 'to excuse the lapse' of not being informed of the ExCo meeting beforehand.
>
> The governor-general took two decisions: he authorised the loan

raising and he raised none of his doubts with Whitlam.[11]

That is an accurate summary of events which does not fully support its own conclusion viz., that Kerr raised none of his doubts with Whitlam. The fact is that Kerr did raise the issue of the questionable legality of the loan in that it did not seem to be for 'temporary purposes'. The import of this is that if it were not for temporary purposes, it should have been progressed through the Loans Council. According to Kerr:

> On 14 December I spoke directly to the Solicitor-General, Mr M.H. Byers. I knew that the Prime Minister did not in general agree that I was entitled to direct advice from the Law Officers, but the matter was urgent and so worrying that I felt I should have some confirmation of the legal consideration given to the matter. The Solicitor-General by telephone confirmed that the Attorney-General had advised the Ministers that the loan contemplated could be regarded as for temporary purposes. He said that he thought the Attorney-General's view was an arguable or tenable one. I spoke to the Prime Minister and told him what I had done about the Minute and what the Solicitor-General had said. He raised no objection to the initiative I had taken in speaking to the Solicitor-General.[12]

If Kerr is to be believed – and Byers, no friend of Kerr's, never contradicted this claim – then Kerr certainly did raise his doubts with the Solicitor-General. It is hardly conceivable that Byers would not report this conversation to, at least, the Attorney-General. Kerr also says that 'I said to the Prime Minister that the purposes did not seem to be temporary to me. He replied that the Attorney-General believed that the point was arguable'.[13] It is not clear whether this was the same conversation. Whitlam denied that the purported phone call to him, following the discussion between Kerr and Byers, took place. That seems unlikely.

Regardless of that, whatever doubts Kerr had about the legality of the loan were a matter for him alone. He had satisfied himself that the issue was not overtly illegal and was justiciable.

---

[11] Ibid., pp. 106-107.
[12] Kerr, op.cit., p. 235.
[13] Ibid., p. 233.

Therefore, there was no basis for him to 'advise and warn' Whitlam beyond the implicit warning in his phone calls to Byers and Whitlam himself. What was he to have said? That he believed the loan was not for temporary purposes and that Whitlam should not proceed with it? As Kerr notes that ship had already sailed, when the Prime Minister and the Attorney-General, supported by the Solicitor-General agreed the point was 'arguable'. Would Kelly and Bramston expect another Governor-General, one without legal qualifications, such as Sir Peter Cosgrove, to press the point even as far as Kerr did?

Kerr again:

> ...when there is a matter before the Council and it involves a legal point which is justiciable, and when that point is covered by the advice of the Attorney-General and the Ministers present are the Prime Minister, the Attorney-General himself, the Treasurer and the Minister specifically concerned, all identifying themselves with that advice and, so informing the Governor-General, the latter has no real alternative but to accept the firmly tendered advice and the determination of the Ministers to proceed to a decision upon it. The Governor-General cannot be his own lawyer in handling business passing through the Executive Council.[14]

The point here is that the doubtful issue was not some obscure point of law, some stumbling block, that only the Governor-General had hit upon and therefore had a duty to bring to the attention of the Ministers. They were already aware of it and had formed a considered legal opinion upon it. There was, thus, no role for the Governor-General to 'advise and warn' beyond what he did by virtue of his questions.

As to signing the Minute, as Kerr points out, this was a clear case of the Governor-General 'acting on advice'. This is something which Kelly and Bramston insist upon *ad nauseam* throughout the book, so no criticism can be attached to Kerr on this point.

Kelly and Bramston continue:

> In his July 1975 record, Kerr said he felt the loan 'could run into po-

---

[14] Ibid., p. 229.

litical and legal trouble' but that Whitlam's position was firm. Kerr wrote that he contemplated whether to resort to the Crown's 'advise and warn' doctrine but rejected this option as useless and impractical since it meant intruding into the policy and politics of the issue.

In his memoirs, Kerr went a step further. 'The purported meeting of 13 December was in my view invalid.' He decided this because his prior consent as governor-general had not been obtained. In effect, he was accusing Whitlam of misleading him and of giving him invalid advice. Yet Kerr conveyed no such concerns to Whitlam on the day. His rationale was that the issue of whether or not the meeting was valid was one 'to be left to the courts'.[15]

On the question of resorting to the 'advise and warn' doctrine, it is worth noting that Kerr regarded recourse to the doctrine as exceptional and a matter of prudent judgement. It is also worth noting the view of Sir Paul Hasluck, quoted in the Australian Parliament House website that:

> For him [any Governor-General] to take part in political argument would both be overstepping the boundaries of his office and lessening his own influence.[16]

As to the validity of the meeting, it is evident that Kerr believed on 14 December that the meeting was invalid.

Kerr subsequently had access to the thinking of Professor Geoffrey Sawyer who believed that the meeting was invalid. However, the situation is rather more nuanced that Kelly and Bramston have painted. From Kerr's own account:

> In any event my legal assumption was, on December 14, and is, that only the Governor-General or the Vice-President may validly call a meeting.

> Sawyer deals with the meeting of 13 December 1974 on the basis that it may not have been a valid meeting because it was not called by the Governor-General or the Vice-President or because the delegation of the power to call a meeting to the Senior Member is invalid. Sawyer says that if this were so 'it is doubtful whether the

---
[15] Kelly and Bramston, op.cit., p. 107.
[16] 'Powers and Functions of the Governor General', *Australian Parliament House Website*.

Governor-General could subsequently validate it'.

> I was asked, as I shall relate, to approve of the meeting after it had been held, and was advised that I could so validly approve. I was advised by the Prime Minister to do so and I did. If my own view and the trend of Professor Sawyer's reasoning are sound it may well be that what I thus did, upon advice, was invalid and had it been tested in the courts this might have resulted in invalidation of the decision. It was never tested and the point became an academic one. It was however one to be left to the courts. For this reason I expressed no view to Mr Whitlam as to the validity of the meeting.[17]

It seems to me that no fault resides with Kerr on this matter. On 14 December he believed the meeting was invalid, but he was advised by the Prime Minister that he could validate it *post hoc* by signing the minute and thereby tacitly approving the meeting. Kerr accepted that, firstly on the 'acting on advice' principle and secondly, on the basis that had he been asked to approve the meeting the previous day, he would have done so. This seems a reasonable position. So, at that time Kerr believed that he *had* validated the meeting and that is why he expressed no view to Mr Whitlam as to its validity. Subsequently, upon the publication of Professor Sawyer's book *Federation Under Strain* in 1977, he became aware of Sawyer's opinion that his action *may* not have validated the meeting. As a result of that he accepted that he may have been wrong in believing he had validated the meeting and that is when he raised the issue, *in hindsight*, of the matter being decided by the courts.

Kerr's predecessor as Governor-General, Sir Paul Hasluck, in his 1985 series of interviews with former Labor Minister, Clyde Cameron, was quite unequivocal that the actions of Whitlam and his Ministers themselves calling a meeting was quite improper. He said it would never have happened in his time, and that if it had, he would have insisted the meeting be reconvened and the matter properly discussed the next day.[18] Kerr was confronted with circumstances that made that impossible, particularly so

---

[17] Kerr, op.cit., p. 225..
[18] 'Reminiscential Conversations between Rt Hon Sir Paul Hasluck and the Hon Clyde Cameron', 1985, https://nla.gov.au/nla.obj-215705852/listen/9-2735~9-2824

early in his term, and he acquiesced to Whitlam's advice. But, as he observed in *Matters for Judgement*, this did cause him some concern. However, the real import of Hasluck's opinion is that Whitlam had treated Kerr in a way he would not have dreamed of treating Hasluck. And Kerr probably suspected this.

Getting back to the loan itself, we cannot suggest that, because of his legal training, Kerr should have been more aware of the legal complexities. If the principle of 'acting on advice' is to have any value it must be consistent and, as I have pointed out earlier, other Governors-General have not had that background.

We now hear about Kerr's reaction to this affair:

> When news of the loan leaked during 1975, with reports of Treasury opposition, Kerr came under collateral attack: he was criticized in public and private for signing the minute and not questioning the government about the policy and process. This had a profound impact on Kerr – he looked complicit in one of the greatest follies in the nation's political history.
>
> In his memoirs, Kerr took his concerns to a new intensity – saying the circumstances of the ExCo meeting were a 'great shock' to him. He felt the government failed to respect him or his office. 'My deepest concern,' he said, was not the legal issue but whether the 'proper attitude' was taken towards his office. The more he learned about the loan, the more he feared Whitlam's attitude was that the governor-general could be 'increasingly ignored'. Kerr says he now worried the office might be 'diminished' during his tenure.
>
> Harders affirmed later that Kerr's 'deepest concern' was whether Whitlam had a 'rubber stamp' approach to his office. He said Kerr worried whether the governor-general could on occasions be 'forgotten rather than being kept fully informed'. John Menadue, the head of the Prime Minister's Department, reveals Kerr's changed behaviour after the ExCo meeting: 'Almost from that meeting on, the Governor-General was very particular about Executive Council meetings and was more careful and probing.'[19]

I have not been able to find evidence that Kerr was criticised

---

[19] Kelly and Bramston, op.cit., pp. 107-108.

in public for signing the minute, although that is not to say it doesn't exist. If it does, it is not readily available, and I doubt it was extensive or that it weighed upon Sir John Kerr in the way the authors have suggested. It would have helped their case if they had cited one or two examples.

But to continue:

> In an effort to save his government, Whitlam convened on 9 July 1975 a special sitting day devoted exclusively to putting on the table all details of the loans affair. It was at that time that Kerr wrote his nine-page document, a methodical and self-justifying missive, explaining everything he had done.[20]

The public interest and outrage over the loans affair was extraordinary. It dominated the media and yet the most Kelly and Bramston can say about this momentous event is that Kerr wrote a 'self-justifying missive' explaining his actions.

Well, they do go on to say:

> During the special sitting day, future Liberal attorney-general Bob Ellicott delivered his withering condemnation of the Whitlam government:
>
> 'I cannot believe that any honest man could advise the Governor-General to approve of that minute if he knew that the borrowings were for 20 years and were to meet the long term energy purposes of the Government. I do not believe an honest man could do it. I believe it was an illegal and unconstitutional act ... I cannot imagine that His Excellency, a lawyer of great eminence, would have approved that minute unless he had received assurances and advice that satisfied him that this was indeed a borrowing for temporary purposes. To satisfy him that it was, was to deceive him ... That is the charge. The action was unlawful, unconstitutional and based on deception.'
>
> Given Kerr's long association with Ellicott, a former solicitor-general, this speech would have had a profound impact on him. While it was an attack on Whitlam, the governor-general hardly appeared

---

[20] Ibid, p. 108.

in a flattering light.[21]

That the speech would have had a 'profound effect' on Kerr is just speculation. And it did not cast Kerr in an unflattering light. It cast him as the victim of the government's duplicity. It stated that he must have been deceived. Ellicott would have understood the basis upon which Kerr signed the minute – that the issue was justiciable – but in this speech he was simply indulging in a bit of political hyperbole.

But now the authors lay another charge at Kerr's feet:

> After the dismissal, however, Whitlam laid a lethal accusation against Kerr: that the protests in his book about the loan were retrospective. Whitlam said of Kerr: 'He became concerned about his complicity in the events of 13-14 December 1974 only when they became a matter of political controversy and when the people with whom he wished to ingratiate himself started ribbing him about it. Legality and propriety had nothing to do with it.'[22]

That is nothing more than an unsubstantiated. And it is hardly lethal. It does not stand up to the most basic scrutiny. Earlier, I quoted Kelly and Bramston quoting John Menadue to the effect that, after the fateful ExCo meeting, 'the Governor-General was very particular about Executive Council meetings and was more careful and probing'. That would hardly be the case if his concerns were manufactured only after the controversy erupted. And, if he really were unconcerned about the loan, why would he have bothered to phone Solicitor-General Maurice Byers to seek his thoughts after he had been assured by the Attorney-General, Lionel Murphy, that the loan was for temporary purposes?

Following the December meeting, two further Executive Council meetings considered the Khemlani loan:

> The loan authorisation was revoked on 7 January 1975 at an ExCo meeting attended by Kerr, at which he said nothing about the process. On 28 January, Kerr presided at another ExCo meeting at-

---

[21] Ibid., pp. 108-109.
[22] Ibid., p. 109.

tended by Connor and Murphy, which re-instated the authority for half the amount. At this meeting, in response to Kerr's question, Murphy gave the same opinion – it could be regarded as being for temporary purposes. In his private notes, Kerr later wrote he concluded 'it would be useless for me to try to discuss policy and of no relevance what my own legal opinion might be.' He did not even ask Murphy to put his opinion in writing. When the meeting broke, Kerr's social discussion with the ministers confirmed their determination on the loan. Kerr decided 'there was nothing I could do about it'. Again, he had not raised any doubts with them.[23]

As regards the second meeting, there is nothing new in this instance other than the fact that it was approved in advance, in which case there would be no reason for Kerr to say anything about the process. And on 28 January, the same considerations that applied on 14 December 1975 also informed Sir John's actions on this occasion. It could be argued that in questioning Murphy again about the legality of the loan, he was, in fact, raising his doubts. As to not requesting Murphy's advice in writing, it was Kerr himself who raised that issue. He seems to accept that he might have erred in not doing so:

> Perhaps it could be said that when it came to the meeting of 28 January 1975 I could have asked the Attorney-General for written advice. My judgement was that the Ministers had acted once on the oral advice and that this was a matter on which it was profitless for me to run violently into a brick wall. I decided that as they and the Prime Minister had clear-cut views there was nothing I could do about it. I had been in office only six months and was learning fast what was possible and what was not.[24]

In fact, there was little point in Kerr asking for a written opinion. He did not see it as his province to critique that opinion and he was certainly correct in surmising that even if he had, this cabal would have ignored the warning implicit in such a request. The only purpose to be served in asking for the opinion would have been to protect Kerr's own back. So, in this instance, at least, he was not acting in a self-serving manner. That he was rather more diffident than, say, Sir Paul

---

[23] Ibid.
[24] Kerr, op.cit., p. 239-240.

Hasluck might have been in the same situation can certainly be put down to the fact that, as he says, he was only newly installed in the job and still, to some extent, feeling his way.

Whitlam now makes another claim:

> Whitlam later mocked Kerr's hypocrisy. How, he asked, could the matter that caused Kerr 'great shock' on 14 December apparently deserve his approval and acquiescence on 28 January? Whitlam was enraged by Kerr's claim that the original meeting was invalid and by his justification for not raising this at the time: that it was a matter for the courts. He branded this a 'monstrous' argument. Whitlam is surely correct: the idea that a governor-general would decide an ExCo meeting was invalid but not raise it with the prime minister is untenable behaviour. At face value, it is an abdication of constitutional responsibility. This is either a post-event fabrication by Kerr or confirmation that Kerr was weak and frightened of Whitlam.[25]

Let me first deal with Whitlam mocking Kerr's 'hypocrisy'. This is disingenuous in the extreme. What shocked Kerr on 14 December 1974 was the way in which the ExCo meeting had been sprung upon him after the event. The fact that a meeting had been called at very short notice without seeking his approval. He was *not* 'shocked' by the fact of the loan itself. He merely expressed doubt as to its legality. There was no hypocrisy in acquiescing to it on 28 January under the same considerations that applied originally. That is, he 'acted on advice'.

Going back to that original meeting, Kerr did note in his autobiography that preparations for the meeting had been underway for most of Friday 13 December, even though the meeting was not called until 7pm. As Kerr tells it:

> There had in fact been preparations by officials during Friday for a possible meeting. On Saturday morning 14 December the Prime Minister did not tell me this and I did not know it. I do not know when those preparations began. In normal practice it is not when a positive decision is made to have a meeting that Government House is notified but when it becomes apparent that a meeting may be

---
[25]   Kelly and Bramston, op.cit., pp. 111-112.

necessary. The Secretary of the Executive Council would normally act at that time. On this occasion he did not.[26]

It is hard to gainsay that. It makes eminent sense. And, although he doesn't say so himself, it is hard to escape the conclusion that Kerr was ambushed. He must have thought so. That would be the basis of the great shock he felt.

As to the validity of the meeting, I have dealt with this earlier. There was no doubt that the 13 December meeting was invalid. It was not just Kerr who thought so. However, Kerr believed, not unreasonably, that he had validated the meeting on 14 December by agreeing to sign the minute. He subsequently conceded, prompted by the 1977 opinion of Professor Sawyer, that he may have erred in this respect but if he had, it would be a matter for the courts because it was already a *fait accompli*.

Kelly and Bramston now offer another claim by Whitlam:

> In assessing Kerr's attitude at the time Whitlam said the governor-general in discussions with ministers in December had been enthusiastically canvassing the loan's potential.[27]

It is difficult to see how Kerr could have canvassed the loan's potential with Ministers during December, since they had all departed for the Christmas recess. That was the reason for the urgency of the 13 December meeting. But in any case, even if Kerr had doubts about the legality of the loan, it would not necessarily preclude him being enthusiastic about what it might achieve if it came to fruition. This is just another gratuitous smear.

They continue:

> Whitlam said that 'at no stage' did Kerr raise with him 'the slightest doubts about any aspect of the matter' though he had 'plenty of opportunities' to do so. Whitlam documented his frequent meetings with Kerr over January and early February and said there was no sign of any tensions. In his book about the crisis, Whitlam said 'it surprises me to discover nearly four years later that Sir John Kerr

---

[26] Kerr, op.cit., p. 231.
[27] Kelly and Bramston, op.cit., p. 110.

was a deeply troubled man at that time'.[28]

But was Kerr 'deeply troubled' at that time? From Kerr's autobiography:

> The affair had a real affect on me because I could not see a good reason why the ordinary practices relating to the Executive Council had been departed from. Despite preparations for a meeting on 13 December the Governor-General had not been brought into the matter; and I pondered the reason why this was so. It seemed to me that what happened ought not to have happened and that it could perhaps be a warning of the risk that the reality of the Governor-General's office might be by-passed and refuge taken in the rubber stamp assumption. I was very much concerned too that what I had had to do might be misunderstood by many in the community as indicating that I myself was indifferent to important government business and subscribed to the rubber stamp theory. Certainly this was not true.[29]

So, Kerr was certainly wary at this time, but he was not 'deeply troubled'. And it is important to make the distinction that what he was worried about was the attitude of the government towards his office. Despite his doubts about its legality, he was not troubled about the loan approval itself.

As I noted earlier, Kerr probably suspected he had been ambushed. But there is a reason he doesn't say anything to Whitlam at this point. It's called human nature. At this stage, Kerr, by nature a friendly and gregarious man, had been in the job six months – a job which was given to him by Whitlam, along with a ten-year tenure and a pension. Kerr had every reason to feel grateful to Whitlam, with whom he was going to have to work for at least two and a half more years. The natural reaction is to give Whitlam the benefit of the doubt and hold fire for the moment. And, as most people would know, this can turn out to be a mistaken course if events do turn for the worse. Generally, this happens in small stages and the hesitation to raise the matter persists until it is too late. Kerr might be criticised for not raising his doubts at some point down the track but, if

---

[28] Ibid.
[29] Kerr, op.cit., p. 239.

he had, would that have altered the course of events? Would Whitlam have taken him seriously?

Let me continue:

> Fraser following Ellicott's line, said the original ExCo minute raised the possibility of a 'deliberate conspiracy to deceive and defraud'. The public servants involved were later called to the bar of the Senate and quizzed. Whitlam laid his own charge against Kerr: if the governor-general had such doubts then, as a man of honour, it was his duty to raise them.[30]

This is just flim-flam on the part of Whitlam, and it does Kelly and Bramston no credit to repeat it here. Kerr did not entertain doubts about the ExCo minute in terms of a 'deliberate conspiracy to deceive and defraud'. That characterisation was just political hyperbole on the part of Fraser. Kerr's only doubts related to whether or not the loan was for temporary purposes and he 'accepted advice' that this was, at least, arguable. In fact, Kelly and Bramston concede:

> Kerr was correct to accept Whitlam's advice, sign the minute and authorise the loan raising. He is correct in saying the substantive legal issue was for the High Court.[31]

However, they go on to say:

> But the contradiction in Kerr's account is unsustainable: he claims to be shocked, offended and worried the office is being diminished yet he says nothing to Whitlam. The contradiction is untenable.
>
> Given the gravity of his concerns, what should Kerr have done? He should have told Whitlam the depth of his concern about the ExCo meeting. He should have asked on the Saturday morning for the attorney-general's opinion to be put in writing. He should not have signed the minute until the written advice was provided. He could have spoken to Connor to get a fuller explanation of the purposes of the loan and spoken to Cairns to get an explanation for the unusual channels being used to raise the funds. He spoke to Byers but

---

[30] Kelly and Bramston, op.cit., p. 110.
[31] Ibid.

missed the main game: the Treasury and the treasurer.[32]

Keep in mind that Kelly and Bramston a few sentences earlier conceded that Kerr was correct to sign the minute. As his autobiography makes clear, Kerr did not have 'grave concerns' on 14 December. The passage above has conflated Kerr's concerns, on 14 December, over the temporary nature of the loan, with other issues of legality and probity that emerged later. It was not Kerr's job to quiz Connor and Cairns about the purposes of the loan and the means of obtaining it. That would be intruding on the politics of the matter. As to getting Murphy's advice in writing, Kerr was in Sydney and had had impressed upon him the urgency and that the players were dispersing for the Christmas recess. Kerr's actions were perfectly reasonable. And, particularly in this timeframe, how could Kerr possibly have gained access to Treasury officials to get their input? And would this have even been proper?

It is telling that Kelly and Bramston, at no stage in this discussion, raise any criticism of Whitlam for what was, at best, a cavalier approach to calling an Executive Council meeting, and at worst (and probably) an ambush.

There follow several paragraphs that describe Kerr's dereliction:

> His personal records, correspondence, journal and memoirs are tedious in the gravity of his concerns yet near empty in tangible actions. These concerns should have been put to Whitlam on the Saturday both orally and in writing. Harders [Secretary of the Attorney-General's Department] nailed the issue: 'I think a Governor-General who had concerns about the ExCo minute and its legality along the lines expressed by Kerr in his book should have raised those concerns at the time with the Prime Minister.' Indeed, if the concerns were genuine at the time, Kerr was irresponsible not to do so.
> This penetrates to the supreme lesson from the loan crisis – Kerr felt he could never influence Whitlam. His writing is thick with self-justification for inaction. In the end Kerr never tried to influ-

---

[32] Ibid., pp. 110-111.

ence Whitlam. Kerr keeps saying that raising issues would be useless and pointless and that because Whitlam and his senior ministers had made up their minds 'there was nothing I could do about it'.[33]

To begin with, I'm not sure how much weight should be placed on the view of Harders, who, as head of Attorney-General Lionel Murphy's department, allowed his own minister to present questionable advice to the Governor-General. Harders would not have been unaware of the concerns of Sir Frederick Wheeler and John Stone, adverted to earlier. Did he, himself, remonstrate with Murphy or Whitlam? Did he, for example, offer to resign over the matter?

Much of the above gives the impression that it refers to Kerr's longer-term relationship with Whitlam, but in fact it is still all about the 13 December meeting. They are just restating points already made and with which I have already dealt. In summary:

a) Kerr was concerned about the way in which the meeting was called,
b) he was doubtful that the loan was really for temporary purposes, however
c) he believed that was for the courts to decide and given the urgency impressed upon him,
d) he 'accepted advice' to sign the minute.

The extract above is sourced to pages 238-240 of *Matters for Judgement*, part of the chapter which deals with the 13 December meeting. If you read that chapter, you will find that it is not tedious with hand-wringing, self-justification for inaction and does not overstate the 'gravity', as Kelly and Bramston do, with which Kerr viewed matters at that time. It simply states Kerr's position. Whether or not you believe any or all of his account, it is not 'thick with self-justification'.

There is more along these lines (which it would be tedious to go into) until we get to October. Despite the impression, which Kelly and Bramston have striven to create, that Kerr's ongoing relationship with Whitlam was replete with incidents in which

---

[33] Ibid., p. 111.

he should have proffered advice but failed to do so, Kerr's autobiography details no other such occasion between 14 December 1974 and October 1975. There is no hand-wringing or agonizing or lack of action on some constitutionally doubtful issue. But, by the middle of October things changed materially:

> Kerr was turning against Whitlam.
>
> His doubts were accentuated on the eve of the supply crisis. In his memoirs, Kerr says that shortly before the 14 October resignation of Connor, he had a conversation with Whitlam in which the prime minister said he would defy the Senate if supply were blocked and 'destroy forever' the Senate's power. Kerr claimed he asked Whitlam whether 'that is the wisest course'. Kerr suggested it might be better to go to an election. He argued that Whitlam was still young and even if Whitlam lost an election, he would have a good chance of returning, as did Harold Wilson in Britain in 1974. He says Whitlam rejected this approach 'out of hand'.
>
> The governor-general believed this was an important exchange. He said it was one of the first conversations when an 'implacable element' began to appear in Whitlam. 'He made it clear that my suggestion was not discussable and never would be,' Kerr says. He gives no date or location for this exchange.
>
> Kerr claimed this view was confirmed when Whitlam came to Government House on 14 October for the swearing in of Senator Wriedt as Connor's successor ... Kerr gave no details of this further discussion with Whitlam. But his conclusion is breathtaking: he decided Whitlam was beyond reach of any argument 'or even discussion'.
>
> Kerr said in his memoirs that these exchanges saw him go as far as he 'could prudently go in the exercise of my right to "advise and warn"'. This is a ludicrous statement. In no way does it constitute a serious example of the Crown's 'advise and warn' doctrine ...
>
> If Kerr had been serious, he would have warned Whitlam that, in any supply crisis, it was the prime minister's ultimate responsibility to resolve the deadlock before funds expired.[34]

---

[34] Ibid., pp. 112-113.

Here we have the first suggestion that the 'advise and warn' doctrine is a duty not merely a right. That may sound like semantics, and it may be arguable that a Governor-General who chooses not to exercise that right when it is called for *and when the relationship between the two is conducive to such an approach*, is failing in his duty. But all the evidence – much of it compiled by Kelly and Bramston themselves – is that Whitlam was immune to advice from his own staff, his Caucus colleagues and the Government's senior departmental advisers. It is more than likely he conveyed that message to Kerr as well. Furthermore, Whitlam was, or should have been, aware of his responsibility to obtain supply appropriated by Parliament. It is a fundamental tenet of responsible government. Kerr's suggestion, that Whitlam's wisest course might be to go to an election, can be construed as a warning. A warning couched in diplomatic terms can be more effective than one bluntly stated. Had Kerr advised or warned Whitlam in stronger terms than he did, does anyone imagine that Whitlam would have taken any notice?

Later:

> A contemporary twelve-page handwritten note in Kerr's papers dated 16 November 1975, reinforces his core claim. Kerr said that from 'the beginning of my relevant talks' with the prime minister before the blocking of supply, 'Mr Whitlam told me would never agree to an election for the House or a double dissolution whilst supply was being denied as a means of getting supply'. The note continued: '[Whitlam] told me he intended to "tough it out" and if necessary to govern without supply ...'
>
> Whitlam, however, disputed the facts in Kerr's memoirs. He said no such discussions took place. He said he would have remembered any reference to Wilson and it was not made.[35]

Whitlam said 'he would have remembered any reference to Wilson and it was not made.' Well, that settles it!

Can anyone doubt that 'toughing it out' was Whitlam's intention?

---

[35] Ibid., pp. 113-114.

In Chapter Seven of *The Dismissal*, Kelly and Bramston describe exactly this strategy and portray it as Whitlam's sacred mission. That being the case, can anyone imagine that Whitlam would conceal this fact from the most important player in the drama? In the event, as we shall see, Whitlam did canvass the possibility of governing without supply by virtue of a loan from the banks.

Continuing:

> Accepting Kerr's version, it does not constitute a serious example of the 'advise and warn' doctrine. Indeed, it reveals the farcical nature of the situation and Kerr's behaviour. These exchanges, if they occurred, were before supply was even blocked.[36]

As I have argued, it is highly improbable that these exchanges didn't occur, and it is of no significance that they occurred before supply was blocked. As Kelly and Bramston themselves report in Chapter Seven of their book, Whitlam was addressing the possibility of supply being blocked and foreshadowing his strategy in a speech in Goulburn on 12 September.[37]

And further:

> Kerr's admission that he never subsequently counselled Whitlam in a frank manner reveals the extent of the governor-general's deception of the prime minister. His justification was Whitlam's intransigence. But that was no justification whatsoever. Having an intransigent prime minister is hardly unique and did not absolve Kerr of his responsibility. Everybody had to deal with Whitlam's overbearing personality: his staff, ministers, party officials, public servants and journalists.[38]

'Everybody had to deal with Whitlam's overbearing personality: his staff, ministers, party officials, public servants and journalists.' Kelly and Bramston make it clear in various instances that Whitlam refused to listen to reason from even his closest advisers. In other words, they *didn't* deal with it.

---

[36] Ibid., p. 114.
[37] Ibid., pp. 97-98.
[38] Ibid., p. 114.

It might be more accurate to say they had to 'cop it sweet'. Kerr did not. And I doubt very much that Whitlam would have suffered, with any equanimity, being 'counselled' by Kerr.

It's ironic that, in a chapter which deals with the Loans Affair – as Alan Reid put it, the 'death warrant' of the Whitlam government – Sir John Kerr should emerge as the villain. Chapter Eight of *The Dismissal*, if I may borrow a phrase from Kelly and Bramston, is tedious with accusations that he failed in his constitutional duty to 'advise and warn'. But, to put it in perspective, the occasions in which Kerr allegedly failed in this respect, cover a single day in December 1974 and a single month in 1975. And in the month of October and early November, there was only one issue on which Kerr supposedly failed, viz., that he should have warned Whitlam it was his duty to obtain supply or risk having his commission terminated. I will deal with this topic in more detail later. I am not a lawyer, and I may be missing some subtlety regarding the 'advise and warn' doctrine, but its importance here seems to be grossly overstated. If Kerr erred in this respect it would seem to be more an error of judgement – the use of implicit rather than explicit warning – more than deception.

Does anyone seriously imagine that wise words to Whitlam from Sir John Kerr about the risk of his strategy, would have fallen on willing ears? Does anyone imagine that things would have turned out differently, other than Whitlam deciding he could do without this meddlesome Governor-General and having him recalled? This is the subject of the next chapter. Kerr's statement, dismissed by Kelly and Bramston, that his suggestion to Whitlam that he advise a double dissolution was 'as far as I could prudently go in the exercise of my right to "advise and warn"', needs to be seen in this context.

9

Kerr's Fear of Recall

One of the major criticisms of Sir John Kerr was that he failed to warn Whitlam of the possibility of his sacking. Presumably that warning would have taken the form of words such as: Prime Minister, I must warn you that it is your obligation to obtain supply. If you fail to do that, I may be forced to withdraw your commission.

One of the reasons he did not do that was because he believed that if he had, Whitlam would have asked the Queen for his recall. That would have had two consequences. The first and obvious one is that Kerr – who from sometime in September (or possibly earlier) contemplated that he might have to dismiss Whitlam – would have certainly been replaced by someone who would act as a rubber stamp. That would seriously diminish the office of the Governor-General. And secondly, it would have drawn the Queen into a political controversy in Australia. And that is something that Kerr went out of his way to avoid.

Kerr was convinced that Whitlam would have moved against him.

Much of this chapter of *The Dismissal* is devoted to examining the evidence for this belief. It commences with a letter that Whitlam wrote to British PM, Harold Wilson, shortly after the election:

> He said: 'I made a fundamental mistake in recommending to the Queen that she appoint a judge as her viceroy. In Australia judges suffer the corruption of knowing that on the High Court they can with impunity make propositions and dispositions of a political

> nature. The Governor-General was persuaded that he could do the same. He deceived me – realizing, I'm sure that I would have been in touch with the Queen if my suspicions had been aroused.'
>
> Whitlam, in effect, was telling Wilson he would have moved against Kerr if he had had any notion of the governor-general's intentions.[1]

The first thought that occurred to me on reading this was that Whitlam regretted appointing a judge as Governor-General, on the basis that he could 'with impunity make propositions and dispositions of a political nature'. And yet he saw no incongruity in his own appointment of Lionel Murphy as a judge on the High Court where, apparently, he could 'with impunity make propositions and dispositions of a political nature'. It seems a double standard to me.

Kelly and Bramston point out that this was after the event and claim that this was Whitlam 'exposing his heart'. Whitlam subsequently denied he would have moved against Kerr, but we will see that assertion must be treated with some scepticism.

They describe Kerr's position:

> Kerr believed he was under threat from Whitlam. He was convinced that Whitlam, if he had any inkling of Kerr's plan to use the reserve powers, would contact the Palace to have Kerr recalled. It is the reason Kerr deceived Whitlam. The governor-general's protection of the Queen from any involvement is the justification Kerr openly offered for his dismissal by deception. He wanted to surprise Whitlam and he did surprise Whitlam.[2]

This is another example of wording chosen to cast Kerr in the worst possible light. If Kerr genuinely believed he was under threat, then to 'keep his own counsel' or to 'keep his powder dry', is not an example of deception – certainly not a sin of commission – but a tactical move to protect his own position. And Kerr's wish to protect the Queen was not merely a convenient *post hoc* justification, as Kelly and Bramston imply, but a genuine requirement of the job, one which any Governor-

---

[1] Kelly and Bramston, *The Dismissal*, p. 117.
[2] Ibid., p. 118.

General would strive to honour.

But Whitlam's memoirs tell a different story:

> In his memoirs of the crisis published in 1979, Whitlam denied outright any interest in removing Kerr: 'At no time during the crisis had the possibility of replacing Sir John Kerr been a significant element in my thinking. I never bothered even to inquire into the legal or practical procedures for so drastic and unprecedented an action. I have not to this day.'
>
> Comments from John Menadue in a document he wrote in late 1975 throw light on this contradiction. Menadue said the possibility that the governor-general might seek to dismiss Whitlam was considered early in the crisis but 'as time passed, [Whitlam] became less concerned with the question'.
>
> Menadue wrote: 'On a couple of occasions I asked him if he had considered the mechanics of contacting Government House if he had to move quickly. He merely said he would have to ring Martin Charteris but believed this was a hypothetical and theoretical possibility which he did not consider likely ...
>
> In short, Whitlam had no contingency plans for Kerr's recall. The reason is he was sure he had Kerr's measure. Seeing Kerr as a weak man, Whitlam never took seriously the idea of dismissal by the governor-general. And, as Menadue indicated, the prime minister also made no plans for a situation in which Kerr moved against him.[3]

So, it seems Whitlam's complacence was not based on a belief in the non-existence of the dismissal power but on the idea that Kerr was a weak man who would not defy him. The authors then quote several sources that confirm the above. But:

> During the crisis, however, Whitlam would periodically joke about having to sack Kerr. 'Yes, he would joke about it,' his principal private secretary, John Mant, said. Mant recalled this took the form of Whitlam saying, "Oh well, I might have to ring the Queen. I might have to ring Westminster about this." Nobody ever took it seriously and I certainly don't think he ever would.' Mant's comment, however, highlights one of the paradoxes of the crisis – Whitlam

---

[3] Ibid., pp. 118-119.

knew that Kerr had a technical power to move against him but he never treated this as a serious option that required any contingency planning.[4]

This quote of Mant is rather curious. In what context did Whitlam make these jokes, apparently to his colleagues? Was he reacting to a suggestion from one of them that he might be dismissed? If so, he could hardly claim to have been totally blindsided by the eventuality. And as to Whitlam knowing that 'Kerr had a technical power to move against him', he also knew that the Opposition and many in the media were urging exactly that. In these circumstances, his insouciance at this possibility seems almost unbelievable. It can only have stemmed from his belief that he could intimidate Kerr into not acting, as Kelly and Bramston have already outlined above. But if that is the case, then Whitlam's amazement that Kerr did dismiss him, if it were true, can only have stemmed from the fact that he misjudged Kerr, *and not* because he was taken totally unawares by Kerr invoking a power that Whitlam claimed was moribund.

The fact that Whitlam never made any plans to have Kerr recalled – on the basis that he didn't think he would ever need to – does not preclude the possibility that he would have acted if he *had* become aware of Kerr's deliberations, as Kelly and Bramston concede:

> What Whitlam might have done had he discovered Kerr's dismissal plan is another matter. His anger and sense of betrayal would have matched the fires of hell.[5]

Kerr had no 'plan' to dismiss Whitlam. It was a contingency Kerr needed to consider, based on Whitlam's own vehement public pronouncements. And the main point is:

> There is, however, no gainsaying Kerr's conviction on this question. In his twelve-page hand-written note dated 16 November 1975, Kerr said: 'On several occasions, sometimes jocularly sometimes less so, but on all occasions with underlying seriousness, [Whitlam] said that the crisis could end in a race to the Palace to see who could

---

[4] Ibid., p. 119.
[5] Ibid.

get there first.

Throughout the crisis Whitlam sought to reinforce his confidence in Kerr with a counterproductive tactic of intimidation, in private and public. This was notable in his public declarations that the governor-general had no option but to act on the advice of the prime minister. The most famous such example was the Government House dinner for Malaysian prime minister Tun Abdul Razak on the night of 16 October, the day the Senate deferred the budget bills. Kerr recollected that Whitlam, referring to the supply crisis, 'said to me with a brilliant smile. "It could be a question of whether I get to the Queen first for your recall or you get in first with my dismissal." We all laughed.'

Kerr said later he saw this supposed joke as 'a very real threat'. He said he felt shattered and that it was another piece of Whitlam's 'psychological warfare'.[6] (emphasis added)

The depth of Kerr's reaction was confirmed by his wife, Lady Kerr, and his Official Secretary, David Smith.

But:

Whitlam later dismissed his remark as flippant, but it would be a mistake to accept that at face value. Anybody familiar with Whitlam knew he used wit, sarcasm and jokes a weapon.[7]

In other words, Kerr not only believed Whitlam might move against him, but he was also justified in that belief. And, on that basis, Kerr had every right to infer that Whitlam knew he risked being dismissed and that he, Kerr, was being warned off. In which case, why would he risk exposing himself by explicitly warning Whitlam. He would have seen this as a futile and provocative gesture. This was a game of cat and mouse and if Kerr did 'deceive' Whitlam, he was himself equally deceived by Whitlam.

We now turn to a claim that does raise some questions in my mind concerning Kerr's actions. It concerns a type-written note

---

[6] Ibid., pp. 119-120.
[7] Ibid., p. 120.

discovered in Kerr's papers in which he reveals that, at the Tun Abdul Razak dinner, he had three conversations with Fraser. The first of these was prompted by an approach from Fraser:

> In the note, Kerr said that before the dinner Fraser told him: (a) he was 'very worried' and would 'welcome any advice I could give him'; (b) that he was relying 'heavily' on the advice of Bob Ellicott ; (c) that he had not decided to block supply until the Khemlani loans affair scandal recurred and 'after that he really had no choice'; and (d) that he thought he could 'possibly have destroyed himself' but 'he had to do it'.[8]

This certainly sounds like Fraser courting Kerr with a view to influencing his actions. Understandable, if not entirely proper, but in no way reflecting badly on Kerr. After dinner Fraser spoke with Kerr about the Ellicott opinion, telling Kerr he wanted him to see it. They then move on to the third conversation:

> Kerr's note said that he had not yet begun 'any process of mediation' between the leaders 'although this has been canvassed during the weekend in the press'. His note said: 'There was one element in my pre-dinner and post-dinner short conversations with Mr Fraser which for completeness I should record.' In a remarkable account, Kerr said:
>
>> Before dinner [Fraser] was undoubtedly wishing me to know that he had confidence in me and that my presence was important and he hoped to have the benefit of my advice. Some intuition led me to make a cryptic remark about things not necessarily remaining the same. He did not understand this – I was referring to the remote possibility that I might not be there, to possible but unlikely dismissal. He did not pick this up and I could not at that time stay and elaborate ...
>>
>> Having thought about it over dinner, I concluded that I should be rather more specific because I felt he was entitled to take into account a bare possibility which he had not seemed to contemplate. I therefore said to him that one conceivable but remote aspect was that as the crisis developed the Prime Minister had the option of considering the degree of his confidence

---

[8] Ibid., pp. 120-121.

in me. He said that it was inconceivable.

His reaction was to say the Queen would never permit it. I told him that that question was one I preferred not to discuss. It was most unlikely but he would have to make up his own mind about it. I did this out of fairness because he could be badly caught by ending up with a Governor-General who would not even consider ever using the reserve power however bad the situation and I had a feeling that the point would in any event break into the press as it immediately did. He should be thinking about it.

There is of course nothing he could do if things moved, as I do not believe they will, in this direction except make a fuss. There would be a very great fuss indeed. I judge that the only circumstances in which my dismissal would be recommended would be if the crisis became really drastic and the Prime Minister feared that I was about to dismiss him. He would under those circumstances undoubtedly try to get in first.[9]

Kelly and Bramston describe this as astonishing and so, in some ways, it seems to me. They list several implications, the most important of which is that it proves that Kerr did believe that Whitlam might act to sack him and that this was valuable intelligence for Fraser, both as to Kerr's attitude towards Whitlam (distrust) and to the fact that Kerr was willing to use the reserve powers. It is hard to argue with those conclusions and it does seem, on the face of it, to be an indiscretion on the part of Kerr.

It is difficult to see that Kerr owed any duty to Fraser other than to treat him fairly. Kelly and Bramston report that Fraser, interviewed by Bramston in 2013, denied that the conversations took place. They conclude:

> With Kerr and Fraser both dead, a degree of uncertainty surrounds this conversation. Yet the explicit and detailed nature of Kerr's note must lend credence to the view that it happened.[10]

---

[9] Ibid., pp. 121-122.
[10] Ibid., p. 123.

Again, that would seem logical but on the other hand why would Fraser deny the conversation? It does not reflect any discredit on him, and, by that stage, he was well past doing any favours for Kerr.

The odd thing is that, on the face of it, it seems an indiscretion on the part of Kerr. And yet Kerr obviously saw no impropriety in these conversations, or he would not have written the note. As Kerr's defence counsel, the only possible explanation I can offer for this apparent indiscretion is that he thought his comment might give Fraser pause, might induce him to be more accommodating towards the government. But I admit it's a long bow.

The next interesting development involves a conversation Kerr had with Prince Charles during the Papua New Guinea independence celebrations in Port Moresby in September 1975, before Fraser had formally blocked supply. This was discovered in his 1980 hand-written journal:

> ... [Kerr] told Charles, the Prince of Wales, the reserve powers might 'need to be exercised' which could 'heighten the risk of recall'. According to Kerr, the Prince said: 'But surely, Sir John, the Queen would not have to accept advice that you should be recalled at the very time should this happen when you were considering having to dismiss the government.'

> Kerr's journal says that after returning to London, Prince Charles spoke to the Queen's private secretary, Sir Martin Charteris, who then wrote to Kerr on 7 October. Kerr says Charteris advised 'that if the kind of contingency in mind were to develop, although the Queen would try to delay things, in the end she would have to take the Prime Minister's advice'. Kerr makes the point he already knew this.

> The suggestion that Kerr told Charles a month before supply was blocked, that he might have to dismiss Whitlam is astonishing. Its credibility is in question. The full account is not mentioned in Kerr's memoirs or in any of Kerr's contemporary notes written during the crisis sighted by the authors. It also contradicts Kerr's golden rule in the crisis – that he did not signal his hand to the Palace. The let-

ters between Kerr and the Palace have not been released.[11]

Well, the letters have now been released and they confirm these discussions. What they show, above all else, is that Kerr did not 'sandbag' the Palace when he dismissed Whitlam. And that Kerr told Charles a month before supply was blocked that he might have to dismiss Whitlam is not so astonishing. The possibility had already been widely canvassed in the media. On 15 September the *Financial Times* editorial, although critical of Fraser's ambivalence on the issue, anticipated that he would block supply and discussed the possibility of Whitlam's dismissal.[12] As did other publications.

But did this mean that Kerr did, in fact, signal his hand to the Palace? Does it mean, as Professor Jenny Hocking claimed, that there was a conspiracy between the Palace and Kerr to dismiss Whitlam?

The answer to the second question is definitively no, as Kelly and Bramston argued in the first place and as they now reaffirm in their later book *The Truth of the Palace Letters*. This is not an issue which I intend to address further.

As to the first question, again the answer must be no. What he meant by 'not signalling his hand', if he used that phrase, was that the decision was his and his alone and he, at no point, sought advance approval of his decision or advised the Palace prior to the event that he was about to withdraw Whitlam's commission. That protocol did not prevent him from discussing the issues, including the use of the reserve powers, with the Palace.

Kelly and Bramston offer further evidence that Kerr was concerned about his possible recall, describing the occasion of a dinner with the Governor of New South Wales, Sir Roden Cutler:

> Around the onset of the crisis, the Kerrs dined at Admiralty House with the NSW governor, Sir Roden Cutler, and his wife. This arose

---
[11] Ibid., pp. 123-124.
[12] 'Exit the Marquess of Queensberry', *The Financial Review*, 15 September 1975, p. 18.

because Kerr had planned an overseas trip – subsequently cancelled – and Cutler, as the senior governor, would have served in his place during the crisis. Cutler recalled: 'At one stage I said to Kerr that there was, of course, the possibility that the Prime Minister might move to dismiss him. He became very activated at this point, saying, "Yes, I know, I know." It was obvious he had given some thought to this possibility.'[13]

What this tells us is that Kerr was not alone in considering that Whitlam might seek to remove him. Cutler, who is elsewhere quoted as being critical of Kerr, clearly believed that it was a possibility.

They continue:

> The governor-general is appointed by the Queen on advice from the prime minister and can be removed by such advice. There is no security of tenure. Kerr and his official secretary, David Smith, had discussed the possibility of Kerr's removal from office. As a result, Smith contacted Charteris to inquire about the process. The advice from Charteris was that a phone call would not suffice. The Palace would require a letter. Charteris later told Paul Kelly: 'You couldn't just pick up the telephone and fix it up that way'. Smith told the authors: 'The message from Charteris was that the Queen would have to accept any advice from the Prime Minister but in the process there could be to-ing and fro-ing.'[14]

Which brings me to another digression. If you will bear with me, I am going to go out on a limb. It is my belief that the view of the Palace – that the Queen would ultimately have to accept Whitlam's advice to withdraw Kerr's commission if he, Whitlam, pushed the point – is wrong. If not wrong in practice and precedent, then wrong in theory and logic.

As I argued earlier, the Governor-General is analogous to a regent. He represents the Monarch but, in all practical respects – in all but name – he *is* the Monarch. According to the Constitution, it is he who exercises the executive powers vested in the Crown. The Monarch him/herself does not

---

[13] Kelly and Bramston, op.cit., pp. 124-125.
[14] Ibid., p. 125.

exercise those powers. It is to the Governor-General alone that the Prime Minister proffers the 'advice' upon which, under normal circumstances, he/she is obliged to act. It seems to me that there is no scope for the Prime Minister to offer advice of this nature to the Monarch. He cannot bypass the Governor-General. So, any advice that he offered the Monarch to remove a Governor-General must necessarily be no more than a request.

The Governor-General is appointed by the Monarch on the recommendation of the Prime Minister. In my view, once that appointment is made, confidence in the Governor-General is the sole province of the Monarch. The mother, having given birth, does not own the child. The gift, having been given, cannot be demanded back. Or put another way, the Governor-Generalship is not the gift of the Prime Minister. It is his duty (or privilege) to recommend a particular person to that role.

That is not to say that the Prime Minister may not recommend recall in the event of criminality, malfeasance, debilitating ill-health etc. But it is hardly logical to suggest that a Prime Minister, who is subject to an exercise of the reserve powers – specified in the very Constitution which it is duty of the Governor-General to uphold – can arbitrarily and self-interestedly insist upon his removal.

Kelly and Bramston make the point later in the chapter that Sir Paul Hasluck, in talking to Sir Martin Charteris 'remarked on the bizarre nature of Australia's system – a Governor-General could sack a Prime Minister without further consideration, but a Prime Minister had no power to sack a Governor-General without recourse to the Queen'.[15]

It is not so bizarre if you consider that that is exactly the situation that applies in the United Kingdom, notwithstanding that convention dictates that the Queen would only exercise her power to remove a Prime Minister in extreme circumstances. The British Prime Minister does not have the power to dismiss the Monarch. And if we consider that the Governor-General,

---

[15] Ibid., p. 133.

once having been appointed by the Monarch, *is* effectively the Monarch, then the same consideration should apply in Australia.

There is nothing in the Constitution about how the Governor-General is appointed. That he is appointed on the recommendation of the Prime Minister is a convention. This anomaly of the Governor-General lacking 'security of tenure' could be managed if the Constitution were amended to protect the Governor-General from opportunistic recall by, for example, establishing that his removal be recommended to the Monarch only on the basis of impeachment by both Houses of Parliament and only for reasons that do not impinge on his *judicious* use of the reserve powers. This sensible arrangement could also be done quickly and easily by legislation, since it is not a matter covered within the Constitution. It was one of the items of consideration during the 1999 republican referendum. There is no reason why it could not be revisited under existing circumstances.

But back to the central theme and a conversation between Whitlam and Kerr on 18 October:

> Kerr said he had a long discussion with Whitlam on 18 October in which the prime minister talked of finding a method to enable the banks to fund government salaries and services, thereby out-manoeuvring Fraser. Kerr claimed Whitlam said, as a result, there would be 'no excuse for removing him and sending for someone willing to advise an election'. Such a remark by Whitlam would have been extraordinarily inept. He denied the conversation took place. The point, however, is Kerr's self-declared state of mind. He asserted that from this point, early in the crisis: 'I never again felt I could talk to the Prime Minister about his policy on Supply.' Kerr said Whitlam told him: 'I can and will break Fraser, if my party stands behind me and it will.'[16]

'Such a remark by Whitlam would have been extraordinarily inept.' Well, Kelly and Bramston have already established that Whitlam's handling of Kerr had been consistently inept, and

---

[16] Ibid., p. 125.

they expand mightily on this theme in the next chapter. But why would this remark be inept? Whitlam had to convince Kerr he had a way of 'breaking Fraser' other than by hoping political and public pressure would force him to back down. This bank loan idea had in fact been seriously explored by Labor, and it makes sense that Whitlam would raise it with Kerr. Whitlam's denial that the conversation took place rings hollow. It is almost certain that it did occur. As we now know, Kerr reported this conversation to the Palace in a letter dated 20 October.[17] It is highly unlikely he would have invented the conversation for them. And if the conversation did take place, then Whitlam's purported remark about Kerr not needing to dismiss him would be the most natural thing in the world. And Whitlam's denial that this conversation took place, puts all his other unverified assertions in doubt.

The fact is that the possibility of Kerr dismissing Whitlam had been vigorously promoted by the Opposition and much of the media for months at this stage. The idea that Whitlam was living in blissful ignorance of the possibility that Kerr might remove him is inconceivable. And flowing from that, the suggestion that he was 'ambushed' is wishful thinking at best.

We now come to a contentious issue – a formal meeting between Kerr and Fraser which was approved by Whitlam:

> A fateful Whitlam-Kerr discussion occurred on 21 October after an ExCo meeting. At this point Kerr was feeling pressure from an intense media campaign for him to become more active. He was worried he may have appeared 'indifferent' to the deadlock. He had been assessing from the start what role he might play. He now asked Whitlam for approval to meet with Fraser to evaluate the situation. Kerr said he merely wished to assess Fraser's intentions. He told Whitlam he believed the crisis was still 'political' and had not crossed the threshold to become a 'constitutional' crisis.
>
> Whitlam agreed. He believed Kerr might be able to help.[18]

---

[17] Letter to Sir Martin Charteris, *The Palace Letters*, 20 October 1975, p. 120.
[18] Kelly and Bramston, op.cit., pp. 125-126.

All that is true except for the assertion that Kerr had been assessing what role he might play. He already knew what his role was. The only undetermined aspect was what decision(s) he might make. Kelly and Bramston go on to say:

> It was, however, an epic blunder. At this point Whitlam surrendered one of his major advantages. The Crown acts on the advice of its ministers. The Crown exists not as a constitutional umpire but as a constitutional guardian. It is the prime minister, not the opposition leader, who advises the Crown and the governor-general. The opposition leader has no direct relations with the governor-general. On those rare occasions when the Crown does mediate with both sides, the solemn responsibility of the Crown is to promote a solution yet keep the Crown impartial.[19]

The above passage clouds the issue. To begin with, Kerr did not seek to meet with Fraser in order to solicit advice from him. He did, probably primarily, wish to re-assure the public that he was taking an interest in the developing crisis. However, his other aim was to assess the probability of Fraser persisting in his strategy and to gauge if he was open to compromise. There was no suggestion he would mediate or try to procure a solution to the impasse. The reference to keeping 'the Crown impartial' is a *non sequitur* in the context of this meeting.

In his own words as reported to the Palace on 22 October, Kerr said:

> I suggested to the Prime Minister that he should agree to me seeing the Leader of the Opposition with a view to raising the question whether the Leader of the Opposition is determined to cross the threshold from a political to a constitutional crisis. He would do this, if he is going to do it, by producing what in the course of time would be a rejection of supply either by active rejection or continued deferral up to the point of time where money runs out. I thought it might be possible subtly to direct a conversation with the Leader of the Opposition to the point where he might see that he has to withdraw from the brink, having done all he could to force Mr Whitlam to an election. He could take whatever political capital he could out of the Prime Minister's refusal to go to the people. This

---

[19] Ibid., p. 126.

would allow the main issue in the country to return to the economic problems instead of being clouded, even dominated, by the constitutional issue.[20]

It was not within Kerr's remit to receive advice from Fraser and equally it would be most improper for him to offer advice to Fraser. Whitlam would have known and counted on Kerr not receiving advice. But, if he thought that on the other hand, Kerr might advise Fraser to back off, he seriously misjudged the situation. The best that Kerr could do would be to accept any hint of compromise or indecision on Fraser's part and, as he said, subtly steer the conversation in a direction which might cause Fraser to rethink his position. As it turned out Fraser offered no such opening, as Kerr revealed in the same letter:

> The Prime Minister agreed to me seeing the Leader of the Opposition, not of course for the purpose of getting advice from him, but simply to do my best to ascertain the likely future course of events … I spent more than an hour with him. He maintained that the intention of his Party was quite firm and irreversible and that if the Appropriation Bills were re-presented, as is happening, they would be deferred as often as they were presented.
>
> He, of course, believes that there is already a serious constitutional crisis but in any event accepts, from what he says and from what the Prime Minister says, that such a crisis is inevitable.
>
> My effort therefore to explore alternative possibilities did not get off the ground but nevertheless, from the point of view of the Vice-Regal office at least, I appear to be showing an interest, looking at things from the point of view of Australia generally.[21]

Kelly and Bramston's assertion that the Governor-General is not a constitutional umpire, but a constitutional guardian seems self-contradictory to me. The Governor-General is certainly not a *political* umpire, and in the encounter between Kerr and Fraser no political advice was offered or received. What was received by Kerr was intelligence that impacted upon his role as a constitutional guardian. In the end, he would make

---

[20] Letter to Martin Charteris dated 22 October 1975, *The Palace Letters*, p. 106.
[21] Kerr, Letter to Martin Charteris, *The Palace Letters*, 22 October 1975, pp. 106-107.

a decision on constitutional *not* political grounds. That makes him a constitutional umpire.

Kelly and Bramston then assert that:

> Whitlam's decision changed the atmospherics of the crisis. It brought Kerr to centre stage.[22]

This is a gross over-statement. Kerr had been at the centre of the crisis since day one, as evidenced by the newspaper reports and opinion pieces of the time. The issue dominated the media for months and Kerr's role had been canvassed in this coverage from the start.

Kelly and Bramston consider this meeting between Kerr and Fraser to be significant. They devote six pages to it, much of which centres around the Opposition's view of Kerr and their tactics to handle him. Their conclusion is that the meeting conferred an advantage on Fraser in the sense that he came away with the impression that Kerr felt threatened by Whitlam. And that, therefore, he would give Whitlam no warning if he eventually decided to dismiss him. That may or may not be true, but it would be fair to say that the meeting also conferred a disadvantage on Whitlam, in that Fraser managed to convince Kerr he would not back down. The weight of this is mitigated by the fact that it only confirmed the strong impression that Fraser himself was giving the public by virtue of his Parliamentary performance and his public pronouncements.

That the Opposition was trying to influence Kerr is not surprising and it reflects no discredit on him. Whitlam was trying the same via his public statements that the Governor-General would do what he told him to.

They conclude their coverage of this incident:

> The Fraser memoirs say: 'Fraser himself was so confident that Kerr would act that he had no fallback, no Plan B. He says today that while he was sure of Kerr, he was not certain that Whitlam would be dismissed. He thought it equally likely that Kerr would give

---

22 Kelly and Bramston, op.cit., p. 126.

Whitlam an ultimatum and that Whitlam would then agree to call an election.' Frankly, this reeks of post-event rationalisation. Towards the end of the crisis, Fraser and Ellicott were predicting a dismissal, pure and simple.[23]

Frankly, that sounds like a perfectly rational assessment. You can predict something and still have reservations. Effectively, Kerr did give Whitlam an ultimatum but, in the event, Whitlam did not concede. But he could have – it was his call. Why he chose not to, I will discuss in more detail later.

Kelly and Bramston then ask: 'Would Whitlam have sacked Kerr?' They advance opinions from various persons on both sides. Fraser and Menadue say 'yes'. Whitlam's secretary John Mant, and Labor Senator Jim McClelland say 'no'. Whitlam himself in later years said he wouldn't have.

They then ask:

> What would the Palace have done?
>
> Sir William Heseltine said: 'None of us felt the Queen would have been bound to act on a telephone call without substantial support in terms of a signed written submission from the Prime Minister'. Charteris said: 'I am sure that written notification would have been required.' The dismissal was much debated at the Palace after the dismissal. Heseltine said: 'After the event we had quite a lot of discussion about this issue and various possible scenarios were canvassed. This included recall, but we considered that some sort of written document would be needed.[24]

The critical point is not whether Whitlam would have moved against Kerr, but that Kerr believed he might – as Kelly and Bramston concede. And he had Whitlam's own words – his jokes about a race to the Palace – to buttress that belief. Kelly and Bramston argue that Kerr conveyed this belief to Fraser, which gave him some advantage. It is an arguable point, but it would not have been decisive in Fraser's thinking. What Fraser relied upon was Kerr's legal and judicial background, his knowledge

---

[23] Ibid., p. 132.
[24] Ibid., p. 133.

of the constitution and his determination to uphold it.

A final point. Kerr's reluctance to have Whitlam move against him was not only based on self-preservation. It was also a determination to keep the Queen out of it. Had Whitlam advised Kerr's removal, the Queen would then be inextricably involved, regardless of whether she recalled Kerr or not. The fact that it might take some time to go through a formal written process is irrelevant. Once the phone call had been made, the Palace would undoubtedly have advised Kerr to take no action to dismiss Whitlam until the matter was resolved. Sir Paul Hasluck, in his memorandum, sets the scene:

> Charteris told me nothing of his conversation with Whitlam but said: "Supposing that, having got to the telephone first, the Prime Minister of Australia, had recommended that The Queen dismiss the Governor-General, what would you have done if you had been me?" I replied that, if one assumed that the Prime Minister was Whitlam and the situation was much the same as the one that we knew in November, 1975, then I would have said in effect that this was not the sort of matter in which action could be taken on a telephone call and that in fairness to The Queen and to himself, the Prime Minister should make a formal submission in writing and transmit it to be placed before The Queen. As it clearly involved constitutional issues it would probably be advisable to have the submission supported by opinion by the Crown's legal advisers and both documents should be prepared in a form that would allow them to be published as giving sound reasons for the action. In the meantime no other measures should be taken either by Governor-General or Prime Minister.[25]

In other words, the Queen would now be at the centre of a dispute between her representative and the Prime Minister, and the political impasse would have continued until it was resolved. There would now be two crises impacting the nation – one political and one constitutional. If Kelly and Bramston think the dismissal of Whitlam was divisive, it would have been as nothing compared to this situation, and the position (and future) of the Monarchy in Australia would have been

---

[25] Hasluck, *The Hasluck Memorandum*, 10 August 1977.

seriously compromised. From Kerr's point of view that would have represented a monumental failure on his part.

In correspondence with me, Professor David Flint offers a clarification of Hasluck's final remark:

> I disagree with Sir Paul Hasluck on one point.
>
> This is that once a Prime Minister puts the case for dismissing the Governor-General with legal advice and in a form which can be published, there is, as it were, a stay of proceedings.
>
> As Sir Paul says, "In the meantime no other measures should be taken either by Governor-General or Prime Minister."
> If that is a wish, a counsel of prudence, that is all very well. But I do think that it cannot in any way be supported as a constitutional ruling.
>
> Indeed, I think it is contrary to the Queen's opinion set out in her reply to the Speaker on his request in 1975 that she overrule the Governor-General. As that opinion clearly states, the Constitution 'firmly places the prerogative powers of the Crown in the hands of the governor-general as the representative of the Queen in Australia.' The opinion also states that '... it would not be proper for her to intervene in person in matters which are so clearly placed within the jurisdiction of the governor-general by the Constitution Act.'
>
> Unless and until the Queen acts on the prime minister's advice, the governor-general is, in my view, unrestrained in acting under the powers vested in him. (I agree that the Queen here enjoys a reserve power. There would be circumstances so unusual that she could decide to reject the advice.)
>
> Thus, before the Queen acts, the governor-general could still therefore dismiss the prime minister.
>
> I agree that the Queen should only be expected to react on a properly drawn submission with supporting advice. These days, it could be delivered by modern means, provided the original is on its way on an aircraft and the modern digital form is delivered in a well-established way that is secure and verifiable.

Incidentally, Gough Whitlam told me well after the event this would not be by a dismissal but by a fresh appointment which would thereby end the current appointment.

Hasluck goes on to say:

> In my view a man such as Whitlam would have enough intelligence to consider his next step very soberly and only to persist with his recommendation if there were good and defensible reasons for it.[26]

By which time the damage would have been done. And, as to Whitlam's response, perhaps it would be more appropriate to rely on his common sense rather than his intelligence. And on the evidence so far, Whitlam's common sense seems to be a questionable proposition.

The only one who could tell us if Whitlam would have phoned the Palace is Whitlam himself. Straight after the event he told Harold Wilson he would have. Later, having had time for reflection and when it then suited his narrative, he claimed he wouldn't have. But what would have stopped him? Certainly not the protestations of his caucus, most, if not all, of whom he regarded as 'pissants'. Then what about protecting the reputation of the Monarchy? Would that consideration trump Whitlam's ego, his republicanism, and his monumental sense of destiny? Based on this extract from *Head of State* by Sir David Smith, you be the judge:

> [On] 11 April 1974, the double dissolution proclamation, counter-signed by Whitlam, and requiring the Governor-General's signature, arrived on my desk. I took it to the Governor-General, Sir Paul Hasluck, and pointed out that, while the proclamation seemed in order, the words which customarily appeared at the bottom of all such proclamations – 'God Save the Queen – were missing from this one. The Governor-General asked me to ascertain the reason for the omission. I telephoned Ewart Smith for an explanation. He told me that the proclamation had been submitted to the Prime Minister in the customary form, but that it had been returned to the Attorney-General's Department with a wavy line drawn through the request to the Almighty and with a notation in the margin in

---

[26] Ibid.

Whitlam's hand-writing – 'We'll have no more of this nonsense.'[27]

It is doubtful that Whitlam's scant regard for the Monarchy would have stayed his hand if he felt threatened.

Kerr's reticence or discretion in his later dealings with Whitlam – the 'deception' that Kelly and Bramston hang so heavily around his neck – is explained by his well-founded fear that Whitlam might move against him.

---

[27] Smith, *Head of State*, p. 253.

10

Whitlam's Blunders

This chapter covers what Kelly and Bramston believe were Whitlam's mistakes in his handling of Kerr. It is predicated on the assumption that the final outcome depended upon who was more effective in manipulating Kerr. That is wrong. It was the *decisions* of Fraser and Whitlam, rather than their rhetoric or attitude to Kerr, that determined Kerr's decision. Their attitudes towards Kerr no doubt provided him some comfort at a personal level. For instance, Whitlam's contemptuous attitude probably ensured that Kerr felt no personal regret at dismissing the man who had appointed him to the role. But that played no part in his decision.

In the end, Fraser won not because he persuaded Kerr that he could sack Whitlam – Kerr already knew that – but because he persuaded Kerr that he would not back down. Of the two antagonists only Whitlam was determined upon a course which was unconstitutional – attempting to govern without Parliamentary approved appropriations. That is what determined Kerr's decision. Whitlam could have stroked Kerr's ego day and night but, in the end, it was his proposed course of action that determined his fate.

That said, had Whitlam paid more heed to Kerr and to his own departmental advisers, he may well have not put himself in that invidious position, so it is worth studying Kelly and Bramston's treatment of this topic. They begin:

> Gough Whitlam had two fixations during the 1975 crisis – that the management of John Kerr was his exclusive domain and that the

governor-general had no option but to act on the prime minister's advice. They saw him overrule advisers, shut his mind to alternative options, lose his judgement and engage in a brand of kamikaze politics that virtually invited dismissal.[1]

Again, just to be clear, Kerr did not withdraw Whitlam's commission because he felt aggrieved and unloved by him. They continue:

> ... Whitlam had an exceptionally narrow view of how Kerr should be advised. 'The advice given by Mr Whitlam in all instances was oral and in the expectation that the Opposition would give way.' Menadue said.
>
> In the end the Whitlam government failed to provide direct, formal written advice to the governor-general on how he should act. This omission seems incredible. It was recommended on a number of occasions by the Prime Minister's Department and the Attorney-General's Department. Giving formal advice to the governor-general during the most serious parliamentary and constitutional crisis since federation would seem the supreme act of prime ministerial logic and common-sense. Yet it never happened.
>
> The reason is that Whitlam's irrational approach towards Kerr resulted in a failure of process and policy from the prime minister. His attitude towards Kerr was patronising, contemptuous and guaranteed to provoke hostility. Whitlam's defective grasp of human nature lay at the heart of the dismissal.[2]

That last sentence may be true, but only in the sense that Whitlam failed to recognise the fragility of his position. Whatever hostility Whitlam may have provoked within Kerr had no bearing on his decision. And again, we come to this question of advice. In the context of the dictum that the 'Governor-General acts on the advice of the Prime Minister' this refers essentially to government policy, timing of elections, appointments and so on. It does not refer to interpretation of the Constitution, which is what we are talking about in the context of this chapter. Kerr did seek constitutional advice from the law officers *vis-à-vis*

---

[1] Kelly and Bramston, *The Dismissal*, p. 135.
[2] Ibid., pp. 135-136.

the Ellicott opinion. He was not obliged, under any convention, to accept that advice, even if he had received it.

Whether or not the Governor-General has the power to dismiss the Prime Minister is not a matter for the Prime Minister to decide. Interpretation of the Constitution is the prerogative of the High Court.

For example, in 2020, the High Court ruled that a person of Aboriginal descent, although not born in this country and not a citizen, could not be regarded as an alien under Section 51 (xix) of the Constitution.[3] Part of the justification for that ruling was that Parliament cannot define the terms in the Constitution. That is the prerogative of the High Court. (As an aside, this seems to me to be another example of the High Court making law. The logic that determined that one class of person i.e., someone of aboriginal descent, is exempt from the commonly accepted definition of an alien as one who is not a citizen because of his/her putative 'spiritual connection with the land', seems perverse to me as it did to three of the High Court judges.)

So, the Prime Minister can, via the agency of the Solicitor General, offer an opinion as to the application of the reserve powers in any given situation but it would carry no more weight than that of, say, the Opposition's shadow Attorney-General. It would certainly not be binding on the Governor-General. Only a High Court judgement could make it binding.

Kelly and Bramston quote Whitlam's principal private secretary, John Mant:

> Asked how Whitlam saw his relationship with Kerr, Mant said: 'As master and servant. Whitlam was Kerr's intellectual superior. He was somewhat contemptuous of Kerr because of his drinking and his pretensions but didn't see him as a class traitor.' Mant said that whatever regard Whitlam might have had for Kerr was 'disappearing' by the time of the crisis. 'I think that Kerr joined the pissant group – which was a large group – and the assumption was that he

---

[3] The High Court of Australia, 'Thoms v The Commonwealth of Australia', Case B43/2018.

would do what Gough told him,' Mant said.[4]

If Whitlam believed that the Governor-General's actions should be dictated by his 'class', then he had a serious misunderstanding of the role. This whole passage suggests that Whitlam did indeed believe the Governor-General was a 'rubber stamp' – an idea that was certainly an anathema to Kerr. And Whitlam should have known that. They continue:

> While declining to provide Kerr with considered advice, Whitlam insisted in public that the governor-general had no independent discretion and must follow what the prime minister wanted. This insulted Kerr's pride and intellect. It would have been offensive to most governors-general. It was Whitlam's job to persuade Kerr to his position but he substituted intimidation for persuasion.[5]

Again, ultimately what Whitlam had to persuade Kerr of, was his ability to obtain supply or, absent that, to continue to govern constitutionally. He knew that dismissal was being urged on the Governor-General by some in the media but also, and more importantly, by the shadow Attorney General, Bob Ellicott QC, in an opinion which had been widely publicised and had been made available to Kerr.

Realistically, it was never in Whitlam's power to persuade Kerr that he did not have the power to dismiss the Prime Minister. But that should not have stopped him trying to convince Kerr that the power should not be invoked in the circumstances pertaining at the time. Kerr offered him the chance to do so when he asked for an opinion on the Ellicott memorandum. In fact, Kerr doubted that the anticipated response from the Law Officers – Solicitor-General Maurice Byers QC and Attorney-General Kep Enderby – would change his mind, but nonetheless it was his duty to seek such advice. And he did. But he never received it. This issue will be covered in more detail later.

Kelly and Bramston then devote some space to emphasising that Whitlam insisted that he would 'manage' Kerr. And that his ministerial colleagues, his party adviser and his senior

---
[4] Kelly and Bramston, op.cit., p. 136.
[5] Ibid., pp. 136-137.

bureaucrats all accepted, despite some misgivings, that Whitlam had things under control. And that, therefore, they declined to push the matter. It is best summarised in this extract:

> At the outset of the crisis on 17 October, interviewed by Richard Carleton on This Day Tonight, Whitlam said the governor-general must 'unquestionably' take advice from his prime minister. Asked if there was any tolerance here, he replied: 'None whatever.' He repeatedly affirmed this position. Menadue said of Whitlam's dealings with Kerr: 'I think his attitude was there was nothing to discuss.' He saw the governor-general as a rubber stamp.[6]

This takes us back to Chapter Eight, wherein Kelly and Bramston take Kerr seriously to task for failing to take Whitlam into his confidence – by not exercising his right to 'advise and warn' on the basis of his belief that Whitlam was beyond reason. The above passage would seem to confirm Kerr's judgement in this respect. If that was the view of Menadue, who knew Whitlam better than most, how could Kerr be expected to arrive at a different conclusion? How could Whitlam subsequently back down from such an unequivocal statement. It would not have been in his nature to do so, and Kerr would have known that.

And if Whitlam really believed he could intimidate Kerr into acting as he dictated, then this suggests he would not hesitate to recommend Kerr's recall, if he ever got an inkling that his dominance over Kerr was not as complete as he had thought.

We now come to a significant development:

> Under Menadue and Harders, the departments, from the outset, were focussed on two techniques: formal letters from Whitlam to Kerr and an innovation in the appropriation bills that would have kept them in the House of Representatives, a decisive event.
>
> The departments were prophetic in raising the idea, as Menadue said, of 'inserting clauses in the Appropriation Bills, insisting the Bills be returned from the Senate to the House before they were presented to the Governor-General for assent'. It would have been

---

[6] Ibid., p. 137.

> unusual but legal. Menadue raised this option in a two-page note to Whitlam dated 2 October. By requiring the bills to be endorsed another time by the House after Senate passage, the effect, as Harders said, 'is that Mr Fraser would not have been able to guarantee to the Governor-General that he could provide Supply.' This is a pivotal point.
>
> It would have made impossible the commissioning of Fraser under the conditions required by Kerr. Labor would have retained control of the appropriation bills. The idea, debated before the crisis was never adopted. Menadue said later: 'As it turned out it was the greatest mistake the government made.'[7]

The greatest mistake the government made? Well, that's debatable but it's certainly a major mistake in the context of the dismissal. The option was eventually dropped because, according to Menadue and Harders, it was feared it would be provocative to the Opposition, effectively inviting them to block supply.[8] I am not sure I understand the logic of this reasoning. A tactic that would render the Opposition's blocking of supply ineffective was dropped in case the Opposition blocked supply?

This is significant because it shows, primarily, that the government was seriously anticipating the refusal of supply but, more importantly, the possibility that the Opposition might be called upon to form a caretaker government on the condition that it approve supply. Nothing could be clearer from this account. And that is exactly what happened. And it could only happen if the Prime Minister were dismissed. At this stage, the claim, addressed in Chapter Three, by Labor ministers and, indeed, the Prime Minister, that they were deceived and ambushed looks increasingly unsustainable.

They continue:

> In the end, Kerr's dismissal of Whitlam depended upon control of the supply bills.
>
> The bizarre feature, however, is the lack of any evidence Whitlam

---

[7] Ibid., p. 139.
[8] Ibid.

was interested. Whitlam's focus was the House of Representatives, not the governor-general or the Senate.[9]

The first sentence is correct. The second is problematic. Kerr recounted to the Palace, in a letter of 20 September 1975, a conversation he had with Whitlam during the Papua New Guinea independence celebrations:

> Another point of importance put to me by the Prime Minister in Port Moresby was that if I were, at the height of the crisis, contrary to his advice to decide to terminate his commission at the time when the public service, defence forces, police and so on were not being paid he would have to tell me that Mr Fraser would not be able to get supply either because new legislation would probably be necessary and it would not pass the House of Representatives. He was, however, frank in saying it may be legally possible for Mr Fraser to revive the bills which have passed the House and then have them passed in the Senate. We were, of course, talking on quite friendly terms in all of this.[10]

Clearly, at this stage Whitlam was aware of the possibility he might be dismissed, and even canvassed the tactics that might be employed by him or Fraser. Earlier Kelly and Bramston castigate Kerr for considering, before the Opposition actually blocked supply, the possibility he might have to dismiss Whitlam. Yet here is Whitlam doing exactly the same thing.

It is strange that Whitlam, having foreshadowed a tactic to frustrate Fraser, did not take the precaution to constrain the bills such that they had to be returned to the House for final approval. And it is also clear that Kerr was alerting the Palace to that same possibility. The Palace cannot credibly claim that it was caught completely unawares, as Kelly and Bramston report in their Chapter One. They continue:

> In his reappraisal of the crisis, Menadue offers another perspective: if it was apparent that a dismissed Labor government could deny supply to Fraser because of its ongoing House of Representatives majority then 'it is most unlikely, in my opinion that the Gover-

---

[9] Ibid., p. 140.
[10] Kerr, Letter to Charteris, *The Palace Letters*, 20 September 1975, p. 15.

nor-General and Mr Fraser would have contemplated the action that was taken'. This seems to be an arguable proposition.[11]

I would suggest that it is more than arguable. It is almost certain that if the 'poison pill' clause had been inserted in the Appropriation Bills, Fraser would have seen no point in persisting. Kerr's letter of 20 September continues:

> One point is that if neither can get supply and public servants etc are not being paid it is said that only an election can resolve the point and if Mr Whitlam will not advise one, I may have to find someone who will. My mind is at the moment open on this.[12]

It is interesting to contemplate what course of action Kerr might have taken if the stalemate continued and Fraser could not guarantee supply. It would seem the only option available to him would be a forced dissolution, but as that did not eventuate there is little point in canvassing it. Suffice to say that Whitlam precluded that option when he visited Kerr on 11 November to advise a half-Senate election. He absolved Kerr of the necessity to consider that option.

Kelly and Bramston then go on to detail that many formal letters to Kerr, outlining the Government's view, were drafted but never sent. They conclude this section:

> No such letter was sent. In the period before supply was blocked this may have been wise. The critical insight, however, is that Whitlam didn't want to write to Kerr at any time, before or during the crisis. He felt it was unnecessary. He said repeatedly in private that 'Kerr would do the right thing'. The prime minister was loath to take any action that conceded it was necessary for him to persuade Kerr. In its essence this was irrational.
>
> Because constitutional practice was for the governor-general to act on the advice of the prime minister, Whitlam had an obvious advantage over Fraser, who was opposition leader, an office with no claim on the governor-general's actions. Yet Whitlam failed to capitalize on this advantage.[13]

---

[11] Kelly and Bramston, op.cit., p. 140.
[12] Kerr, op.cit., p. 15.
[13] Kelly and Bramston, op.cit., p. 141.

Here again, in that last paragraph, we have a conflation of two distinct categories of advice, which I have covered earlier. There is formal 'advice' on matters of government (legislation, elections etc) – which convention dictates the Governor-General acts upon *in normal circumstances*. In this context, the word 'advice' is a euphemism for 'instruction'. I suspect it came into this use as it would be regarded as unseemly to 'instruct' the Monarch. And there is informal advice designed to clarify some issue with the Governor-General, which is genuinely advice in that the Governor-General is not obliged to accept it. In this chapter we are talking about the latter and the Prime Minister is not the only source for it, which the earlier paragraph seems to concede.

On 16 October 1975, the Professor of Law at Sydney University, Professor Patrick Lane, wrote in the *Sydney Morning Herald*:

> There is no question – and there is a strong convention, it is no humbug – that by convention the Governor-General usually follows the advice of his ministers. And there is no question that the Governor-General has a discretion, a personal discretion. Evatt said so in his book The King and His Dominion Governors. Hasluck more recently said the same thing, that the Governor-General follows the advice of his ministers usually but he insisted that he had an ultimate discretion. Moreover, he made the point that the Governor-General, in the sort of circumstances we may find ourselves in, can take advice from people other than his ministers – from the Chief Justice and eminent counsel. And having received that advice, Hasluck said that a Governor-General then had a solemn responsibility 'to make a judgement on whether a dissolution is needed to serve the process of good government by giving to the electorate the duty of resolving a situation which the Parliament cannot resolve for itself'.

So, Sir Paul Hasluck, former Governor-General and one of Kelly's and Bramston's witnesses for the prosecution of Sir John Kerr, clearly makes the same distinction that I have above. And he has no problem with the Governor-General seeking advice (as opposed to instructions) from the Chief Justice.

Kelly and Bramston rhetorically ask what Whitlam should have done:

> Whitlam should have visited Kerr after the Senate's initial vote to force an election. That would have been on 16 or 17 October. He should have given Kerr formal written advice at the outset explaining his government's support for the doctrine of responsible government as embodied in the Constitution and explaining that he had no obligation, legal or financial, to buckle before Fraser at that point and recommend an election. He should have offered to make the solicitor-general available to Kerr for direct consultations. This was necessary given Whitlam's belief that Kerr must not consult with the chief justice. Far better that he talk to Byers than Barwick.[14]

Talking to Byers would not obviate the need or the right to also talk to Barwick. The idea is that the Governor-General should receive the best advice, not the most convenient. And this logically dictates that, ideally, he should receive advice from multiple sources.

It is true that, at that point, there was no Constitutional imperative upon Whitlam to advise an election. But it is difficult to see how the authors could base their argument on an appeal to the doctrine of responsible government.

According to the website Australian Politics, responsible government is defined as:

> Responsible Government is the term used to describe a political system where the executive government, the Cabinet and Ministry, is drawn from, and accountable to, the legislative branch.[15]

In other words, the government or ministry is responsible to the Parliament. And the Parliament comprises two equal Houses – the House of Representatives and the Senate. They have different powers but equal status. Or put another way, the government is not responsible to the House of Representatives only. Whitlam was responsible to Parliament to obtain supply. He could not obtain it elsewhere.

---

[14] Ibid., p. 141.
[15] Politics, D., & Terms, K. (2022). Responsible Government - AustralianPolitics.com. Retrieved 19 May 2022, from https://australianpolitics.com/democracy/key-terms/responsible-government

They continue:

> Beyond this, Whitlam should have engaged Kerr as a personality. He should have spent time with Kerr, being encouraging and supportive, without jokes, put-downs or patronizing asides. Kerr was a social being, he loved conversation, and Whitlam, since his survival was the issue, should have been prepared to make concessions on this front.[16]

This suggests that Kerr was a reed, capable of being bent to the will of the politician who loved him most. And that he would make his decision based on that. There is no basis for this suggestion. Despite his easy-going personality, Kerr was essentially an intellectual being and was guided by his own knowledge and the advice he received, not his treatment by either Fraser or Whitlam.

At this point, the authors cover the topic of the Ellicott opinion. Bob Ellicott QC was the Shadow Attorney-General. He had penned an opinion, which was made public on 16 October, that the Governor-General had the power to dismiss the Prime Minister and that, in the current circumstances, he should exercise that power immediately.

Kerr was given a copy of that opinion. Ellicott asked to speak to the Governor-General about it, but Kerr declined to see him:

> 'I decided not to do this and told Mr Smith to say that I had read the document but that, in the circumstances, thought I should not talk to him about it,' Kerr wrote in a 21 October note. In a later note Kerr surmised that Ellicott only wanted 'to indicate that the statement was not meant to put pressure on me'.

> But in a conversation with Troy Bramston in 2014, Ellicott said his memo had purpose: to persuade Kerr to dismiss Whitlam. Ellicott, like Kerr, regarded himself as an expert on the reserve powers. Ellicott recalled: 'Fraser said to me that Kerr would like to see the legal opinion. And I said: "Yes." I couldn't see why the Governor-General couldn't have it. Everybody else had it. Let's be frank, when I put it out there, I put it out there for the Governor-General to read.

---

[16] Kelly and Bramston, op.cit., p. 141.

> We wanted it to influence his thinking. We were politicians. The person who's going to make a decision was the Governor-General.'
>
> Ellicott's opinion put dismissal at the heart of the matter. This was its significance, yet Whitlam and Labor never grasped the point.[17]

Dismissal was always an option – it was not the heart of the matter – and the press grasped this very early on. That the Ellicott opinion was designed to influence Kerr's thinking is not unusual and does not reflect adversely on Kerr. The opinion did not alert Sir John to a course of action open to him that had not occurred to him before. In fact, it played almost no part in the decision, other than, possibly, to bolster Kerr's confidence.

What it should have done, as Kelly and Bramston point out, is alert Whitlam and Labor to that possibility. As, even more so, should the request from Kerr to have the opinion of the Commonwealth Law Officers.

As to the opinion itself, Kerr essentially agreed with it, since it accorded with his own knowledge of the reserve powers, derived, in part, from his study of Evatt:

> Kerr disagreed with Ellicott's view on immediate action. He did not agree that he should ask Whitlam for advice on a solution. Nor did he agree with the view that if the advice was not adequate, he should dismiss Whitlam. Kerr wrote: 'If Ellicott were hoping that his document would influence me to act immediately or very soon after supply was blocked, it in fact had the opposite effect. I strongly felt that time should be allowed to pass and action, if needed at all, should await the last possible moment. Ellicott took the opposite view.
>
> But on the core point, the dismissal power, Kerr agreed with Ellicott: that he had the power to dismiss Whitlam if the crisis were not resolved.[18]

This hardly accords with one portrait of Kerr, painted right from the start of *The Dismissal*, as a scheming opportunist just

---

[17] Ibid., p. 142.
[18] Ibid., p. 143.

itching to flex the Vice-Regal muscles.

On 21 October, Kerr asked Whitlam to provide him with a response to the Ellicott opinion. Whitlam agreed and asked Attorney-General Kep Enderby to arrange it.

Solicitor General Maurice Byers QC promptly wrote an opinion and passed it to Enderby where it languished for some days. According to Kelly and Bramston:

> The attorney-general and his advisers wanted 'to see it strengthened'. There is no evidence Whitlam saw it as a priority. Sexton [Enderby's adviser] said Enderby felt the opinion 'conceded too much'. … On 28 October, Kerr saw Harders [Head of the Attorney-General's Department] at a reception for a public service board course and asked when the advice would be ready. By 1 November, Harders had become agitated. The deadlock had lasted nearly three weeks. The government had provided no advice to Kerr despite his request thirteen days earlier.[19]

This suggests that the Attorney-General was not seeking the objective advice of the Solicitor-General, but a politically tainted opinion.

Despite the agitation of Harders, it took until 6 November before Enderby presented the opinion to Kerr. He proffered a 28-page document signed by Byers but not by himself. He explained to Kerr that it was not the final document, and he was only showing it to Kerr at this stage as an indication of the advice that the Prime Minister would be giving him. He crossed out Byers' signature. No final opinion was ever given to Kerr.

Kelly and Bramston summarise the opinion thus:

> The Byers opinion addressed the dismissal issue. He said the Senate power over supply had never been exercised, a fact suggesting the convention claimed by Whitlam against its use did exist. Byers said, given Whitlam's refusal to bend, the issue was a forced dissolution by the governor-general. Yet the rarity of forced dissolutions 'cast the gravest doubt upon the present existence of that prerogative'. Byers said it was incorrect to resort to the dismissal power when

---
[19] Ibid., p. 146.

supply was blocked. This was a conflict between the two houses and the Constitution in section fifty-seven provided a specific resolution for such a deadlock.[20] (emphasis added)

I have argued earlier that the fact that a power had not been used, or had only been used rarely, in a period as short as seventy years cannot possibly suggest that the power no longer exists. These are powers that are intended to be used rarely or, preferably, never. I would argue that whatever may be thought of the vestigial nature of the reserve powers in the United Kingdom, the fact that the Australian Constitution, in 1901, enshrined them, however ambiguously in law, establishes that in our polity they exist. That is not to say that their use should not be informed by precedent and convention, where appropriate, that applies throughout the British Commonwealth.

Here Byers was referring to a 'forced dissolution', which is a dissolution in which the Crown acts to procure an outcome which it desires.

I have also argued that the purported 'convention' against the Senate bocking supply was ephemeral best, and therefore Byers' opinion on this aspect was certainly tainted by a bureaucratic mindset to say the least. It was not rigorous legal argument.

Byers was quite correct to say the dismissal power should not be used when supply was blocked. He was responding to the Ellicott opinion that said Sir John should act immediately, an opinion which Kerr did not accept. But, in the end, Whitlam was not dismissed because supply was blocked but because he, Whitlam, could not find a way to legitimately overcome that obstacle.

As to Section 57, it does indeed a provide a specific solution to a deadlock between the Houses. It's called an election. And that could only come about if the government advised it, or the Governor-General forced it.

Section 57 says that if a deadlock arises between the Houses i.e.,

---

[20] Ibid., p. 148.

a refusal of the Senate to pass legislation approved by the House a second time after an interval of three months, the Governor-General *may* dissolve the Senate and House of Representatives simultaneously. Byers argued that Section 57 did not apply because, on 6 November, the requirement that three months elapse between two rejections of the Appropriations Bills by the Senate, had not been met. And that therefore, the Governor-General did not have the discretion to force a dissolution.

And that is true. Normally such a deadlock would involve legislation, the blocking of which would not involve a disruption in the normal functions of government. And it would always involve the Prime Minister of the day advising a double dissolution, as Whitlam did in 1974, or refraining from resorting to Section 57, as Prime Minister Kevin Rudd did in 2009, when his Carbon Pollution Reduction Scheme legislation was twice rejected by the Senate. It is hard to imagine a situation where a Governor-General would force an election on an unwilling Prime Minister over this type of deadlock.

Although it did not change Sir John Kerr's view, it is worth looking at the draft Byers opinion. Essentially, it was intended to respond to the Ellicott opinion which postulated that the Governor-General had a *duty* to immediately seek an assurance from the Prime Minister as to how he intended to obtain supply and, absent a satisfactory answer, to dismiss him.

In short, Byers argued that:

a) the blocking was designed with the express purpose of forcing an election (rather than, as is normal, to kill a legislative initiative that the Opposition vehemently opposes),
b) that in these circumstances there was no obligation, either constitutionally or conventionally, for the government to resign, and
c) the government had no intention to resign, and
d) there was no obligation on the part of the Governor-General to intervene, and
e) the provisions of Section 57 did not (yet) apply, and therefore,

the only option for the Governor-General's intervention would be by means of a forced dissolution (that would operate under Section 5).

Kerr agreed with all these conclusions. However, Byers also argued that:

> the Senate was constrained by convention from exercising its power to reject bills in respect of appropriations, and
> with regard to forced dissolutions, the 'rarity and the long years since their exercise cast gravest doubt upon the present existence of that prerogative'.

Kerr did not agree with these propositions. In respect of forced dissolutions, Byers quoted Senator Eugene Forsey of Canada, considered to be one of the world's experts in the Westminster constitutional system. This is quite a complex question and Kerr examines it closely in Chapter Fourteen of his memoir *Matters for Judgement*. In Chapter Eighteen, in his coverage of the Byers opinion, he argues that Byers misunderstood Forsey, who was referring to a 'true' forced dissolution, in which as Kerr describes it 'a dissolution is forced upon a government at the Governor's personal wish, for his own personal reasons'. This had occurred in New Brunswick in 1856. Kerr agreed that: 'Nowadays of course no Monarch or Governor would contemplate such a course' and he agreed with Byers that it 'was very rare indeed and now almost inconceivable'.[21] But Forsey also listed at least eight other instances of other forced dissolutions that were not of this nature, the last being the dismissal of the Lang government in NSW in 1932. In fact, Forsey, who was both a social progressive and a constitutional conservative, was very supportive of Kerr's actions, and wrote encouragingly to him after the event.

As to the 'convention' of the Senate not blocking supply, this ground has been extensively covered earlier in this book.

So, the Byers opinion told Kerr what he could not do. It did not offer him any useful information as to how Whitlam intended

---

[21] Kerr, op.cit., p. 305.

to overcome his political problem. That was the other essential advice Kerr needed.

That came in the form of another brief from Enderby, also presented on 6 November, concerning a plan to borrow money from the banks to tide the government over until the results of a proposed half-Senate election might give Whitlam the numbers he needed to pass his supply bills. Kelly and Bramston deal with this in a later chapter so I will reserve my coverage of this aspect for the moment.

They conclude this chapter:

> There is no evidence the Byers opinion, delivered when it was and the way it was, had any impact on Kerr. Indeed, it represented a view Kerr had rejected in coming to his decision for a dismissal.
>
> The refusal to provide formal written advice – which would have necessitated a response from Kerr and hence a dialogue – was a function of Whitlam's blind dogmatism and belief that because Kerr was weak intimidation would suffice. It is false to assume such advice would have saved Whitlam but it would have changed the atmospherics, perhaps significantly. The flawed 'advice' saga testifies to Whitlam's irrational approach to Kerr. By shunning engagement and persuasion, Whitlam failed to respect Kerr as a man and treated him with contempt as a governor-general.[22]

All true as far as it goes. Here is Kerr's reaction:

> I must say that to receive, on 6 November, from the Attorney-General of Australia, on two crucial areas of policy, and at a critical time, those two unsigned, draft 'opinions' was not particularly helpful. I found the lack of properly provided assistance deeply disquieting.[23]

And:

> In the crisis I was entitled to real information, help and advice but not receiving them. I prepared therefore to cope with the situation myself.[24]

---

[22] Ibid., p. 149.
[23] Kerr, op.cit., p. 303.
[24] Ibid., p. 308.

The authors concession that 'it is false to assume such advice would have saved Whitlam, but it would have changed the atmospherics, perhaps significantly' could be more accurately stated as 'it is safe to assume such advice would *not* have saved Whitlam'. It was not the manner in which the advice was presented (unsigned draft), but the contents of that advice that determined Sir John's course of action.

What he inferred from this informal 'advice' was that Whitlam did not intend to resign in order to resolve the deadlock, that he intended to govern under a financial arrangement that was highly problematical, both practically and constitutionally, and that Kerr could only intervene using a reserve power that *probably* no longer existed.

It is not clear what 'changing the atmospherics' means, but the whole tenor of this chapter suggests that Kerr was materially influenced by Whitlam's personal attitude towards him. That is an unjustified slur. Whitlam could have loved Kerr to death, but if he had finally and formally proffered the same advice that was in the two draft opinions, then Kerr would still have acted exactly as he did.

In conclusion let me observe that the Whitlam described in Chapter Ten of *The Dismissal*, seems very much the same man that Kerr described as 'beyond reason' and feared may advise his recall, if forewarned that Kerr might dismiss him.

11

Anthony Mason and the Arch of Opinion

This is a rather odd chapter that covers the discussions between Sir John Kerr and Sir Anthony Mason, a judge of the High Court. This issue was raised in an earlier chapter in conjunction with that of Kerr's consultation of the Chief Justice, Sir Garfield Barwick. Here the authors explore the relationship between Kerr and Mason more deeply.

They commence with the observation that Kerr, in his 1978 memoir *Matters for Judgement*, referred to the existence of an unnamed adviser. Kerr said:

> My solitude was tempered by conversation with one person only other than the Chief Justice. The conversation did not include advice as to what I should do but sustained me in my own thinking as to the imperatives within which I had to act, and in my own conclusions, already reached, as to what I could or should do. The person with whom I spoke was not and has never been mentioned in any of the speculations about persons I might have consulted. The substance of our conversation is recorded and will some day, when for history's sake the archives are opened, be revealed.[1]

As has been revealed, that person was Sir Anthony Mason, a close friend of Sir John. Mason was appointed to the High Court in 1972, was promoted to Chief Justice by the Hawke government in 1987 and retired in 1995. He was regarded as a pre-eminent jurist, having presided over the 1993 Mabo case. He was highly regarded by both sides of politics.

---

[1] Kerr, op.cit., p. 341.

Kelly and Bramston note:

> In the Kerr papers there is a pivotal document, including earlier drafts, titled 'Conversation with Sir Anthony Mason during October – November 1975' ... It was written in 1981, although it includes another note written on 21 October 1975, during the crisis. In one version, Kerr has a revealing descriptor denoting the importance of this document for future historians: 'If this document is found among my archives, it will mean that my final decision is that truth must prevail and, as he played a most significant part in my thinking at that critical time, and as he will be in the shades of history when this is read, his role should be known.'

> Yet a shadow fell across Kerr-Mason relations. It troubled Kerr for many years after the dismissal. He wrote of Mason: 'I feel that although he and I differ not at all about the facts of what happened between us and are still very good friends, he would be happier for the sake of the Court if history never came to know of his role.' Kerr's implication is that Mason preferred to keep their dialogue unknown to the public and judicial colleagues. Mason disputes this statement: he said he told Kerr his condition for the release of their discussions and Kerr did not reply.[2]

One of the main issues here is the propriety of Mason, a sitting High Court judge, discussing the use of the reserve powers in a specific (rather than an abstract) context with the Governor-General. To begin with it would be natural for Kerr to want Mason's role known as it would bolster his case that he had not acted in a cavalier manner but had carefully considered his options with input from a highly qualified friend.

On the other hand, it would be natural that Mason would want his role kept secret. He knew that the decision would be controversial and that a certain amount of opprobrium would accrue, primarily, to Kerr but also to anyone else involved in the decision. That reflects no discredit on Mason, who had a career to protect and nothing to gain from shouldering any of the abuse. He would have known that a future Labor prime minister would never consider elevating him to Chief Justice

---

[2] Kelly and Bramston, op.cit., p. 151.

if his role became known. He would also have known that a Liberal prime minister, especially Fraser, would also be very loath, from a public relations point of view, to appear to reward Mason for his part. Whether protecting the reputation of the Court played any part in Mason's reticence is questionable. If he thought his involvement would have adversely impacted the Court, perhaps he should have refrained from becoming involved in the first place.

The condition that Mason claims he imposed upon Kerr for the release of their discussions was that Kerr must include the fact that Mason had told him he should warn Whitlam that he may terminate his commission and therefore give him the opportunity to go to the election as Prime Minister. We will cover this question in more detail later but let me observe here that inclusion of that slightly mitigating (from the point of view of Whitlam supporters) point is hardly likely to have weighed to such an extent that it would have saved Mason's career. And Mason would have known that.

The suggestion here is that Kerr decided to refrain from making their discussions public, not to honour a request from Mason, but to avoid having to make public what Kelly and Bramston refer to as a damaging fact. That sounds unlikely to me. All Kerr's writings suggest he would have dearly loved the fact of these discussions to come out. As to not acting on Mason's advice – which was that he should warn Whitlam, and allow him to consider his position, before handing him his dismissal, Kerr had his own response to that – only part of which rests on his belief that Whitlam would act to have him recalled – and would no doubt have been happy to make his own case in defence of that particular criticism. It was, after all, a charge which had been levelled against him by a number of other figures. It must be admitted, of course, that the charge would be more damaging having been levelled by a friend.

As to the propriety of their discussions, Kerr has no doubt about it, otherwise he would not have arranged for it to come out, albeit after his death. Clearly his legacy meant much to him. Kerr could not be accused of treachery or deception in respect of these discussions.

And I'm sure also that Mason was satisfied as to the propriety of his conduct. His reticence, as I have suggested, would have been based on his natural inclination to not pointlessly damage his career.

But if there *was* any impropriety, the prime offender would have been Sir Anthony Mason. Kerr wanted all the help he could get and what better source than his trusted friend? He would have been content to let Mason make the judgement as to whether or not his role as a High Court judge precluded him from talking to Kerr in this way. So, the harshest criticism that could be levelled against Kerr in this respect is that he allowed his friend to potentially compromise himself.

The fact that Mason was the background adviser came out when Sir Garfield Barwick revealed the fact in an ABC interview in January 1994. Author Gerard Henderson then confirmed that Kerr had earlier told him about Mason's role. However, according to Kelly and Bramston, it was not until 2012 that the full extent of their discussions became public, courtesy of researcher Jenny Hocking in her biography of Whitlam. She had gained access to Kerr's papers in the National Library.

As Kelly and Bramston tell it:

> In explaining the purpose of his document outlining Mason's role, Kerr wrote: 'In, say, fifty years' time the personalities concerned will have largely disappeared into history and the nature of the friendship between Mason and myself and of his part in my thinking in October-November 1975 will not, without this note, be known to history.'

> This is a man determined to have Mason's role made public. It is impossible to miss an element of resentment towards Mason at what Kerr felt was his reluctance to have his role revealed. Kerr wrote of Mason:

> 'I start by saying simply that I regarded him (I still do) as a liber-

al-minded and progressive man and lawyer, of judgement and wisdom, as well as of learning and all-round intellectual quality and believed that no one could better, by conversation, help me to sort out my own thoughts on the constitutional powers of the Governor-General in the constitutional crisis of 1975 ... His opinions and his role in his talks with me at that time would certainly be regarded as significant by many who have engaged in controversy about events of that time and from my point of view it is unfortunate that they are unknown ... It is only the magnitude of the 1975 crisis itself which makes it historically important what happened between Mason and myself. But it is truly relevant because my conversation with Mason helped me to fortify myself for the action I was to take.'

These comments reveal so much. Kerr needed help in the crisis. He felt lonely and confided in his memoir about the burden of 'intense mental solitude'. He needed a trusted figure as sounding board and adviser. Kerr could see the controversy to come; it required resilience and strength and he sought counsel from a trusted friend to help him translate his words to deeds ... With Mason, Kerr found a meeting of minds sealed by friendship and trust. Kerr believed it was important for Mason's role to become public and for people to know that a prestigious figure such as Mason had fortified him in the dismissal decision.[3]

I have included that rather long extract because, in its entirety, it effectively demolishes the persona, carefully constructed over the best part of ten chapters in *The Dismissal,* of a scheming manipulator intent on making his mark in history by dismissing a duly elected prime minister. It is clear that Kerr agonised over his decision. He knew it would be controversial and that he would attract violent criticism. As Sir David Smith tells it, on the morning of 11 November:

As he returned the documents to their folder, the Governor-General gave a heavy sigh. He was well aware of the responsibility which he now carried, but he was prepared to be true to the oath of his office and to do his duty. He knew he would be execrated by the Labor Party and its supporters for the rest of his life, and he had told me so in just those words, but he knew he had a responsibility to put to the people, for their decision, the issue which the Parliament had

---

[3] Ibid., pp. 153-154.

failed to resolve. We then left the study to prepare for the events of the day.[4]

This is not the reaction of a self-serving *bon vivant* who loved the trappings of office and hobnobbing with royalty. Of one who was about to put the finishing touch to the coup he had so cynically and deceptively planned for months.

Kerr's notes stated that his discussions with Mason, regarding the crisis, covered the period 12 October to 9 November. However:

> Mason, however, offers a different version. He says their first conversation about the crisis was much earlier, in August at Yarralumla
> ...
> Referring to their August meeting, Mason says: '[Kerr] mentioned that an occasion might arise for him to exercise the Reserve Powers, dismiss Mr Whitlam and commission Malcolm Fraser to form a caretaker government for the purposes of securing supply and holding an election.' This is an extraordinary statement from a then serving judicial officer about events of which the public (and Whitlam himself) was otherwise unaware.
>
> The political mood in August was not focussed on dismissal. Indeed, Whitlam had not yet made his declaration that he would defy the Senate if supply was blocked. There was virtually no public debate at this time about a possible dismissal. It was not on the radar. Yet this statement suggests Kerr's mind had focussed on a dismissal option many weeks before the crisis. That is what makes this statement from Mason so extraordinary.[5]

So now we are back to Kerr the schemer. Mason's claim about what Kerr said at the August meeting is indeed extraordinary in that it foretold exactly what was to eventuate – if it was made in exactly those bald terms. It is possible Mason was paraphrasing a more nuanced or complex proposition by Kerr.

Be that as it may, it's possible this early discussion took place not in August as Mason claims but in early September. Later in

---

[4] Smith, *Head of State*, p. 244.
[5] Kelly and Bramston, op.cit., pp. 155-156.

this chapter, Kelly and Bramston reveal that on another issue, Mason's recollections were inaccurate:

> Mason also provides more details than Kerr of their 12 October discussion. Yet Mason's account of this discussion is inaccurate because he referred to events that had not yet happened ... Mason also referred to the Ellicott opinion, yet this opinion was made public only on 16 October four days later. Mason's timing is confused.[6]

So, it is not beyond the bounds of possibility that Mason also got the date of this first meeting wrong. It could have been in early September, in which case the idea that Whitlam would defy the Senate may not have been widely canvassed in the public arena, but it was certainly known to Kerr. On 12 September, Kerr wrote to Sir Martin Charteris:

> I feel reasonably sure that the Prime Minister believes that if there is to be an election at this stage the loss for his party would be devastating and the Opposition would gain control of both Houses. In this situation he is not in the mood, to coin a phrase, 'to go quietly'.
>
> The press this morning carried a story to the effect that he was going to 'tough it out'. By this it is meant to say simply that only the House has the political right to decide about the Budget. If the Senate refuses to pass it, the theory is that the Prime Minister will not accept that as a ground for coming to me for a dissolution of the House of Representatives or indeed for a double dissolution. He will simply say that the responsibility for funds running out must be borne by the Opposition. He will send the budget back to the Senate and if necessary will do so again and force them to reject it more than once. Then there will be a battle in the country about who is responsible for the ensuing mess – failure to meet obligations, pay public servants, the Defence Forces and so on.
>
> This morning I had here in the house a delegation of Canadian parliamentarians and they were all openly saying that the Prime Minister had quite clearly enunciated this strategy in a speech he made to them yesterday.
>
> I am also keeping my mind open to the constitutional issues. If the

---

[6] Ibid., p. 157.

Prime Minister and the Leader of the Opposition get into a battle in which the Senate has defeated the Budget, the Prime Minister refuses to recommend a dissolution, my role will need some careful thought though, of course, the classic constitutional convention will presumably govern the matter.[7]

So, if the first discussion between Kerr and Mason took place in early September, Mason's statement was not quite so extraordinary except as to the accuracy of his prediction – and that could be put down to *post hoc* paraphrasing.

In fact, the Governor-General's dismissal power was canvassed in a *Canberra Times* editorial dated 4 July 1975, admittedly not in relation to the blocking of supply but in relation to the Loans Affair.[8] The possibility that Fraser might be Prime Minister in 1976 was raised in a number of publications in August; and such speculation could only have been based on a projection that Fraser, despite his prevarication, would block supply and that, consequently, Whitlam would advise an election which he would lose. In those circumstances it would not be unreasonable for Kerr to, as early as August, contemplate the possibility that he might have to use the reserve powers.

We now come to Mason's advice to Kerr that he should warn Whitlam:

> Mason, moreover, claimed that in this discussion he told Kerr 'that in my view the incumbent prime minister should, as a matter of fairness, first be offered the option of holding a general election to resolve any dispute over supply between the two houses and be informed that if he did not agree to do so, his commission would be withdrawn'. Mason said that he pointed out to Kerr the 'advantage' of the incumbent prime minister going to the election rather than facing the poll as a dismissed prime minister. 'Sir John did not question my view then, or at any time in his discussions with me,' Mason wrote.
>
> This statement is damaging to Kerr because it suggests he got sound

---

[7] Kerr, Letter to Marin Charteris, *The Palace Letters*, 12 September 1975, p. 33.
[8] *The Canberra Times*, July 5, 1975, *The Palace Letters*, p. 67.

advice and did not heed it.[9]

The authors point out that no reference to this advice is to be found in Kerr's papers, but that this might be explained by Kerr having a motivation not to include it. That is unlikely because Kerr was remarkably frank and thorough in his private writings, as Kelly and Bramston themselves reveal. Let's assume, however, that Mason did give this advice. He says he gave it on a number of occasions, most notably during their final discussion on 9 November.

Mason said:

> On our arrival at Admiralty House in the evening, in response to my inquiry, Sir John told me that the prime minister had left Kirribilli House earlier in the day. Sir John also said that he had spoken to the chief justice and would be seeing him the next morning. Later, at the end of dinner, Sir John told me that he would see Mr Whitlam and simply hand him a letter of dismissal. I then said that before doing so he should say that he had no alternative but to dismiss the prime minister unless he was willing to hold a general election.
>
> Sir John replied "I know that". I told him that, if he did not warn the prime minister, he would run the risk that people would accuse him of being deceptive. I also said that he would need to consider the possibility that the prime minister might ask for time to consider his position and, if so, what response should be made.[10]

If Kerr did intend to simply hand Whitlam his letter of dismissal, as he reportedly told Mason he would, then perhaps he did, after all, accept Mason's advice, because, according to his own account he did not do that. He first ascertained if Whitlam's position remained unchanged and then said 'in that case' he *had decided to* terminate Whitlam's commission. This hiatus gave Whitlam the opportunity to back down. This is Kerr's defence against the charge he failed to warn Whitlam. Whitlam rejected this version of the interview, however, I will argue that Kerr's version is the more likely. This issue is examined later in this and further chapters.

---

9 Kelly and Bramston, op.cit., pp. 156-157.
10 'Text of statement by Sir Anthony Mason', *The Sydney Morning Herald*, 27 August 2012.

The charge that Sir John Kerr had a duty to warn Whitlam that he might be obliged to terminate his commission, and that he failed in this duty, is cited as one of Kerr's most serious failings in the whole crisis. But is it really that significant an issue? Let's consider what would have happened if Kerr had given that warning at, say, the time the Ellicott opinion was released. One of two things could have happened. The first is that Whitlam could have advised the Palace to recall Kerr and that the Palace would have agreed. This is what Kerr feared and what, no doubt, impelled him to not provide this warning at that stage. And it would not matter to Kerr even if he were not absolutely certain of Whitlam moving against him. He could not risk even a chance of that happening.

That said, it is highly unlikely that Whitlam would have acted overtly against Kerr at that stage. The public would not have liked it and the Opposition would have had a field day. Whitlam could however have quietly set the process in train by preparing the documents in advance of them being needed. He could have called the Palace on Monday 10 November and warned them that he may be advising Kerr's removal the following day and that he would need a quick resolution. Once that call had been made, Kerr's fate would have been sealed. Even if it took a day or two to formalise his recall, he would have been instructed immediately by the Palace to take no action against the Prime Minister. Under those circumstances, Whitlam would have demanded Kerr's resignation unless he were prepared to accept his (Whitlam's) advice. Indeed, it is hard to imagine that Whitlam, forewarned, would not have taken this step. From what Kelly and Bramston tell us about the nature of his feelings toward Kerr, he would have enjoyed ambushing him in this way and ensuring a compliant Governor-General into the future.

On the other hand, if Whitlam did none of those things, it would suggest he still believed he could intimidate Kerr into doing whatever he, Whitlam, advised.

And he would have done exactly what he did do in the event. Having listened to Kerr's warning, he would have stood firm and tried to outbluff Fraser. He certainly would not have caved at that point. Eventually, he would have been compelled to call on Kerr with some advice aimed at ending the crisis. Presumably that would have been on 11 November. His advice may have been for a double dissolution, or he may have decided to persist with the half-Senate election and the problematical bank loan. It is probable he would not have made up his mind on this until the last minute, hoping or believing that Fraser would have caved by then. If he then found that Kerr was not to be intimidated and, brandishing a dismissal notice, refused to accept advice for a half-Senate election, Whitlam could then modify his stance and advise a double dissolution.

So, in what way is this scenario any different from what actually played out on 11 November? Sir John Kerr says, in *Matters for Judgement*, that having ascertained that Whitlam was intent on governing without supply and having told Whitlam that, based on that, he had decided to withdraw his commission:

> The documents duly signed, were face downwards on my desk. I now knew there would be no changed advice, only the certainty of constitutional disruption if any time were allowed to elapse. I therefore made my final decision to withdraw his commission and hand him the signed documents. He could still say, 'Let's talk about this. If you are determined to have an election, I would rather go to the people myself as Prime Minister.' Had he done so I would have agreed, provided he agreed by action there and then. I was not prepared to run any further risk.[11]

Kelly and Bramston cover this point in a later chapter. They say:

> Kerr constructed this argument as a face-saving device. He pretended that at the precise moment of his planned political execution Whitlam could have remained prime minister. This claim was designed to rebut criticism that Kerr had betrayed the convention of the Crown by conducting a dismissal by ambush and without prior discussion of the situation with Whitlam. It is not believable.[12]

---

[11] Kerr, op.cit., p. 358.
[12] Kelly and Bramston, op.cit., p. 223.

On the contrary, it is eminently believable. To begin with, we must dispense with the notion that Kerr's *aim* was to dismiss Whitlam. I have made this point earlier. Kerr's *aim* was to secure supply to the Crown by means of a general election. His *means*, in the absence of Whitlam advising such an election, was to replace Whitlam with someone who would, viz., Fraser.

If we can get past that Kelly/Bramston mindset, we then look at the nature of the two men involved. Kelly and Bramston have written the script.

Whitlam is the egotistical, yet principled, ideologue intent on destroying forever the claimed power of the Senate to frustrate the will of the 'people's' House. They tell us, in Chapter Seven of *The Dismissal,* that:

> Whitlam intended to teach Fraser that using the Senate to break convention was not cost free. His plan was to transform the issue from Labor's unpopularity to the integrity of Australia's democracy.[13]

This is the man that Kelly and Bramston tell us despised Kerr and had no doubt about his ability to bend Kerr to his will. This is 'crash through or crash' Whitlam.

And yet we are to believe that, at this pivotal moment in his career, he was prepared to meekly accept dismissal at the hands of a man who he, apparently, held in contempt? Are we to believe that he would not attempt to use the supreme self-confidence and bluster he successfully employed against all his parliamentary and departmental colleagues, to overcome this final obstacle to his noble mission?

That proposition is, frankly, unbelievable.

And if we are to adhere to the Kelly and Bramston portrayal of Kerr, are we to believe that the greedy and adroit opportunist that we discovered in the first ten chapters of *The Dismissal* – the obsequious toady intimidated by Whitlam – would *not* have crumbled in the face of such an onslaught and withdrawn his

---

[13] Ibid., p. 99.

termination? Hardly likely, I would have thought.

However, if we disregard that fatuous caricature and look at the real man, the same consideration applies. Kerr accepted the appointment as Governor-General because he saw it as an important and fulfilling job of work. It was the next stage in his career, not a sinecure bestowed at the end of his career as a reward for distinguished service. He negotiated an extended tenure. Is it likely he would risk it all just for the dubious pleasure of dismissing Whitlam? Would he have rejected the chance of resolving the crisis in a non-controversial way? Would that not have added lustre to his career?

The proposition that Kerr would have rejected any such change of heart by Whitlam is, again, inconceivable.

Which leads us to the obvious question. Why didn't Whitlam back down and agree to advise a double dissolution?

And the obvious answer is that he decided that the advantage of going to the election as Prime Minister was outweighed by the advantage of going to the election as the victim of an 'undemocratic coup'.

The polls had improved somewhat for Labor on the back of the Senate's intransigence, but Whitlam would have known that this factor would pretty much disappear once the election campaign was under way. The focus would have returned to the government's incompetence and dysfunction. The best way to counter that would be to elevate the debate, above petty politics, to a consideration of the very preservation of democracy. It would have been a big ask – and in the end it failed – but by then it was all Whitlam had.

As to Mason's suggestion on 9 November that Kerr should provide prior warning and give Whitlam time should he request it to consider his position, that was no longer a viable option. By 9 November the game had changed. Kerr was no longer an umpire, but a player and he needed, and had every right, to not concede any advantage to Whitlam. As I have argued above, Whitlam had all the time he needed in the 11 November meeting to make a snap decision.

There follows an examination of some aspects of Kerr's account of his discussions with Mason versus Mason's recollections. There are some differences which are neither here nor there, such as whether Kerr had sent Mason a copy of the Ellicott opinion and asked him to provide his view of it. But the significant issue concerns discussions about when to consult with Sir Garfield Barwick.

It seems this issue first arose during the 20 – 21 October discussions:

> According to Kerr, he and Mason spoke about 'the desirability of seeking Barwick's formal advice'. It is obvious that any resort to Barwick was in the context of the reserve powers. Kerr wrote: '[Mason's] assessment was that I should only do so if I felt otherwise at liberty to take this step, if I had assessed (a) what advise I really needed and (b) what [Barwick] would be likely to advise. Today he said he believed it possible that Barwick believed and would advise immediate radical action, dismissal etc. He agreed with me that to get such advice would be disastrous at this stage.' While confirming Kerr's account, Mason claimed he did not use the words 'radical' or 'disastrous'.
>
> This is evidence that Mason was advising Kerr on how to deal with Barwick on the issue of a Whitlam dismissal. And the crisis was not yet a week old.[14]

That Mason claimed he did not use the words 'radical' or 'disastrous' is neither here nor there. Kerr would have simply been paraphrasing Mason, in his own words.

However, this is illuminating in that it shows that Kerr didn't really want or need Barwick's advice. What he wanted was his imprimatur on the final decision. This is a tactical move that Kerr was well within his rights to employ. It was an important public relations move designed to reassure the public that Kerr was not a maverick operating his own agenda.

---

[14] Ibid., pp. 139-140.

Of course, there is an element of pragmatism – some might even call it cynicism – about this because no-one would imagine that Kerr would have solicited the opinion of Lionel Murphy, had he been Chief Justice at the time.

As to the crisis being 'less than a week old', two considerations apply. Firstly, as I have already shown, talk of Whitlam's dismissal had already been widely canvassed, most notably via the Ellicott opinion. And, secondly, the crisis only had three more weeks to run. Events moved very quickly, and it was incumbent on Kerr not to be caught flat-footed. Kerr already knew there was a deadline before the money ran out. And that deadline applied even if Whitlam were to advise, or agree to, a general election.

This section concludes:

> The Kerr-Mason dialogue would culminate on 9 November, the day Kerr decided to engage Barwick to give the dismissal legal sanction and began preparing the documents for the dismissal.[15]

This is a deceptive form of words. It suggests that Barwick was the ultimate decision maker. That he gave approval for Kerr to dismiss Whitlam. That is not true. He merely gave it, as his opinion, that the course Sir John Kerr had determined upon was within his power. That provided cover for Kerr. It confirmed, for the benefit of the public, that his decision was not based only upon his own understanding of the Constitution. If there had been another Chief Justice at the time, for example Lionel Murphy, that cover might not have been available to Kerr. But that would not have changed his decision.

We come now to the title of this chapter. This comes from a note in Kerrs papers:

> 'There is one final point I should like to make. Mason is the keystone in the arch of opinion which was at the time important to me on the Reserve Powers of the Crown. That arch consisted of Evatt, Bailey [a distinguished solicitor-general], Sir Garfield Barwick, Bailey's successor Mason, Mason's successor as Solicitor-General,

---

[15] Ibid., p. 160.

Ellicott (on all points except timing) and Forsey, the great Canadian authority.' ...

Kerr's 'arch of opinion' is an artificial concept and probably had a dual purpose. It refers to individuals and scholars who helped to shape his attitude towards the crisis and, in retrospect, it is a list of the luminaries Kerr invoked to sustain his role before history.[16]

Rather than being an artificial concept, the arch is actually a useful analogy which simply highlights that support for Kerr's position came from both Right (Barwick, Ellicott) and Left (Evatt, Forsey) and that Mason – as Kerr's close friend and probably politically neutral – bridging the two arms, provided a 'leavening' influence.

To take the analogy a step further, the arch is an inherently strong construction. Kerr clearly sees himself standing atop this arch, which testifies that the weight of informed opinion on the existence and use of the reserve powers is overwhelmingly on his side. Which, getting back to a point I made much earlier, means that Kerr's position, legally and constitutionally, is impregnable. And that leaves only the motivation and the way he exercised those powers as grounds to attack him. And I hope I have shown that, however mightily they have striven to construct a damming case against Kerr, Kelly and Bramston have constructed a house of cards.

The remainder of this chapter covers some peripheral issues – Kerr's desire to have Mason's role become public, Mason's reticence and Kerr's respect for that, Whitlam's apparent *post hoc* acceptance of Mason's role when it became known. The authors are certainly critical of Mason. They highlight Mason's hypocrisy at Kerr's funeral, at which he read the eulogy:

> After the singing of a Welsh hymn, Mason addressed the congregation. He called Kerr a man of 'exceptional talents' but did concede a flaw – at times he 'seemed pre-occupied with the need for self-justification'. Mason has avoided such a flaw. There was no mention of Mason's own role in the events of 1975.[17]

---

[16] Ibid.
[17] Ibid., pp. 163-164.

There's that phrase 'self-justification' again and this time from a friend. With what we now know, that seems exceptionally gratuitous.

They note that there are precedents for a Chief Justice advising a Governor-General but none for a normal High Court Judge. They conclude:

> There is no question Mason has sought to keep his role a secret from public view. He could have disclosed it, certainly after retirement from the High Court. It was only the availability of Kerr's documents from the National Archives that prompted Mason's August 2012 statement, the only detailed statement he has ever made. It came long after Kerr's death, thereby denying Kerr, his friend, the chance to answer the contradictions that Mason identified.
>
> If it was not for Kerr's documentary time bomb Mason's role might never have been fully revealed. Kerr was not to be denied. He unmasked the full extent of the Kerr-Mason dialogue from the grave.[18]

In the grand scheme of things, the differences between the two accounts are neither here nor there.

Kerr clearly saw no impropriety, at least on his part, in consulting Mason. As to Mason, it is arguable that he should not have become involved. As I said earlier, I believe he was equally comfortable in his role. But he knew it would attract a degree of censure and controversy if it came out. He would have seen little point in risking that and cannot be harshly blamed for his reticence.

And again, Mason's involvement was only peripheral to the decision, which was Sir John Kerr's alone.

---

[18] Ibid., p. 164.

12

Kerr's Decision

This chapter goes over a lot of ground already covered – Kerr's failure to 'advise and warn', Kerr as Fraser's dupe, Whitlam's misjudgements and cluelessness, and so on. But it also introduces discussion on the alternate financial arrangements that Whitlam proposed in order to govern without supply. And it goes into more detail about compromises proposed by Kerr.

But before going into detail, it is important to make the point that, in this chapter, Kelly and Bramston concede that, on 11 November, neither Kerr nor any other Governor-General could have accepted Whitlam's advice for a half-Senate election and continuance in office based on the dubious promise of funds loaned by banks. One of the reasons for this was that the money already appropriated by Parliament would have run out before the election would be finalised. In the face of that inconvenient truth, they must fall back on all the specious half-truths, inferences and sophistry that they have already canvassed in the earlier chapters.

They begin:

> Sir John Kerr's decision to dismiss the Whitlam government was the consequence of two events – Fraser's month-long command of his own forces in blocking the budget and his superior reading of the governor-general's mind and character. Fraser's tactical management of Kerr was perfect, a blend of public persuasion and private threat. In retrospect, Whitlam seems clueless. He shunned any compromise, failed to devise an effective strategy and was blind to his alienation of Kerr.[1]

---

[1] Kelly and Bramston, *The Dismissal*, p. 167.

This sets the scene that suggests Kerr danced to Fraser's tune. Later they say:

> Fraser won because his grasp of the power realities in the 1975 crisis was superior to that of Whitlam. In the end, Kerr acted upon Fraser's view of those realities and repudiated Whitlam's view of them.[2]

Do you see the subtle sleight of hand at work here? The suggestion that Kerr could have jumped either way, but that Fraser's superior handling of him secured the decision in his favour. The fact is that Kerr's and Fraser's views on this matter *coincided,* not that Fraser converted Kerr to his way of thinking. Kelly and Bramston themselves say so later in the same paragraph:

> As a constitutional and political fact, Fraser's view was correct and Whitlam's view was wrong. And Kerr acted on this basis.

So, at best, Fraser's influence, such as it was, could do no more than attempt to counter whatever pressure he, Fraser, might have imagined Whitlam was subjecting Kerr to. As we now know – and as Kelly and Bramston acknowledge – Whitlam was totally ineffective in bringing pressure to bear on Kerr and therefore Fraser's blandishments were irrelevant. The only way in which he influenced Kerr's thinking was in convincing him that he would not back down. In the end, he also convinced Whitlam of that fact. This was a political consideration. Once that belief was cemented in Kerr's mind – and it was a not unreasonable belief – Kerr acted on his own view of the *constitutional* aspect of the crisis.

They continue:

> Whitlam misread Kerr. But his greater blunder was to misread the basic power equation. Whitlam failed to realize he had only a finite time to break Fraser before supply was exhausted. Once this time expired then Whitlam, his strategy having failed, would need another strategy. Labor was optimistic for most of the crisis period from 16 October to lunchtime on 11 November. This is because

---

[2] Ibid, p. 168.

the polls were running Labor's way and it assumed, sooner or later, Fraser would crack. Fraser's political achievement was immense: as leader, he held his side together for nearly a month.[3]

If Whitlam's strategy was to 'tough it out', to stand on principle in order to finally break the power of the Senate to frustrate the will of the House of Representatives, then he necessarily had to push it to the limit. He had to run the clock down. Which is what he did. Once that strategy failed, he needed a new aim. That was to remain in government and his strategy for that was to advise a half-Senate election with the aim of gaining control of the Senate and governing, by means of a dubious loan arrangement, for a period without Parliamentary supply. As Kelly and Bramston point out, that strategy was doomed to fail.

Kelly and Bramston say Labor believed the polls were running their way and, because of that, they believed Fraser would crack. But if they did believe this, why would they be shy of going to an election, rather than proposing the controversial bank loan proposal? Probably because as Kelly and Bramston also say:

> Fraser's judgement was that bad polls over supply were unavoidable, but once the crisis was resolved and an election called, the opposition's polling dominance would return. This is exactly what happened. Labor's pollster, Rod Cameron, from ANOP, told Labor's national secretary David Combe that the government must not confuse public support on the supply issue with its standing in an election. They were separate: Labor would still lose an election.[4]

If Labor were aware the polls would not stand up during an election, why would they not think Fraser would come to the same conclusion? Why would they pin their hope on Fraser cracking?

Fraser had some issues holding his troops together, as Kelly and Bramston recount, but in the end all that mattered was that he did hold them together. They also recount how Labor, in the

---

[3] Ibid., pp. 168-169.
[4] Ibid., p. 170.

person of new Treasurer Bill Hayden, and others, spelled out, in great detail, the damaging effect lack of supply would have. They observe:

> The question of 'who's to blame' was pivotal. Convinced he was prevailing, Whitlam's mood became more dogmatic. On 21 October, during the second great parliamentary debate over supply, Whitlam said Fraser's action, if successful, would divide the nation 'and leave a legacy of bitterness unequalled since 1916', a reference to the conscription plebiscite. Hardening his position, Whitlam ruled out not just any House of Representatives election as sought by Fraser but any half-Senate election 'until this constitutional issue is settled'. Whitlam felt he was turning the screws on Fraser, denying Fraser anything but ignominious retreat.[5]

Here Whitlam is stating very publicly what he told Kerr privately. This declaration would seem to be 'a line in the sand' behind which Whitlam could not credibly withdraw. If he believed it would be *ignominious* for Fraser to retreat, would not that same consideration apply to him? Certainly, Sir John Kerr made that inference.

In that speech, Whitlam went on to frame the battle he had joined, as a defence of the constitution:

> 'The message from the Senate constitutes an act of constitutional aggression ... Not for the first time is government of the people, for the people, by the people – and in our case the people's house – at stake. In the words of Lincoln ... let me say to the Leader of the Opposition and his followers: You can have no conflict without yourself being the aggressor. You have registered no oath to destroy the Constitution, while I have the solemn one to preserve and defend it.'[6]

Again, it is clear that Whitlam no longer saw this as a political issue but one of principle. Or, at least, that is the position he adopted. For him to back down from this and advise an election as a matter of mere political expediency, would be a massive humiliation in his mind.

---

[5] Ibid., p. 171.
[6] Ibid., pp. 171-172.

On 29 October, the House passed the supply bills for the third time. On the same day, an article was published in the *Sydney Morning Herald*. It was written by Sir Norman Cowper, a leading Sydney lawyer who for many years was the Chairman of the Australian Institute of Political Science. Kerr had worked with him on the Board for the Council on New Guinea Affairs. Kerr included it in *Matter's for Judgement,* and I reproduce it in full here because it is an excellent summary of the real constitutional position:

When the rhetoric and rodomontade are brushed aside, the essential matters are clear enough.

(1) The cardinal rule is that the Governor-General acts in accordance with the advice he receives from the man who commands a majority in the House of Representatives –
the Prime Minister.

(2) If in extraordinary circumstances he rejects that advice, his only course will be to dismiss the Prime Minister, send for the Leader of the Opposition, commission him to form a ministry, and grant him a dissolution, at least of the House of Representatives.

(3) The present Prime Minister's claim that the removal of a government from office before the end of the term for which it has been elected would be a blow to Parliamentary government and democratic institutions is manifestly untenable. Indeed, the power of removal (the reserve power of the Crown) may be the only safeguard against the destruction of democracy. A government which finds its management of a country disastrous and a rising tide of public opinion against it may in its determination to remain in office resort to illegal actions which are the negation of democracy; and only the exercise of the Governor-General's power to dismiss it will save the country from an unconstitutional dictatorship.

(4) If the Prime Minister were dismissed, but his party won the ensuing election, the Governor-General's office would be in jeopardy and, no doubt, the Queen would be asked to recall him and replace him by someone nominated by the (former) Prime Minister. Furthermore, salutary warnings would have been given to future Oppositions and Governors-General as to the unwisdom of forcing

an election against the wishes of the elected government.

(5) If, however, the result of the election were victory for the former opposition party, the actions of the Governor-General would have been vindicated, and the present spate of talk about alleged conventions would be seen to be of little force or value.

(6) In view of (4) and (5), a Governor-General could not be expected to reject the Prime Minister's advice and dismiss him unless he was satisfied:

(a) that the business of government had broken down and the continuance in office of the Prime Minister would result in administrative chaos, flagrant breaches of the Constitution and other illegalities, and

(b) that it was highly probable that the votes of the people at the ensuing election would uphold his action.

It was because these conditions existed in New South Wales in 1932 that Sir Phillip Game was able to dismiss Mr Lang and restore orderly government to the State.

(7) The Executive Council minute purporting to authorise the borrowing of a huge sum for 20 years for grandiose schemes of long-term mineral development as being a borrowing for 'temporary purposes' was a flagrant breach of the Financial Agreement which is part of the Constitution. In my view, however, this does not by itself satisfy condition (a) above.

(8) The rejection or deferral of Supply is undoubtedly within the power of the Senate under Section 53 of the Constitution, but it is a power to be exercised only in very exceptional circumstances.

(9) The circumstances alleged as exceptional are: incompetence in the management of the economy, the breach of the Financial Agreement, dismissal of Ministers for misleading Parliament and, generally inept and dishonest government. Whether those circumstances exist to such an extent as to justify the confusion, hardship and breakdown of orderly government which the refusal or deferral of Supply will entail is a question which I would answer no, but which the Opposition has answered yes.

(10) If it persists in holding up Supply it may force the dismissal of the Government but will run the grave risk that its actions will antagonize public opinion and lead to the loss of the ensuing election. There is,

perhaps, some indication that this swing against the Opposition has begun.

(11) On the other hand, the continued refusal of Supply may put the Government in such difficulties that it cannot carry on without committing gross illegalities and flouting the constitution, in which case if the Governor-General were reasonably assured that the people would support him, he might well decide to dismiss the Prime Minister and force an election.

(12) Other possibilities are:

(i) That the Prime Minister, believing that the refusal of Supply has caused a revulsion of opinion in favour of the Government, will himself advise a dissolution.

(ii) That the Opposition, deciding that the revulsion of opinion has prejudiced its chances at an election, or that the consequences of refusal of Supply are too damaging to the economy or inflict too great a hardship on the whole community, decides to pass the Supply bills, or

(iii) That a compromise will be reached.

For a constitutional lawyer, it is the most interesting confrontation since Federation.[7]

Kerr set great store by this article, although he repudiated the notion that his decision should be influenced by the likely outcome of the election – as well he might. I am not a lawyer, but I am surprised that so eminent a lawyer as Cowper should put this view. And, also, that the result of the election would vindicate Kerr's decision or not. Kerr's actions were to procure an election, not an election outcome. He acted on principle. What the people chose to do at that election has no bearing on that principle. Or put conversely, it would have been unconscionable for Kerr to abandon principle on the chance that the electorate might return the Whitlam government. He was aware, though, that such an eventuality would cost him his prized job. Indeed, it makes it that much more unlikely that the scheming self-serving manipulator that Kelly and Bramston have created, would have made the decision he did.

---

[7] Kerr, *Matters for Judgement*, pp. 287-288.

Kerr's vindication rests on the fact that a damaging political stand-off was resolved by that most democratic of institutions – an election – without resort to illegalities and no damage was inflicted upon our body politic.

The import of this article is that it spelled out, very clearly, as early as 29 October, the prospect that Whitlam might be dismissed and, also, that attempting to govern without supply would be legally and constitutionally fraught. If it never occurred to Labor that Kerr, a conservative and careful jurist, would also think the same way, then they must have been unusually obtuse.

On 30 October, the first of Kerr's two attempts to help find a solution was instigated. One of the things the Opposition feared was that a half-Senate election would be called early (it was due before mid-1976). That would not normally affect the numbers in the Senate until the new Senators took their place in July 1976. But in this case, the High Court had earlier approved the inclusion of two new Senators from each of the two Territories. These would take their place immediately upon election, offering Whitlam the possibility of a brief period in control of the Senate.

From *The Dismissal*:

> On 30 October, Kerr had lunch with Whitlam and McClelland at Yarralumla after an ExCo meeting. While the Governor-General did not see himself as a mediator in the crisis, he felt the need to test the leaders on a compromise. It involved Fraser making the major concessions. The idea was that Fraser might grant supply if Whitlam agreed not to hold any half-Senate election until close to mid-1976, which meant Labor would forego any option of constituting the so-called interim Senate before 1 July and gaining temporary control of the Senate. Fear of this possibility had been a factor in Fraser's decision to block supply.[8]

Kerr thought that if the Opposition were having second thoughts, it might appeal as a face-saving exit. They would

---

[8] Kelly and Bramston, op.cit., p. 172.

have a guarantee of not facing a hostile Senate until, at the earliest July 1976, only some seven months away.

It is not clear to me why this would be attractive to Fraser, even if he were looking for an escape. Nonetheless, according to Kelly and Bramston:

> At lunch, Whitlam authorised Kerr to speak to Fraser on this subject. He made an appointment to see Fraser as soon as lunch broke. It was their second official meeting during the crisis. On 2 November, three days later, Kerr made a five-page handwritten note of his talks on this issue. He floated the idea but Fraser seemed unimpressed. Kerr's notes, however, have Fraser saying that if he 'had a watertight guarantee that the Senate would not meet, even for a day, till after July 1, once the election was held, he would be prepared to consult his colleagues about granting supply on these terms'.
>
> Kerr said he would discuss this position with Whitlam if Fraser had no objections. Fraser agreed. The governor-general's notes say he put this proposition to Whitlam that evening. Kerr wrote 'but [Whitlam] said he could give no undertaking that carried the implication that he got supply by making promises. Nothing but absolute surrender by the Senate was a possibility from his point of view.'[9]

So even as late as 30 October Whitlam was offering no encouragement that he might be inclined to soften his stance. In *Matters for Judgement*, Kerr, says that he considered it a possibility that the Opposition might be looking for some way of retreat:

> A compromise proposal which I had in mind would, I thought, by offering a way out, at the same time test the degree of strength in their stand.[10]

It seems to me that testing the resolve of the Opposition was really the primary motivation for this initiative. It was a critical factor that Kerr needed to consider in his deliberations. Kelly's and Bramston's take on this is:

> There are several conclusions from this event. Kerr said in his

---
[9] Ibid., pp. 172-173.
[10] Kerr, op.cit., p. 288.

memoirs he was offering Fraser 'an opportunity for retreat'. This is also the impression Whitlam and McClelland got from the lunch. Indeed, McClelland got excited and told Paul Kelly, at the time that 'this is the Governor-General's solution'. In fact, Kerr probably thought it had little chance. Fraser was careful. The proposal, in effect, meant a defeat for him. He got virtually nothing in return, since any chance of Labor temporary control of the Senate was remote. Yet, managing Kerr cautiously, Fraser kept the proposal alive. The only interpretation from Kerr's note is that Whitlam killed it. Kerr was unsurprised by this – he understood Whitlam believed the Senate would crack, and he would settle for nothing but total victory.[11]

I do not know why Fraser didn't just reject the proposal out of hand. It is not clear to me in what way Fraser's counter proposal was 'managing Kerr'. He needed to convince Kerr that he was not after a way out, and the best way to do that would be to reject the suggestion outright. It is possible he anticipated that Whitlam would reject his compromise, and this would help cement in Kerr's mind that Fraser was determined but reasonable, whereas Whitlam was just unreasonable. Nonetheless, the fact that Kerr was prepared to float this idea, suggests that, rather than being hell-bent on sacking Whitlam, he would have much preferred a negotiated settlement.

Kelly and Bramston sum up Whitlam's miscalculation:

> Whitlam's fatal misreading of the power dimension of the crisis was apparent in two areas – the half-Senate election tactic and the alternative financial arrangements. These are two of the most extraordinary aspects of the story highlighting the monumental ineptitude of the government.[12]

The importance of the half-Senate election hinges on the fact that, normally, it could be held at any time, but the new Senators would not take their seats until 1 July 1976. But, in this particular election, four newly created Senate seats for the Australian Capital Territory and the Northern Territory would be filled immediately after the election result was called. Thus, if Labor could gain three of those seats and/or regain the seats

---

[11] Kelly and Bramston, op.cit., p. 173.
[12] Ibid.

of Bunton and Field, it could temporarily gain control of the Senate and pass its Supply bills. It was a long shot, but it was worth considering by Whitlam. However, Whitlam resisted this option until it was too late. As Kelly and Bramston report:

> In Kerr's twelve-page handwritten note of 16 November (which includes revisions made on 13 September 1976), he explains his thinking about the half-Senate election, revealing the extent of Whitlam's folly. Kerr said: 'At a fairly early stage it would have been possible for Mr Whitlam to decide on a half-Senate election and so to advise me whilst the crisis was still a political one and not a constitutional one ... My own view was that Mr Whitlam made a tactical mistake in not having an early Senate election when there was money and I was under no deep need to make a final decision about supply ... Had he come to me in the second half of October and asked for a half-Senate election in November I should probably have been bound to take his advice because the Senate election would have been over before a real supply crisis arose.
>
> In short, Kerr would have granted Whitlam a half-Senate election in the early stage of the crisis but not on 11 November, because that would see the exhaustion of supply before any vote.[13]

The half-Senate election was not guaranteed to produce a result for Whitlam. But, as Kelly and Bramston point out, the blocking of supply would be the dominating issue of that election and may cause people to vote against the Opposition's tactic knowing that the result would not change the government either way. They could vote for a principle now and reserve their vote against the government, if that was their inclination, until the next general election. Whitlam would have been counting on a protest vote in his favour and it may well have worked.

But what the above extracts tell us is that Kerr was focussed on the securing of supply not dismissing Whitlam. As Kelly and Bramston note:

> No responsible governor-general, Kerr or anybody else, would have accepted this advice on 11 November, because supply could not be guaranteed for the campaign.

---

[13] Ibid., pp. 174-175.

Kerr wrote in his 16 November note:
> The other fundamental mistake made by Mr Whitlam was to believe, as he apparently did, that whatever happened I would do exactly what he advised and let him govern without supply and without going to the people. I should like to make it clear that at all times during the crisis Mr Whitlam stated in the clearest terms that he intended to govern without supply and that he would never recommend a dissolution of the House or a double dissolution because supply had been denied.

This statement by Kerr is credible precisely because by seeking a half-Senate election to be called on 11 November, Whitlam was assuming he could govern, at least for a time, after supply was exhausted.[14]

So here we have Kelly and Bramston conceding that Kerr could not accept Whitlam's advice on 11 November. Which brings us back to the rubric that the Governor-General must always act on the advice of his Ministers. Clearly, Kelly and Bramston do not accept this premise. The alternative interpretation is that the Governor-General acts *only* on the advice of his Ministers. Thus, in this situation, Kerr's detractors argue that his only other option was to refuse to accept Whitlam's advice for a half-Senate election and warn him that if he were not prepared to advise a dissolution of at least the House, Kerr would dismiss him and appoint someone who would. It is theoretically possible that Kerr could have found another Labor minister who would proffer such advice but that is highly unlikely. That minister would be signing his own political death warrant. And, of course, Kerr was convinced Whitlam would move against him if he was given time to re-consider.

They continue:
> What Whitlam did, however, was frighten Kerr. He persuaded Kerr that he was an unreasonable prime minister, and he cracked Kerr's nerve when he should have been calm, friendly and reassuring in dealing with the governor-general.[15]

---
[14] Ibid., p. 175.
[15] Ibid., pp. 175-176.

In typical fashion, this passage is worded to demean Kerr. Whitlam certainly persuaded Kerr he was an unreasonable prime minister but the suggestion he 'cracked Kerr's nerve' is nonsense. Kerr was not on Whitlam's side in this political confrontation. He owed nothing to Whitlam in a political sense. He was not one of Whitlam's troops who needed to be reassured in the face of the oncoming battle.

Kerr's aim was always to ensure that the government would not be forced, or allow itself to be cornered, into attempting to govern without supply.

Kelly and Bramston themselves point out:

> [Whitlam's] options from mid-October were (1) to 'tough it out' or (2) 'to tough it out' with a half-senate election. But if those options failed there was only one fall-back – to admit defeat and call a general election as Fraser demanded.[16]

Whitlam believed he could avoid this fall-back with an alternative financial arrangement in which the banks would loan the government money to tide it over until the half-Senate election had been completed. There were three serious problems with this plan. Firstly, its legality was questionable, although the Law Officers (the Attorney-General and Solicitor-General) provided informal advice that it was. Secondly, it was highly unlikely the banks would come to the party. And thirdly, there was no guarantee that the half-Senate election would result in Labor gaining control. In which case the problem of supply would remain unresolved.

Realistically, it could only have been contemplated as a bluff – to convince Fraser to back down. Indeed, former Treasurer Bill Hayden is reported in *The Dismissal* as saying:

> 'I had large doubts, although I could bear with the proposal as a political bluff, a legitimate political tactic. I am afraid I would have retreated from any effort to have it go much beyond that. In my view, the system could only function briefly and not happily and

---

[16] Ibid., p. 176.

would have broken down early in the New Year.'[17]

The scheme would have been challenged by the State governments, and the banks, if they could satisfy their boards that the risk was acceptable, would also, of course, require interest to be paid. And that could only occur if Parliament approved such a payment in advance – something that Fraser would never have agreed to. As Kelly and Bramston observe: "This was not a sustainable solution to the crisis."[18] And they provide a detailed account of its shortcomings.

It is hard to imagine that Whitlam really believed he could pull this off. Kelly and Bramston point out that, in the mind of Sir John Kerr, it effectively undermined Labor's position:

> The conclusion Kerr drew was the opposite of what Whitlam wanted: the governor-general felt the talks with the banks were a clear sign that Whitlam's efforts to obtain supply by cracking the senate had been unsuccessful ... At no point did the governor-general regard the measures as an alternative to supply ... In his letter to the Palace of 20 October, Kerr ... wrote in conclusion, that Whitlam's purpose was to circumvent the denial of supply so 'there will be no excuse for me to demand evidence from him that he can get supply and no excuse for removing him and sending for someone willing to recommend an election'.
>
> In short, Kerr had a conspiratorial view of the scheme. This letter shows, again, that Kerr saw Whitlam's dismissal as an option from the start ... and offers the view that the scheme, in fact, was designed to prevent him from doing his job.[19]

Again, this passage is worded to cast Kerr in the worst possible light. It implies that Kerr saw his job as being to sack Whitlam. In that letter, Kerr did not offer the view that 'the scheme was designed to prevent him from doing his job'. He did *not* use those words, although the text above clearly implies that he did. Here is the full text of that section of the letter:

---

[17] Ibid., p. 177.
[18] Ibid.
[19] Ibid., pp. 178-179.

> By this technique he believes he can defuse the issue – no one or almost no one will suffer and Mr Fraser will be outmanoeuvred. More important the crisis will, he argues, thus be kept at the political level. There will be no real constitutional crisis, because despite the denial of supply he will still be able to govern and there will be no excuse for me to demand evidence from him that he can get supply and no excuse for removing him and sending for someone willing to recommend an election.[20]

What Kerr was saying was that the scheme was designed to obviate the need for his intervention, not to 'prevent him from doing his job'. Kelly's and Bramston's misleading paraphrasing of Kerr is, frankly, dishonest. This may seem nit-picking on my part, but the repetition of this meme throughout *The Dismissal* is fundamental to the blackguarding of Kerr. He cannot be faulted on technical or legal grounds, as Kelly and Bramston concede. Therefore, he must be condemned on motive.

If Whitlam had been able to convince Kerr that the alternative financial arrangements were a legal and viable means of circumventing the Senate, then Kerr would have granted Whitlam his half-Senate election on 11 November. That would have been a big ask because, as we have seen, even Labor members such as Treasurer Bill Hayden were doubtful about it. Kerr was highly unlikely to rush in where Hayden feared to tread.

Kerr's concurrence was even more unlikely if you consider that the idea was first floated sometime before 20 October and yet the banks were not invited to discuss the measure until 4 November, at a meeting scheduled for 6 November.[21] It was on 6 November that the Attorney-General Kep Enderby tendered to Kerr an unsigned *draft* Law Officer's opinion on the proposed financial arrangements. According to Kerr:

> The document stated that the Government would announce the introduction of legislation to enable it to pay interest to the bankers and would give an undertaking, subject to legislation being passed,

---

[20] Kerr, Letter to Martin Charteris, *The Palace Letters*, 20 October 1975, p. 120.
[21] Kerr, *Matters for Judgement*, p. 292.

to pay interest at a rate to be struck. The opinion also stated that the banks would be encouraged by the Government's promise to introduce the necessary legislation, passing of which would ensure that their interest would be paid. It seemed to me extremely unlikely that the Senate would pass such legislation whilst it was continuing to block supply. If it were going to do that, thus aiding a scheme of governing without supply, it might just as well grant supply.[22]

At this stage the banks had not even been consulted. The opinion was virtually worthless. That it was unsigned was unsurprising. It is hard to imagine that Byers would have put his name to this opinion. This was the same occasion on which Enderby also tendered the draft Law Officer's opinion on the Ellicott memorandum, striking out the Solicitor-General's signature as he did so.

Kerr must have felt he was being made game of. To be treated with such cavalier impropriety would, in my view, have absolved him of the need to be overly fastidious regarding the niceties normally accorded the Prime Minister by the Governor-General. At this stage, as I have observed earlier, Kerr was a player, no longer an umpire.

A few days earlier, on 3 November, Fraser made a compromise offer to Labor through the Governor-General. This was an idea floated by Victorian Liberal Premier Rupert Hamer. Fraser offered to pass supply if Whitlam agreed to hold a House of Representatives election at the same time as the half-Senate election due before July 1976. Whitlam rejected the offer out of hand.

Kelly and Bramston describe this as 'one of the most overlooked yet most decisive events in the crisis'.[23]

In fact, it was decisive only to the extent that it further confirmed in Kerr's mind the intransigence of both Whitlam and Fraser, that the political crisis would (if it had not already) evolve to a constitutional crisis and that he would have to play the decisive

---

[22] Ibid., pp 301-302.
[23] Kelly and Bramston, op.cit., p 179.

role. As far as Fraser's position is concerned, he left Kerr in no doubt:

> Mr Fraser said that this as far as the Opposition parties were prepared to go and that if rejected they would unfailingly stand firm on the refusal to pass supply.[24]

In the circumstances the offer was a generous one and Kerr could hardly doubt that, it having been rejected by Whitlam, Fraser's resolve would only harden.

Kelly and Bramston say of the offer:

> It was designed to cast Fraser as Mr Reasonable, always a hard call. The problem, as Fraser knew, was that this concession would make him look weak. Fraser suspected that Whitlam would interpret the offer as proof that he was crumbling, a correct conclusion. He suspected, therefore, that Whitlam would reject the offer, another correct conclusion. Having rejected Kerr's compromise, Whitlam would now reject Fraser's compromise.[25]

Whether Whitlam saw the offer as a sign that Fraser was weakening is moot. In his own account, Whitlam accepted that the offer was genuine but stated that, aside from the principle concerned, the issue he had with it was that it would effectively result in a six-month election campaign, with all the adverse consequences to stable government that would flow from that.[26]

Kelly and Bramston report:

> For Whitlam, only total victory would suffice. This event confirms Whitlam's real objectives during the crisis went far beyond avoiding an immediate election. Those objectives were, first, to break the Senate's power over supply for all time and ensure no opposition would repeat the tactic – in effect, to alter the power balance between the houses and impose a constitutional change on the system of government. Second, he sought to damage Fraser permanently and, by achieving a complete victory, ensure the opposition was discredited in a way that would alter the atmospherics of politics in

---

[24] Kerr, op.cit., p. 291.
[25] Kelly and Bramston, op.cit., p. 179-180.
[26] Gough Whitlam. (1983). *The truth of the matter.* Ringwood: Penguin, p. 87.

Labor's favour. Given these objectives, it made sense for Whitlam to reject the compromise but with a critical proviso: he had to be sure that Kerr would comply. And Whitlam assumed this.[27]

This is a significant passage. Among other things it suggests that, if, on 3 November, Whitlam were to reject pragmatism in favour of principle by refusing Fraser's rather generous offer, then when the crunch came on 11 November, he would see any advice for a general election as a humiliating failure on his part. Even if Kerr took the risk of himself being sacked by warning Whitlam that he would be dismissed if he refused to advise a general election, it is unlikely Whitlam would have acquiesced. And, as I have argued earlier, he did have that opportunity at the 11 November interview.

Flowing from that, the implication in the above passage that, lacking Kerr's concurrence, Whitlam would have modified his stance is problematical. It is clear that Kelly and Bramston believe this was not mere rhetoric on Whitlam's part. That being the case, once it was obvious to Whitlam that he had failed to break Fraser, the only way to achieve his aim would be to win a general election. And he could only win it following a campaign that put the Senate's actions at centre stage. And the best way of doing that would be to make himself a martyr by being dismissed. I have made this point before and will make it again on every occasion in this book that it is apposite.

Now we come again to the question of Whitlam's putative astonishment that Kerr withdrew his commission – the so-called ambush. Concerning the discussion between Whitlam and Kerr on 3 November, Kelly and Bramston report:

> Kerr claimed that during this discussion Whitlam said the only way an election would be obtained was if Kerr 'were willing "to do a Philip Game"'. If true this remark would be reckless, almost taunting the governor-general, the implication being 'you wouldn't be bold enough to sack me'. This was a phrase Whitlam sometimes used; he had used it in private discussions at the time with a number of people. If Whitlam said this to Kerr, it could only be interpreted

---

[27] Kelly and Bramston, op.cit., p. 181

as foolhardy intimidation. Interviewed in 1995, Whitlam said: 'I never spoke about Game to him.' It was a denial but not a comprehensive denial.[28]

Whitlam's denial is not to be believed. He certainly broached the subject. Kerr noted in his 6 November letter to the Palace that:

> [Whitlam] later said that the only way an election for the House would occur would be if I dismissed him.[29]

And if Whitlam had used the Philip Game reference before, why would he not have said it to Kerr on this occasion?

As Kelly and Bramston concede this could only have been seen by Kerr as attempted intimidation. And yet they manage to sheet home equal fault to Kerr, on the basis that he did not respond. As he said in his memoirs 'I made no comment'. They say:

> He seemed proud of his silence. But that silence meant he allowed Whitlam to reject Fraser's compromise on the false assumption that Kerr acquiesced in Whitlam's approach.[30]

Whitlam had already taken the kid gloves off, repeatedly asserting in public that the Governor-General would do what he told him to do. It was a power-struggle, and it was Whitlam who had made it so. At this stage Kerr could hardly be expected to 'cop it sweet'. If Whitlam, in making the statement about Philip Game, rather than trying to intimidate him, had actually been seeking to gauge Kerr's attitude to dismissal, then in the absence of some reassuring words from Kerr, his silence said, as clearly as any words could, 'it may well come to that'. Any normal person would have read it that way. And Kerr would have expected Whitlam, of all people, to be at least as perceptive as the normal person. Remaining silent seems to me the least provocative way of conveying this message.

But, if you will pardon the crude metaphor, this was a

---

[28] Ibid., pp. 181-182.
[29] Kerr, Letter to Sir Martin Charteris, *The Palace Letters*, 6 November 1975.
[30] Kelly and Bramston, op.cit., p. 182.

monumental mud-wrestle between two political street-fighters. When the contestants started to break the rules, the referee, necessarily, had to get 'down and dirty' and some mud would inevitably stick. But in the overall scheme of things, Kerr's missteps, if that is what you judge them to be, were small beer. They made no difference to the overall outcome – politically, constitutionally or socially.

Further:

> Indeed, it is tempting to think that Kerr understood what he was doing. Kerr was happy to let Whitlam destroy himself. Kerr, as the key player, had the best vision. He knew what was unfolding ... He wasn't going to talk honestly to Whitlam. He would let Whitlam carry the full consequences of his misjudgement. This was the real meaning of Kerr's conviction that Whitlam had 'no claim' to know his thinking and that Kerr had no obligation 'to advise and warn him'. Whitlam did deceive himself, as Kerr said later. But Kerr also sought to fool Whitlam. His silence at this point was an elaborate deception of Whitlam and sinister in its implications.[31]

Well certainly Kerr understood what he was doing but in what way was his silence 'sinister'? Are they really suggesting that a calming word from Kerr would have achieved what none of Whitlam's closest colleagues or confidantes could – make him see reason? Are they suggesting that if Kerr had said to Whitlam words to the effect of 'don't count on me not doing a Philip Game' that would have given Whitlam pause? Kerr believed that if he had taken that course, Whitlam would have moved against him. Whitlam, well after the event, says he would not have. But we only have his word for that and, as Kelly and Bramston pointed out earlier in their book, some of Whitlam's closest advisers believed he would have. That might have been an irrational act, but Kelly and Bramston themselves have pointed out, emphatically, that Whitlam was indeed acting irrationally at this time.

In the above passage, Kelly and Bramston have paid little attention to Kerr's own defence against this charge. To begin

---

[31] Ibid., pp. 182-183.

with Kerr did not say he had no obligation to 'advise and warn' – at least not in *Matters for Judgement*. It's true he did imply there was no obligation but rather that it was his right to do so. Here is what he said:

> Whereas the Governor-General cannot take advice from, nor advise, the leader of the Opposition, the doctrine in relation to the Prime Minister, that the Governor-General may 'advise and warn', permits the giving of some advice, but it has its limitations in practice. A wise man would not be volunteering it often.[32]

In this view he is supported by Walter Bagehot, quoted on the Australian Parliament House website:

> To state the matter shortly, the sovereign has, under a constitutional monarchy such as ours, three rights—the right to be consulted, the right to encourage, the right to warn.[33]

On this reading there is no 'obligation'.

Let me give you Kerr's own defence. Following a list of the four occasions on which Whitlam had alluded to the possibility that Kerr might dismiss him, he says:

> From all these statements it was obvious Mr Whitlam accepted that I had the reserve powers and might conceivably use them. He never questioned me on my views. Since his statements made it plain that he was well aware of the reserve powers and of the risk he might run by his policy, I had no reason, nor impulse, to volunteer a statement to him of what he clearly knew. I believed, quite starkly, that if I had said anything to Mr Whitlam about the possibility that I might take away his commission I would no longer have been there. I conceived it to be my proper behaviour in the circumstances to stay at my post and not invite dismissal. I elected, as the only neutral and intelligent course to follow, that I should keep silence about my thinking unless and until I decided I must act.
>
> If Mr Whitlam or any other Minister was deceived he deceived himself.[34]

---

[32] Kerr, *Matters for Judgement*, p. 289.
[33] W. Bagehot. (1965). *The English constitution*. London: Fontana. p. 111.
[34] Kerr, op.cit., pp. 309-310.

This reinforces the fact that Kerr genuinely believed he might be recalled. That had implications beyond mere job security on his part. It went to the relationship between the Queen and the Australian government. Kerr's principal fear was that the Queen would personally be caught up in an Australian political scandal. No one can doubt his sincerity on this point. He continues:

> As to Mr Whitlam's complaint that I gave no indication I was contemplating recourse to the reserve powers, I say simply that when I was in a position to tell him what I intended to do, I told him, leaving him an opportunity to indicate to me what his response would be.[35]

What Kerr is referring to here is his claim that, on 11 November, if Whitlam had backed down in the face of his dismissal and advised a general election Kerr would have accepted that advice. On any objective assessment of the two men and on human nature in general, this claim is incontestable. And further:

> From the time when Mr Whitlam began publicly to hammer the theme that I had no choice but to adopt his advice he disqualified himself from being offered a running account of the development of my thinking until such a time as it had crystallized in a way which might affect him positively. The Prime Minister has no claim to be made privy to the Governor-General's inmost mind. My clear belief was that Mr Whitlam being fully aware of the reserve powers of the Governor-General, was concentrating on techniques to ensure that I would not bring them into play.[36]

At some point the relationship between Kerr and Whitlam would, inevitably, become adversarial unless Whitlam modified his stance. Kerr clearly believed that it had already entered this phase. He says:

> I knew that failure to invoke the reserve powers in a situation calling for their use would be detrimental to those powers. Mr Whitlam was not entitled to receive a running report on how I was wrestling with the problem he had set. Any guesses he made on this this, he

---

[35] Ibid.
[36] Ibid.

made on his own responsibility.

> It could perhaps have been different if he had asked me. I should have had to think very carefully about what I should tell him of the shape of my developing thought. But he did not ask. Mr Whitlam's failure to ask my view of the reserve powers must, I have always believed, have been deliberate avoidance. How natural it would have been to open up the question with me, if he had wanted to know. He never did ask that or any other question on what was going on in my mind.[37]

Kelly and Bramston differ with Kerr on his obligation to 'open up' to Whitlam, and the point is certainly arguable. But the travesty of their coverage of Kerr's defence – that they offer up two out-of-context quotes – is all of a piece with their treatment of him throughout *The Dismissal*. It does them no credit. In particular, the use of the word 'sinister', which connotes illegal or conspiratorial conduct, is gratuitous at best.

And keep in mind that, at this point, Kerr had yet to receive any briefing regarding the alternative financial arrangements. There is no way that, on 3 November, he could have offered Whitlam any useful advice since, at that stage, the government had given *him* no substantive advice on either of the two main issues – the Ellicott opinion, and the alternative financial arrangements.

There follows an account of the proposal to pressure Liberal premiers to not issue writs for a half-Senate election but as it has already been covered and is not germane to Sir John Kerr's decision, I will not cover it further.

But then comes another example of egregious misrepresentation of Sir John's motives:

> During the Cup festivities, Kerr stayed at Government House in Melbourne where he discussed the situation with [Sir Roden] Cutler and Victorian governor Sir Henry Winneke. It was not a meeting of minds. Cutler said that he and Winneke believed Kerr should 'call Whitlam in and explain the situation' then 'ask Whitlam to consider his position and tender advice'. That meant warning Whitlam and

---

[37] Ibid., pp. 310-311.

giving him the chance to go to an election as prime minister. *It was anathema to Kerr.* He told Cutler that Winneke didn't understand the situation. Hamer said later that Winneke told him Kerr's dismissal of Whitlam was wrong and that Whitlam should have been warned.[38]

The claim that Winneke's view – that the dismissal was 'wrong' – lacks context. Did he believe it was wrong in principle or wrong because Kerr failed to warn Whitlam in the manner that Winneke thought proper? If the latter, then I have already presented arguments to counter this. But the real offence is the suggestion, in the italicised words, that allowing Whitlam to go to the election as prime minister was 'anathema to Kerr'. This is a serious and deliberate misrepresentation. As Kerr said, had Whitlam relented on 11 November and offered to advise a general election, Kerr would not have proceeded with the termination of his commission and would have allowed him to go to that election as Prime Minister. What was 'anathema' (a rather emotive and inappropriate descriptor) to Kerr was the risk that Whitlam would move to have him recalled.

In fact, as Kelly and Bramston reveal earlier, at a dinner, around the onset of the crisis, at Government House in Sydney, Sir Roden Cutler recalled:

> 'At one stage I said to Kerr that there was, of course, the possibility that the Prime Minister might move to dismiss him. He became very activated at this point, saying, "Yes, I know." It was obvious he had given some thought to this possibility.'[39]

And, following that conversation, no doubt Kerr's mind was even more exercised by this possibility, it now having been reinforced by Cutler. It was clearly not just some sick fantasy in Kerr's fevered brain.

On 6 November, Kerr had a final meeting with Fraser to again put his earlier proposition regarding a delayed half-Senate election. Kerr says Fraser was not at all interested. But he did have some advice for Kerr:

---

38 Kelly and Bramston, op.cit., p. 184.
39 Ibid., p. 125.

Now Fraser made his big play. He felt Kerr was sympathetic. He knew Kerr was worried about job security. He knew Kerr believed in the dismissal power. Fraser felt he had convinced Kerr the opposition would not crack. It was time to push Kerr over the edge. His fear was Kerr's weakness. David Kemp said: 'Fraser told me on November 1 that Kerr was being very weak: he will not act until there is chaos all round.'

The two men were alone. The crunch was coming. Fraser said: 'I now told the Governor-General that if Australia did not get an election the Opposition would have no choice but to be highly critical of him. We would have to say that he had failed his duty as Governor-General to the nation. I made it clear that the Opposition would have to defend its actions to the people ... if there wasn't an election the Opposition would need to explain itself ... I told him we'd be saying he had failed in his office because he had not given the people an election.'[40]

The implication from this passage is that Fraser pressured Kerr into making the decision he did. The problem is, we have only Fraser's word for these reported threats. They are sourced to an interview with Paul Kelly in 1995, long after Fraser had abandoned any support for Kerr, and at a time when he was trying to restore his own reputation by ingratiating himself with the Left. What Kerr reported of this conversation is:

> Mr Fraser was not interested at all. He said that the Senate had shown its firmness and would continue to do so, that he realised he could not advise me but felt he should say that if I failed to act in the situation which existed I would be imperilling the reserve powers of the Crown forever; he accepted that the discretion was mine but inaction on my part, with supply running out, the Senate firm on deferral, and the Government asserting a right to govern without supply, would destroy the reserve powers.[41]

Kerr's version sounds more likely. That would be a persuasive argument if Fraser thought Kerr might 'weaken'. What Fraser claims he said sounds strangely aggressive, considering he was trying to woo Kerr. As Kelly and Bramston say, Fraser knew

---

40 Ibid., p. 185.
41 Kerr, op.cit., p. 297.

Kerr believed in the reserve powers. If he really believed that when the crunch came Kerr might weaken and act against his own instincts, what would be a more effective tool at this stage – a sledgehammer or a nutcracker? Kelly and Bramston have told us how subtle and crafty Fraser was. Do they really think he would have been so ham-fisted on this occasion?

From what we know of Kerr, the purported words would have been, if anything, counterproductive. But, in any case, the suggestion here, viz., that Kerr made his decision under duress from Fraser, is clearly nonsense. And it is at odds with the other Kerr persona – the scheming manipulator intent on dismissing Whitlam – that Kelly and Bramston have been at pains to develop. You know, the one to whom it was anathema to give Whitlam the opportunity of going to the election as Prime Minister.

The fact that Kerr had been discussing his options with Sir Anthony Mason for some weeks tells us that he needed no advice from Fraser on the reserve powers. And yet Kelly and Bramston have the temerity to tell us:

> Fraser, in truth, was advising Kerr and he was threatening Kerr. Fraser was telling Kerr he must accept his responsibility as governor-general. The political message was obvious. If Fraser failed he would blame Kerr. Kerr would be depicted as a weak governor-general who succumbed to Whitlam's intimidation and refused to do his duty. *Kerr understood.*[42]

The clear implication of the italicised words is that Kerr buckled under Fraser's threat. That he made his decision under duress. The fact is that whatever Fraser said or whatever influence he thought he had on Kerr's decision, that influence was restricted to convincing Kerr, as he had Whitlam, that the Opposition would not fold. Nothing more.

If Kerr were to base his decision on the imperative to avoid criticism, he could hardly have made a worse choice. Kerr knew he would be viciously criticised by Labor because of his

---

[42] Kelly and Bramston, op.cit., pp. 185-186.

decision. And that is what eventuated. We know that the Left are much better haters than the Right.

There is more on this theme:

> Fraser also told Kerr the Coalition would win the election. He said once the crisis was over, public opinion would swing strongly against Whitlam. It was vital reassurance. Fraser was telling Kerr the public would vindicate his actions at a subsequent election.[43]

Kerr does not record that revelation in *Matters for Judgement*, however it's safe to assume that Kerr would have treated this prognostication, if it occurred, with some caution. Fraser could not *know* he would win. Kerr may have reached the same conclusion himself, but Fraser's assurance would hardly be a decisive factor in his decision. This is just further grist to the mill of Kerr playing the part of Fraser's patsy. As I have pointed out earlier, Kerr, himself, rejected the notion that the outcome of the election would be vindication of his decision or form any part of it.

Yet they persist with this theme:

> [Tony] Staley (a Fraser confidante) said that ... 'Kerr liked winners ... Things about his life suggested he would go with the establishment or conservative side, as long as they were going to win.'[44]

This was sourced to an interview between Staley and Troy Bramston in 2015. As a commentary on Kerr's motivation or state of mind in 1975, it is virtually worthless.

They complete this passage thus:

> In the end, Fraser was appealing to Kerr to do what he knew was right. None of this means that there was any warmth or affinity in the Fraser-Kerr relationship. The men had little in common. Staley said that years later in their talks, Fraser 'said to me he thought Kerr was "weak and lonely, always seeking reassurance". He made it pretty clear to me that he had exploited that in his character.'[45]

---

[43] Ibid., p. 185.
[44] Ibid., pp. 186-187.
[45] Ibid., p. 187.

Again, this is sourced to the 2015 interview. It is likely that the reference to Kerr 'always seeking reassurance' dates to the period after the dismissal, not prior to it. And therefore, it has nothing to do with the decision itself. Kelly and Bramston say Fraser was appealing to Kerr to do what he *knew* was right. But just because Fraser *thought* that Kerr might fall short when the crunch came, does not mean that Kerr would have done so. From everything we know, Fraser seriously misjudged Kerr in that respect. His discussions with Sir Anthony Mason attest to this.

This is just Fraser aggrandizing himself. His treatment of Kerr, as we have seen in Chapter One, even in the immediate aftermath of the change of government was shabby. He was keen to dissociate himself from Kerr as quickly as possible, in order to rehabilitate his own reputation, and that self-serving mission only intensified over the years.

After the 6 November meeting with Fraser:

> Kerr told Whitlam the same day that Fraser was not compromising. The prime minister said he would probably advise a half-Senate election to be held on 13 December. Kerr, unlike most of the Labor Party, realised this was a sign of serious weakness. Assessing the situation he now faced, Kerr said that 'if I acquiesced' then 'the election would be held after the money ran out'. Obviously, Kerr would not agree to Whitlam's half-Senate election proposal. But he avoided saying this to Whitlam. He let a deluded Whitlam think he would have got his way.[46]

In the end, Kerr could not accept the proposal for a half-Senate election because the money would have run out *and* the proposed alternative financial arrangements to overcome this hurdle were unworkable and probably unconstitutional. But on 6 November Kerr did not *officially know* this, because at that stage he had not received any advice on the arrangements. So, it was only natural that Kerr would keep his counsel when Whitlam told him he would *probably* advise a half-Senate election. He could hardly rule out accepting such advice until

---

[46] Ibid.

he had heard the full story.

Kelly and Bramston often accuse Kerr of ambushing Whitlam. It would seem to me that offering inconclusive advice to the Governor-General, at almost the very last minute, was something of an ambush. Particularly when you consider the advice was unsigned. In other words, Whitlam was asking Kerr to agree to an arrangement to which not even the government was prepared to put its official imprimatur.

Kelly and Bramston then recount the visit of Hayden to Kerr on the same day, ostensibly to explain the workings (not the legality) of the alternative arrangements. They quote Hayden as saying that the Governor-General appeared little interested in what he had to say. I would imagine that Kerr already had a pretty good idea of the shortcomings of the arrangement and Hayden, who is earlier quoted as saying he himself had grave doubts about the scheme, could hardly be expected to do a convincing job selling it to Kerr. But the visit did yield some intelligence which should have been useful to Whitlam:

> Hayden had no history with Kerr. He wasn't an old mate. He wasn't steeped in the romance and sophistry of the good old days. He looked Kerr in the face and he knew. This man wasn't on side.[47]

Here's another cheap shot at Kerr, an eminent jurist. By what measure could his professional life to date be categorised as 'romance and sophistry'. When it comes to sophistry, Kelly and Bramston could teach Kerr a thing or two. Be that as it may, they continue:

> In a story the stuff of legend, Hayden said: 'I left [Government House] with a sense of agitation. I went straight to Whitlam's office instead of going out to catch a plane to return home. Whitlam was in a meeting so he came out of his office ... He was standing against the wall, even more larger than life. I said to Gough, "My copper instincts tell me that Kerr is thinking of sacking us and calling an election" – or words to that effect. Gough looked at me. He was fiddling his spectacles around in his hand. He said to me, "No comrade. He wouldn't have the guts for that."'

---

[47] Ibid., p. 188.

> Whitlam was beyond logic. In order to convince Kerr, he had convinced himself. If Hayden drew this conclusion from one chat with Kerr, then what had gone wrong with Whitlam's instincts?[48]

'In order to convince Kerr, he had convinced himself'? Is that piece of amateur psychology a convincing explanation for Whitlam's apparent equanimity? Did egotism and hubris combine to produce a 'fatal chemistry' in Whitlam's character? What had gone wrong with Whitlam's instincts? Possibly nothing. Perhaps Whitlam had already recognised the impossibility of his position and had determined upon a deliberate a strategy to *induce* Kerr to sack him. That, of course, is merely speculation on my part. I do not assert it as fact, as Kelly and Bramston do with so much of their speculation regarding Kerr's motives.

No matter how convinced Whitlam might have been that he had Kerr's measure, why would he not, at the very least, quiz Hayden to find out exactly what had caused him to get the impression Kerr was ready to sack them? It would be the natural human reaction. Why would he not ask what was Kerr's response to the alternative arrangements? Why, in fact, did he not originally instruct Hayden to report back immediately after the meeting? Presumably because he did not care one way or the other what Kerr thought of the arrangement. He was just going through the motions.

The remainder of this chapter in *The Dismissal* deals with the putative ambush.

The authors look at the timing and come to the conclusion that both Kerr and Whitlam, independently of each other, decided that 11 November was the decisive day. But, as usual, they manage to find fault with Kerr's reasoning. Kerr decided a decision had to be made on 11 November as that was the latest date on which an election could be called in time to be complete before supply ran out. But that was too early for Kelly and Bramston:

---

[48] Ibid.

> On timing, he decided the issue must be resolved by a pre-Christmas general election and that meant a decision by 11 November. The government still had supply for another fortnight. Moving before supply was exhausted was a significant disadvantage to Whitlam. Kerr believed he had discretion on the timing question and said he had waited till 'the national purse was almost empty, which was as long as, for the safety of the country, I could'. His justification, explained in the official dismissal documents, was that he was 'satisfied' Whitlam could not obtain supply, that is, that the opposition would not crack. In truth, Kerr did not know and he could not know this, because neither Fraser nor Withers nor anybody else in the opposition knew. It was a day-by-day, hour-by-hour operation.[49]

Two thoughts occur from the above passage. The first is that, at this stage of the crisis, 'disadvantage to Whitlam' was not a consideration that would, or should, have entered Kerr's calculations. That would have been taking a politically partisan position. And secondly, when Kerr said that he was 'satisfied' that Whitlam could not obtain supply, he was not claiming that he knew it for a fact. In this context 'satisfied' means that he did *not* know it for a fact but that, on all the evidence before him, he *judged* it to be so. Making judgements is what he was being paid to do. And his further judgement – that it would be better to have the issue resolved before the money finally ran out – seems unassailable to me.

But Whitlam brought the matter to a head:

> Yet Whitlam, by deciding on a half-Senate election, was also forcing the issue. The reality was that Kerr could not wait beyond 11 November because Whitlam was seeking a half-senate election on that date. Kerr had to either grant the election or impose another solution that day. Whitlam and Kerr both made 11 November the decision day.
> The reality was that the Senate had held long enough. That is all that mattered. It had held long enough to drive Whitlam into seeking a half-senate poll and forcing Kerr's hand.[50]

So, Kerr's judgement that Whitlam could not obtain supply

---

[49] Ibid., pp. 188-189.
[50] Ibid., p. 189.

turns out, in the space of two paragraphs, to be correct. Or, at the very least, Whitlam, also, was 'satisfied' he could not obtain supply. One of the charges brought against Sir John Kerr is that he should have waited a bit longer to give the politicians further time to resolve the issue. Clearly Whitlam felt that time had run out, so why should Kerr be denied that same judgement?

They then make a strange accusation:

> For Kerr there was a personal element at work – witness Kerr's statement that he would not stand idle and allow Whitlam to engage in 'the effective smashing of the power of the Senate on supply and of the Reserve Powers of the Crown'. Kerr felt Whitlam was threatening the Constitution. He felt Whitlam was reckless in his campaign, in effect, against the Senate and the reserve powers. He saw himself as their guardian against a dangerous prime minister.[51]

It is not clear to me why protecting the Constitution would represent a 'personal element' for Kerr. Surely, protecting the Constitution was, at least implicitly, very much part of his job description?

Kelly and Bramston then go onto exonerate Kerr:

> The pivotal assumption on which Kerr relied was that a government denied supply had to either advise a general election or resign. This was constitutional and parliamentary orthodoxy. Kerr was correct in deciding the alternative financial arrangements were not a satisfactory option. Because Whitlam had refused to advise a general election or resign, Kerr's decision to force the issue was justified.[52]

Unfortunately, his redemption does not last long:

> The fatal defect was how Kerr forced the issue. He decided on a dismissal without warning. Few constitutional authorities would agree with the view that if supply is blocked and a prime minister does not resign or advise a general election, he must be dismissed without prior discussion. The first stage of Kerr's intervention had to be to counsel Whitlam about the situation and for the governor-general to explain the options.

---

[51] Ibid.
[52] Ibid.

> The reserve powers must be the final resort. They cannot be used before every other option is exhausted. Yet because Kerr decided not to warn or confide in Whitlam and give him the chance of going to an election as prime minister, he settled upon an even more extreme position – dismissal by ambush. It was spectacular in its unorthodoxy. Even worse it was the action of a coward. The belief, indeed the obsession, that governed Kerr's approach from start to finish, was that Whitlam, if given any inkling, would advise the Queen to remove him. 'I had not the slightest doubt that if he felt the need the Prime Minister would seek to have me recalled before I could dismiss him,' Kerr said.[53]

Let's deal with the 'ambush' first. If Kerr really wanted to ambush Whitlam, in other words deny him the opportunity to advise an election, he would have sent his Official Secretary, David Smith, to Parliament House to announce Whitlam's dismissal without first notifying Whitlam. That would have been highly controversial and very poor form – but that is the nature of ambushes. You eliminate any possibility of escape. Of course, Kerr would not, and did not, do that.

It is difficult to believe that Whitlam – who apparently held Kerr in contempt and believed he could be dominated/intimidated – seeing at risk his sacred mission to 'destroy the power of the Senate once and for all', would have just crumpled at this final hurdle. It is quite conceivable that Whitlam would have seen going to the election as a victim – rather than as a Prime Minister who bowed to pragmatism in order to save an incompetent government – as much the better way to prosecute this mission. And it is equally difficult to believe that Kerr would not have accepted the advice for an election and allowed Whitlam to go to the election as Prime Minister, if that is what he wanted.

As to Kerr's action being that of a coward, Kelly and Bramston concede that Kerr really believed Whitlam might move against him. And, as we have seen earlier, that belief was reinforced by Sir Roden Cutler. It was also buttressed, *post hoc*, by several of

---

[53] Ibid., pp. 189-190.

Whitlam's own confidantes. Kerr's concern was not primarily for his own position, but that any attempt to remove him, while he was exercising the prerogatives of the Crown, would bring the Monarchy into disrepute. Given his respect for the Monarchy, that would have been unthinkable. He would have seen it as a massive failure on his part. Kelly and Bramston concede this point in their following paragraph but, again, they deploy the idea that Kerr, in order to justify this defence, needed to 'know' that Whitlam would move to recall him: "The truth is, despite his claims, Kerr didn't know what Whitlam would do."[54]

That is a nonsensical argument. It suggests that, in all respects, Kerr could only act on what he knew for certain and was constrained from making any judgements about what might happen. Under those circumstances, the post of Governor-General would be reduced to a ceremonial role only.

Kelly and Bramston argue that, by failing to warn Whitlam, Kerr took a partisan position and thereby, by his own action, compromised the position of the Monarchy. That logic only applies if you hold to the view that Kerr's aim was simply to dismiss Whitlam, and that Whitlam did not have a chance to reverse Kerr's decision i.e., he was 'ambushed'. I have argued that both these premises are false.

They conclude:

> Kerr reduced the issue to an elemental power struggle; he decided to dismiss Whitlam before Whitlam had a chance to dismiss him. This was exactly how he reasoned. It was the essence of his position. In the process he debased the office and the obligations of the governor-general to be an impartial and unifying figure.[55]

Kerr decided to dismiss Whitlam because he could not obtain supply. In order to resolve the issue of supply in a clinical fashion, it was necessary that Kerr circumvent any unforeseen complications, such as a call from Whitlam to the Palace. Which, by the way, Whitlam foreshadowed in his throwaway

---

[54] Ibid., p. 190.
[55] Ibid., p. 191.

comment at the 16 October dinner for the Malaysian Prime Minister.

Australians are divided politically all the time, and this was essentially a political division. It is not the role of the Governor-General to unite us. It is the Constitution that unites us above political division. The role of the Governor-General is to uphold the Constitution, and this he did.

13

Manipulating a Willing Chief Justice

At this point, the prosecution has almost completed its case, but in this chapter, it revisits ground already covered, albeit adding a few more titbits of evidence against the accused.

The chapter commences:

> The governor-general now sought the authority of Sir Garfield Barwick, the chief justice of the High Court, for his dismissal of the prime minister.[1]

The word 'authority' in this context would normally refer to Barwick's legal eminence, but it was chosen deliberately to convey the impression that Kerr was seeking Barwick's *permission*. Someone legally qualified would immediately understand the difference, but the untutored reader probably would not. It is yet another example of the verbal trickery employed by the authors to create a negative picture of the accused. What Kerr was seeking was advice or confirmation that his course of action was constitutional. And that course of action was *not* simply to dismiss Whitlam. It was to dismiss Whitlam if he failed to advise an election, and to appoint Fraser in his place on the proviso that he pass supply and then advise an election for both Houses.

They continue:

> Kerr was astute in his management of Barwick. He wanted assurance and insurance, and he got them both. ... he and Mason had canvassed the resort to Barwick and its timing. They knew when

---
[1] Kelly and Bramston, *The Dismissal*, p. 192.

the time came that Barwick would affirm the dismissal power. Kerr had long admired Barwick. He now sought a de facto alliance with him. Kerr knew the combination of the governor-general and chief justice, united on the dismissal issue, would constitute an almost certain guarantee of a successful operation.[2]

There is no doubt that Kerr knew that Barwick would affirm the dismissal power, because he knew the man. But the above extract is a mischaracterisation of the relationship between the two men in this context. Kerr knew his proposed course of action would be controversial and unpopular in some quarters. He knew that much of the adverse reaction that he anticipated would be based on a lack of understanding of the constitutional issues. But he did not make an 'alliance' with Barwick. They were not 'united' on the dismissal issue. It was not a joint decision. The decision was Kerr's. As they reveal later:

> 'I did not want anything more than constitutional advice,' Kerr says he told Mason. 'I did not want Barwick's views on what I should do but only on what I could do.' ... Kerr said of Barwick: 'If he were willing to confirm the existence of my powers this would be a great help generally in enabling people to understand the unusual powers involved and rarely used.
>
> In short, Barwick's legal authorisation, in addition to helping Kerr, would assist public acceptance of the dismissal.[3]

There's that word 'authorisation' again, this time misused more blatantly. 'Authority' is ambiguous. 'Authorisation' is not – it can only mean permission.

Barwick did not give Kerr permission to dismiss Whitlam. Kerr got his authorisation from the Constitution.

As to Barwick's involvement being 'an almost certain guarantee of a successful operation', that is serious overreach. Barwick's involvement no doubt buttressed Kerr's resolve and, more importantly, gave the public assurance that Kerr had not acted as some constitutional maverick. But it did not in any

---

[2] Ibid., pp. 192-193.
[3] Ibid., p. 196.

way affect the outcome. And again, I must re-iterate that the 'operation' was *not* the dismissal of Whitlam *per se* but the securing of supply to the Crown.

The suggestion that in seeking Barwick's advice, Kerr was attempting to hijack or recruit the High Court to his agenda, is nonsense. The fact that Barwick gave advice in his private capacity, albeit acknowledging the cachet of his position, did not impose any constraint on the Court itself. His involvement would not have prevented any party from mounting a High Court challenge to the decision. In fact, Kerr must have been quite confident of his constitutional position, because by taking advice from both Barwick and Mason, he was pretty effectively emasculating the Court from his point of view. Two judges that agreed with him would have had to recuse themselves, leaving four judges of unknown disposition and one guaranteed to be hostile, Lionel Murphy.

And if Murphy had been Chief Justice, would Kerr have sought *his* advice? Of course not. In this event i.e., lacking advice from the Chief Justice, would Kerr have proceeded with his course of action? Despite Barwick's professed belief that he 'stiffened' Kerr to the task, it seems more than likely to me – from a thorough reading of both *The Dismissal* and *Matters for Judgement* – that he would have done so. In that case, the opinion of the Chief Justice is neither here nor there in relation to the outcome. Barwick's advice was, to put it crudely, essentially a *post hoc* public relations exercise.

The next few pages of *The Dismissal* cover the exchanges between Kerr and Sir Anthony Mason, including areas where their accounts differ. We have addressed the propriety of Mason's involvement earlier and it serves no useful purpose to recapitulate this question or the discrepancies between Kerr and Mason's account as they are largely irrelevant to the broader question.

One incident, however, is worth examining:

> Mason, however, explained something that Kerr did not mention –

that they had two meetings that day [9 November]. He said that at the end of the first meeting, he volunteered to Kerr that it was 'unfolding like a Greek tragedy'. At this point Kerr called out to Lady Kerr, who was upstairs. She walked downstairs and, Mason said, Kerr explained to her what he had decided to do. Mason said the decision 'was bound to be controversial and attract strong criticism'. He recalled Kerr saying: 'Tony, you don't know these people. I do. It will be much worse than you think.' At this point, Mason said, Kerr invited the Mason's to dinner that night at Admiralty House.[4]

There are two implications from this. The first, and lesser, is that Kerr had made his decision before speaking to Barwick, suggesting that Barwick may have overstated his influence on Kerr. The second is that Kerr was well aware of the storm he would unleash and yet was prepared to go ahead. This does not sit well with the image that Kelly and Bramston have tried to portray of a self-serving sybarite addicted to the trappings of office and the high life – someone prepared to bend with the breeze and take the easy way out. And if, as Kelly and Bramston elsewhere postulate, Kerr was determined to make his mark on history by a single decisive act, he would have well known that his legacy would be severely tainted. That too does not fit the character of the adroit opportunist that we met in Chapter Five.

We now come again to the question of Kerr warning Whitlam he risked dismissal:

> At the end of their dinner, Mason said he and Kerr resumed their discussion of the dismissal. Kerr told him the plan was to see Whitlam and simply hand him a letter of dismissal. According to Mason's account: 'I then said to him that before doing so he should say that he had no alternative but to dismiss the Prime Minister unless he was willing to hold a general election.' It is the pivotal point: Mason was saying Whitlam had to be warned. Mason said Kerr replied: 'I know that.'
>
> Mason said: 'I told him that, if he did not warn the Prime Minister, he would run the risk that people would accuse him of being deceptive. I also said that he would need to consider the possibility that the Prime Minister might ask for time to consider his position and,

[4] Ibid.

if so, what response should be made.' He said that Kerr made no comment on this.

Mason's advice was prudent. But Kerr made no reference to these statements. It is a critical omission. He depicted Mason as a vital confidant and said their discussions 'sustained me in my own thinking'. Yet Mason's account had him, in effect, giving Kerr advice that was not followed. As Mason said, allowing Whitlam the option of going to the election as prime minister was the key issue. But the governor-general denied Whitlam this option. The question, therefore, is whether the Kerr-Mason dialogue is different on the fundamental point from Kerr's depiction. Given Mason insisted this was his advice to Kerr the question becomes: why did the governor-general refuse to act on such advice?[5]

I have already argued that Whitlam could have asked for time to reconsider his position at the time Kerr handed him the letter of dismissal. How much time would he have needed? A few minutes at the most. That could be done in the Governor-General's office. What Mason meant by 'reconsider his position' was 'accept the inevitability of a general election'. Allowing Whitlam to leave Yarralumla to 'consider his position' would have allowed him time to develop an alternative strategy, such as contacting the Palace to advise Kerr's recall – which is, in fact, what Kerr feared. Kerr did not 'deny' Whitlam the opportunity to go to the election as Prime Minister because Whitlam never asked him.

As to Kerr refusing to act on Mason's advice in this respect, one may seek advice and find it valuable without accepting it in full. Mason's advice on this was not holy writ and Kerr was well within his rights to reject part of it – if, in fact, it was offered. We only have Mason's word for that.

They go on to discuss another discrepancy between the accounts of Mason and Kerr. Mason claims that Kerr asked him to draft a dismissal letter, which he did do, although Kerr did not use it. Kerr claims that what he asked for was a summary of the reasons for the dismissal.[6] Kelly and Bramston are critical

---

[5] Ibid., p. 197.
[6] Ibid., p. 198.

of Mason for having drafted a letter but the fact of that and the discrepancy between the accounts is irrelevant in the grand scheme of things. But this assertion needs comment:

> The incident, however, revealed Kerr's obsession with involving the High Court and his colleagues on the bench in his dismissal project. He wanted protection at every step. It transcended mere insurance and became a psychological need. He seemed to need others to give him the strength to implement his decision.[7]

Again, we see emotive language in what purports to be a history. There is no evidence that Kerr was 'obsessed' with involving the High Court. They provide no evidence as to how Barwick's advice would 'protect' Kerr. It would not preclude a High Court challenge. No-one makes a decision this momentous without seeking advice. And the reference to Kerr's psychological needs is nothing more than uninformed speculation. Is either Kelly or Bramston qualified in psychology? And finally, I must again insist that Kerr's 'project' – their word not mine – was *not* the dismissal of the Prime Minister.

Now Barwick enters the picture. Kelly and Bramston reveal that Kerr and Mason had, in October, discussed Kerr approaching Barwick and decided that he would do so only after he had decided to intervene. They say:

> He wanted the dismissal to be watertight. The issue was the timing. If Kerr had approached Barwick too early, then Barwick's advice might contradict his own plans.[8]

Here they are intimating that Kerr and Mason feared that Barwick would urge Kerr to act immediately i.e., in accordance with the Ellicott opinion. And that may well be so, because Barwick held the view that, under our Constitution which gives the Senate power over money bills, the government is responsible not just to the House of Representatives but to the Parliament as a whole. That is, it must retain the confidence of both Houses. He argued that a government which loses a vote of no-confidence in the House, or fails to secure supply from

---

[7] Ibid.
[8] Ibid., p. 195.

the House, must resign. He further said that the Senate's refusal to grant supply is its vote of no-confidence. He took the view that availability of funds was not the issue. The issue was lack of confidence by the Parliament in the government:

> It should be emphasised that the question was not at any time whether there were funds which the ministry could lawfully use in carrying on government. The critical question was whether the ministry so far retained the approval of Parliament as to be able to secure from it supply.⁹

He saw it as a matter of constitutional principle rather than a pragmatic consideration, in which case there would be no justification in the Governor-General delaying matters. According to Kelly and Bramston:

> By 9 November, however, Barwick felt that Kerr should have already acted. He believed Kerr was being too generous to Whitlam. That he was too soft. Barwick inclined to the view that the governor-general should have acted by 25 October – when the crisis was only ten days old. He was a chief justice with strong opinions and a closed mind on the issue.¹⁰

It would be strange if a Chief Justice and former minister did not have strong views on most subjects. And as to him having a closed mind on the issue, that is just speculation. They could only come to this conclusion if they could point to counter-arguments that were put to Barwick but which he rejected out of hand.

Whether or not Kerr and Mason knew that this was Barwick's view is not clear. Shadow Attorney General Bob Ellicott QC, who wrote the opinion that Kerr had asked Whitlam to provide advice upon, did not go that far. Kerr certainly did not subscribe to the Barwick purist position, if, for no other reason than that the public were more likely to be receptive to the pragmatism argument. He knew they would expect him to give Whitlam the opportunity to see sense.

---

⁹ Garfield Barwick. (1983) *Sir John Did His Duty*, Wahroonga: Serendip. pp. 53-54.
¹⁰ Kelly and Bramston, op.cit., p. 199.

Nonetheless, the reason Kerr delayed consulting Barwick was more likely designed to emphasise that it was his decision and his alone, rather than to forestall an unwanted opinion that advocated action. As we have already seen, Kerr made it clear to Mason that he did not want Barwick's advice on what he *should* do – he had already made that decision – but that what he was proposing to do was constitutional.

We are given an account of Barwick's mindset and preparation he undertook during the development of the crisis. In this respect the only criticism that can be made of Barwick is that his objectivity, having been a Minister in the Menzies government, may have been in question. That goes to the value one may put upon his advice, not the fact of him giving it. What is of concern to us here are the events that unfolded over the few days from 9 November.

Kerr phoned Barwick on the evening of 9 November and told him he had come to certain conclusions and arranged for Barwick to come to Admiralty House in Sydney the following morning. This Barwick did and he was asked if he would be prepared to provide advice as to the constitutionality of what Kerr proposed. Upon consideration, Barwick decided that, since this was a matter which in his opinion could not come before the High Court, he was free to do so. According to Kelly and Bramston:

> Barwick told Kerr he was able to advise him. He specified two conditions: that his call to Admiralty House that morning should be published in the vice-regal engagements and that his advice would be exclusively in writing. Both were prudent. Kerr accepted them. There would be no secrecy about their meetings.[11]

This is correct. The insistence that there be no secrecy about the meeting seems odd at first sight because if Kerr were intending to use the advice of the Chief Justice as support for his decision – as he was – then the fact of the meeting would become public very shortly thereafter in any case.

---

[11] Ibid., p. 200.

There would be one reason only to keep the meeting secret until after the decision. And that would be to avoid any possibility that Whitlam might get wind of the fact that Kerr had been talking privately to Barwick at a time when things were quickly coming to a head. Whitlam had specifically warned Kerr not to consult Barwick. Had Whitlam not treated Kerr so cavalierly he might have picked up this piece of intelligence. If Kerr were truly intent on 'ambushing' Whitlam, would he have left this clue? It's a minor point, I concede. In fact, as Kelly and Bramston later reveal, the media did contact Whitlam's office on the morning of the 11 November alerting him to this vice-regal notice: "But the prime minister, while a little puzzled, was unmoved."[12]

Perhaps he had already decided on his response – to allow himself to become a martyr.

In the event, Barwick wrote his opinion which was delivered to Kerr late Monday afternoon. Kerr makes no mention, in *Matters for Judgement*, of any other contact with Barwick, however, Kelly and Bramston discovered in Barwick's file a record of a phone call earlier in the day:

> However, Kerr had rung Barwick earlier, at 2.25pm, and had spoken to an associate of the chief justice. This phone call was unknown until the discovery of these notes by the authors in Barwick's file. It revealed Kerr's nervousness and his extreme sensitivity about what Barwick might write.

Barwick's associate wrote in a note to the chief justice that:

> The Governor-General just phoned and asked that the following message be sent in to you: 'I don't want to prevent by anything I do the possibility of compromise so therefore if [Barwick] would feel at liberty to use the phrase that he was contemplating using in a slightly different form, I would have some flexibility and therefore if he used the phrase 'the course of action which you have decided to take unless immediate compromise is reached' or some-

---

[12] Ibid., p. 206.

thing like that. But whatever you say is OK by me.'

> Kerr was offering drafting instructions to Barwick for his formal advice to the governor-general. The text reveals how awkward Kerr felt doing this. Not surprisingly, Barwick was hardly responsive. He made no mention of any possible 'compromise' that would avert intervention. In 2013 Troy Bramston asked Malcolm Fraser for his reaction to the news that Kerr was suggesting how Barwick draft his letter, Fraser said: 'For the governor-general to suggest to the chief justice what should be in the letter, if he was going to write a letter, was totally inappropriate.'[13]

At a superficial level this passage raises some question about the propriety of Kerr's action. Certainly, Fraser's response suggests so. But why question Fraser on this matter, rather than another retired judge or Governor-General? By 2013 Fraser had long since abandoned Kerr to his fate and was intent on maintaining the rehabilitation of his own reputation that he had been working on so assiduously since leaving office.

In fact, this is something of a storm in a teacup. It is clear from the above note that Kerr and Barwick discussed the wording of his advice during their face-to-face meeting. Hence the reference to 'the phrase that he [Barwick] was contemplating using'. No doubt the first thing they discussed was the central issue of Kerr's proposed course of action and would have determined that they essentially agreed with each other on that matter. Then it would be natural to discuss the form of words that Barwick might employ. Given that Kerr had defied Whitlam to consult Barwick in the first place, he was now into tactics not niceties. This incident had no bearing on the outcome. But in order to give some heft to their theory that this was a conspiracy, they employ hyperbolic language such as Kerr's 'extreme' sensitivity. It was, in fact, merely a pragmatic inclination to make sure that Barwick did not constrain his flexibility.

The real import of this phone call is to suggest that Kerr was by no means intent on sacking Whitlam, hence his desire to

---

[13] Ibid., pp. 200-201.

have an opinion worded such as to leave open the possibility of compromise on the part of Whitlam. It seems to me that Kerr probably knew that Barwick would be more uncompromising than he himself would be. Kerr must have hoped that, presented with a *fait accompli*, Whitlam might back down at the last moment. The use of the words 'immediate compromise' suggests that he did contemplate that Whitlam might back down at the last minute and that he would, in fact, have accommodated Whitlam and allowed him to go to the election as Prime Minister if he had asked. Exactly as he stated in *Matters for Judgement*.

The authors then turn to Barwick's contention, which we examined earlier, that an Australian Prime Minister needed the confidence of both Houses of Parliament. They describe this as a 'technical, legal interpretation' and describe it as a 'flawed statement' because 'the issue of "confidence" in Australia is defined by command of majority support on the floor of the House of Representatives'.[14] Tellingly, they do not provide any reference to this definition. It certainly does not appear in the Constitution.

It is a circular argument. They claim that Barwick's opinion was wrong because what he was arguing was wrong. Barwick's position was that confidence is not defined by majority support on the floor of the House only, but that a government needs the confidence of both Houses. Barwick's view was one judge's interpretation of the Constitution. I am not a lawyer, but it seems, at least, arguable to me. Nonetheless, I do suspect that if this question – 'confidence' being required from both Houses, not the dismissal itself – had come before the full bench in 1975, Barwick might have found himself writing the dissenting opinion. That does not, of itself, make his opinion flawed. But this whole question is academic because Kerr did not, apparently, subscribe to that view and he did not act upon it.

They also claim that Barwick exceeded his brief by advising Kerr that his proposed course of action was consistent with his 'constitutional authority and duty'. They say:

---

[14] Ibid., p. 201.

Barwick could not help himself. The notion of 'duty' went far beyond the issue of constitutional powers.

It invites an irresistible conclusion: that Barwick, fearing Kerr might retreat, wanted to stiffen him. If the dismissal became his 'duty' then retreat was unacceptable. Barwick told Paul Kelly he felt Kerr desired 'that the cup would pass from him'. Barwick's view was 'not that [Kerr] was weak but that he was tempted to temporise'. Barwick, by contrast saw himself as a strong man willing to act.[15]

What Barwick was effectively saying was that Kerr, in the circumstances that prevailed, no longer had a discretion in the matter, assuming that those circumstances did not change. What they are suggesting here is that Barwick did what Kerr had specifically wanted to avoid – being told what he *should* do. But that is merely a reflection on Barwick's character. Everything in *Matters for Judgement* and the bulk of *The Dismissal* suggests that Kerr acted on his own initiative. He had made his decision before he called Barwick. I have no doubt that Kerr would have preferred 'this cup pass from him' but that does not mean he would have backed down without Barwick's support. Whatever influence Barwick thought he might have exerted on Kerr, effectively his involvement was confined to the provision of advice. And Barwick was not saying that Kerr's duty was to dismiss Whitlam. He was saying that his duty was to protect the Constitution.

We are now told of a curious incident:

> After Kerr received and read the letter, he rang Barwick, late on Monday afternoon. By this time, the court had risen and Barwick was back in his chambers. This call reveals Kerr as a manipulator, almost playing with Barwick. The chief justice told the story:
>
>> I received a telephone call from Sir John Kerr. He acknowledged receipt of my letter and then said he was curious to know what the former Solicitors-General would have thought of the matter ... he knew what one of them, Robert

---

[15] Ibid., p. 202.

Ellicott, thought because he had publicly stated his views. But he would like to know what the other retired Solicitor-General, Sir Anthony Mason, thought. He asked me if I would mind asking him. I said I did not mind doing that ... I went downstairs to Sir Anthony's chambers. Sir Anthony had been sitting with me during the afternoon though he was then unaware of what had passed between Sir John and myself earlier that day. I told him what had occurred and I told him the substance of my letter. I told him that Sir John had asked me to ask him his view and I was now doing so. He said he quite agreed with the view I had expressed and I may say he did so without any reluctance.

Barwick then rang Kerr to convey Mason's view. In 1994, during an ABC interview, Barwick said he saw this as 'a great sign of weakness' in Kerr because he needed further reassurance from Mason, a man 'who was friendly with him'.

In truth, Kerr was manipulating Barwick. The chief justice did not know that Kerr had been secretly consulting with Mason on the approach to Barwick. The chief justice did not know that Kerr and Mason had discussed what advice Barwick would likely offer. Obviously, Kerr knew what Mason thought. He didn't need Barwick to tell him. He decided, however, to stage this event. Why? Probably to ensure Barwick knew Mason's views, to ensure Barwick would never suspect the Kerr-Mason dialogue and would always believe that Kerr had only discovered Mason's view via Barwick himself and not by any direct Kerr-Mason contact. In his note, Kerr said that he and Mason kept their dialogue from Barwick 'because he might be offended that I had not approached him earlier, and before talking to Mason'.[16]

This incident is the basis for the misleading title of this chapter – Manipulating a Willing Chief Justice – which seems oxymoronic. It is designed to again smear Sir John Kerr's character. The Cambridge Dictionary defines manipulation as 'controlling someone or something to your own advantage, often unfairly or dishonestly'. Effectively it means influencing someone to act in a way in which they might not otherwise.

---

[16] Ibid., pp. 202-203.

Kerr could be said to have deceived Barwick on this minor point, but his phone call could not, remotely, be described as manipulation. It did not cause Barwick to make any decision or take any action that would affect the outcome of Kerr's decision. As Kelly and Bramston point out, the phone call was almost certainly designed to protect Sir Anthony Mason and was probably made at his request.

The next few pages of *The Dismissal* deal with the propriety of Sir Anthony's conduct and, as I have dealt with this matter in an earlier chapter, I will pass over it here.

Back to Kerr:

> Kerr ... like a general on the eve of battle, was cautious, calculating and obsessed. He contemplated the coming moment of dismissal, the moment when he would destroy Whitlam's hopes and expectations.[17]

Here we have more speculation as to Kerr's state of mind – another of those ubiquitous little triptychs. He contemplated the coming moment of dismissal, the moment when he would destroy Whitlam's hopes and expectations. Really? They say this is all clear from Kerr's writings but give no references. Again, this is worded to give the impression that the aim of the whole exercise was the dismissal of Whitlam and that this was a personal quest. It is much more likely that Kerr, rather than relishing the demise of Whitlam, contemplated the moment when he would put at risk all that he himself had worked for.

We now learn about a call that Kerr made to Barwick on the morning of 11 November, a call that neither man revealed in their memoirs:

> The governor-general told Barwick that Whitlam and Fraser were now in a meeting. It was likely he would see Whitlam about 1pm. Barwick's note reads:
>
>> [Kerr] said he had to consider the possibility that the Prime Minister might have cabled the Queen informing her that

---
[17] Ibid., p. 206.

> he, the Prime Minister, had lost confidence in the Governor-General and perhaps seeking the withdrawal of his commission. He said that whilst that was an eventuality which might seem far-fetched it had to be recognised as a possibility. He said that nonetheless he proposed to follow the course which he had outlined to me upon which I had given him advice.

> Dismissal of Kerr was the last thing on Whitlam's mind that morning. That Kerr could not purge from his head the notion of Whitlam approaching the Queen, even at this late stage, testifies to the depth of his pre-occupation about his own dismissal.[18]

Kerr did not know what was or was not on Whitlam's mind that morning and he cannot be blamed for that. The claim that Kerr could not purge from his head the notion of Whitlam approaching the Queen is designed to paint Kerr as paranoid. And yet, his own words to Barwick dispel that idea. He told Barwick it might be far-fetched, but the possibility could not be ignored. And the reason it could not be ignored is because, as we have seen earlier, Whitlam himself, on several occasions, had canvassed that very possibility, most notably at the dinner for Malaysian Prime Minister Tun Abdul Razak.

During this call Kerr told Barwick that if he was asked by Whitlam if he had consulted Barwick, he would tell him that he had. He also asked if he should make Barwick's letter available to Whitlam, if requested by him during the forthcoming meeting. Barwick suggested that as the letter had been confidential to Kerr, he should withhold it until he had completed his action, and thereafter it should be published. In the event, Barwick's opinion was published on 18 November.

Their comment on this is:

> It is unsurprising that Kerr contacted Barwick on the morning of 11 November to brief him on events and seek his tactical guidance on the release of the advice. That was being prudent. It reinforces the fact that Barwick's role spilled over into the management of Whitlam. It is also unsurprising that neither mentions the call in

---
[18] Ibid., pp. 206-207.

their memoirs. They were finalizing the rituals for Whitlam's political execution.[19]

The decision as to when Barwick's advice would be made public had nothing to do with 'the management of Whitlam' nor his 'political execution'. I imagine it was all to do with maximising the effectiveness of that advice in educating the public as to the legal and constitutional basis of Kerr's actions – which encompassed not only the withdrawal of Whitlam's commission but the commissioning of Fraser as caretaker Prime Minister, the approval of supply and the calling of the election. The public needed to be given time to absorb the fact of these events. I suspect Barwick did not want his advice to be lost in the noise of the immediate aftermath of the events of 11 November and would prefer that it be brought to light after the initial fuss had abated, when it could be considered objectively.

The authors then continue their mischaracterisation of Barwick's role:

> In the end, Kerr won the ultimate seal of approval – authorisation of the chief justice. He proceeded to the dismissal fortified by Barwick's advice, his strength and his advice. Above all Kerr wanted the best guarantee that the High Court would not interfere if Whitlam tried to contest the dismissal. While Barwick had written in his private capacity, his authority as chief justice was stamped on Kerr's action. Indeed, it was written on High Court of Australia' letterhead from the 'Chambers of the Chief Justice'. It was of immense assurance to Kerr who said that on the Monday night 'the loneliness of the decision ... was one of the most burdensome experiences I have known'.[20]

Again, we have the implication that Barwick 'authorised' Kerr to act. That is simply untrue. Barwick advised Kerr that, *in his opinion*, the course of action that Kerr had already decided upon was constitutional. As to Barwick's involvement guaranteeing the High Court would not intervene, that is just nonsense. Barwick may have been the Chief Justice but on the Court, he was 'the first among equals'. It is impossible to imagine

---
[19] Ibid., p. 207.
[20] Ibid., p. 208.

that if the Court were petitioned by Whitlam the other judges would decline to hear him just because Barwick – who would, of course have had to recuse himself – had given advice. Do Kelly and Bramston expect us to believe that Justice Murphy, for one, would have denied leave to appeal? Judges regularly recuse themselves from cases on the basis of a real or perceived conflict of interest.

And it is worth looking at the quote from *Matters for Judgement* in its entirety:

> The loneliness of the decision I was engaged in making in these final days was one of the most burdensome experiences I have known. Most policy or executive decisions are made with the aid of advisers or colleagues as to what can and what should be done. There are others to consult and to offer counsel. But the decision to dismiss the Prime Minister could only be made by me. It was a time of immense mental solitude.[21]

In other words, Barwick confirmed Kerr in his thinking about what *could* be done, but the consideration of what *should* be done was Kerr's and Kerr's alone.

They continue:

> That Barwick entered the dismissal project with enthusiasm is beyond question. Barwick wrote in his memoirs: 'To the extent that [Kerr] respected and accepted my opinion, it can be said that I had some influence in his pursuit of the course on which he had decided.' In truth, Barwick lusted after such a role. Ellicott got it right: 'Barwick gave Kerr comfort. It wasn't the thing that triggered the dismissal.' What Barwick didn't realise was that Kerr had manipulated the chief justice, reading Barwick even better than Barwick had read himself.[22]

Again the 'dismissal project'. And Kelly's and Bramston's assertion that Barwick 'lusted' after the role is simply more speculative hyperbole, designed to foster the idea of a conspiracy. But, in the context of the above paragraph, the claim that Kerr had manipulated Barwick makes absolutely no

---

[21] Kerr, *Matters for Judgement*, pp. 347-348.
[22] Kelly and Bramston, op.cit., p. 208.

sense. In what way did Kerr influence Barwick, who apparently 'lusted' to be involved, to do something he would otherwise not have done? This verbal legerdemain is intended to smear Kerr as an untrustworthy character. This is Machiavellian Kerr at work here.

They conclude the chapter:

> Barwick had no regrets. He was proud of his role. He was a willing chief justice. And he was brilliantly recruited by Kerr.[23]

Well, was he manipulated or not?

Earlier, Kelly and Bramston asserted that:

> Kerr knew the combination of the governor-general and chief justice, united on the dismissal issue, would constitute an almost certain guarantee of a successful operation.[24]

The 'operation', if that is what you wish to call it, was done and dusted on the afternoon of 11 November, long before Barwick's opinion was even released.

In summary, the involvement of Mason and Barwick was a sideshow.

Mason's involvement, at his own discretion, was to act as a sounding board for Kerr. Barwick's involvement, at his own discretion, was to provide an assurance to the public that Kerr had not acted unconstitutionally. Nothing more.

Barwick did not 'authorise' Kerr to dismiss Whitlam. The decision was Kerr's alone. Barwick's involvement did not protect Kerr from a High Court challenge. And Barwick's advice, despite the impression Kelly and Bramston would have you believe, was not simply the product of a 'closed mind.' The weight of *eminent* legal opinion, on the constitutionality of Kerr's actions, from all sides of politics – Evatt and Forsey from the left, Barwick from the right, Gibbs and Mason from somewhere in the centre – falls heavily in Kerr's favour.

---

[23] Ibid., p. 209.
[24] Ibid., pp. 192-193.

14

The Dismissal

We finally come to the events of 11 November:

> When dawn broke over Canberra on the morning of Tuesday, 11 November 1975 to herald a warm spring day, John Kerr was ready to strike. He had resolved to terminate the Whitlam government if the impasse was not broken. Everything had been meticulously planned. … He weighed several scenarios that could occur with his official secretary, David Smith.[1]

Here is the perfect image of a calculating political assassin, bringing to fruition the results of months of plotting. Here is what Sir David Smith recorded:

> Before the Governor-General went upstairs to change into formal morning dress for the ceremony at the War Memorial, we finished checking the various documents that he might require later that morning, and ran through the various scenarios that could occur. As he returned the documents to their folder, the Governor-General gave a heavy sigh. He was well aware of the burden of responsibility which he now carried, but he was prepared to be true to his oath of office and to do his duty. He knew he would be execrated by the Labor Party and its supporters for the rest of his life, and he told me so in just those words, but he knew he had a responsibility to put to the people, for their decision, the issue which the Parliament had failed to resolve.[2]

It seems to me there is a country mile between the two different personas offered above – one by a party which is determined that nothing of honour should remain to Sir John Kerr's

---

[1] Kelly and Bramston, *The Dismissal*, p. 210.
[2] Smith, *Head of State*, p. 244.

memory, and the other by a respected civil servant who knew the man well and had observed his behaviour and demeanour throughout the crisis. Smith's description rings true and fits with all we know of Kerr from his own memoir. And although Smith does not detail what the 'various scenarios' were, it is more than likely that one of them included Whitlam backing down after he had been presented with his termination notice. Here is what Sir John Kerr said about these deliberations:

> Immediately Mr Whitlam arrived, before he put his proposal to me about a half-Senate election, if that were his intention, I would ask him whether any change had occurred as regards the deadlock on supply. If the answer were 'no' I would tell him that I had decided to withdraw his commission. This in itself would not amount to a legally effective withdrawal. That would not occur until I told him I had terminated his commission. Whether I would do this or not was to depend on his reaction. If his reaction, as I expected, were to indicate that he would have me recalled, I would decide to act upon the documents on my desk and tell him he was no longer Prime Minister, handing him the documents.
>
> If, contrary to my expectation, he did not do this but changed his mind, offering to recommend a dissolution so that he could go to the people as Prime Minister, I would get that advice formally from him there and then, and act upon it immediately I had secured supply. Supply would certainly be granted if he were willing to advise dissolution. The people would still be called upon to decide the issue the two leaders had failed to settle, but the Labor Party would remain in office, with Mr Whitlam as Prime Minister, until elections were held. If Mr Whitlam wanted to he could walk out of my office as Prime Minister to conduct the coming election campaign.[3]

Kelly and Bramston casually dismiss this claim that Kerr would have allowed Whitlam to remain as Prime Minister had he agreed to advise an election. But it is a logical claim based both on human nature in general and on Kerr's personality in particular. Kerr wanted an election, not Whitlam's scalp, which, as he knew could well come at the cost of his own. From that moment on, the Governor-Generalship would become

---

[3] Kerr, *Matters for Judgement*, p. 346.

a poisoned chalice and Kerr knew it. Would the venal, self-seeking sybarite that Kelly and Bramston have crafted welcome that outcome? Would the temporiser that Barwick described as 'wishing this cup might pass from him' have passed up this chance to achieve just that?

Kelly and Bramston finally inject a note of perspective:

> Kerr's plan went beyond mere dismissal. He had to commission Fraser, ensure supply was secured and dissolve the parliament for the election.[4]

Well of course Kerr's plan 'went beyond mere dismissal', although you wouldn't know it from reading most of *The Dismissal* up to this point, particularly the references to the dismissal 'project' in the previous chapter. Everything Kerr did he did with the aim of securing supply to the Crown, and he had determined that the only way to do this was by an election. Whitlam's dismissal was merely a means to this end.

They then go on to recount 'the feeling among senior Liberals was if 11 November passed without an election, then Fraser's plan might unravel and the Liberals might need to surrender'.[5] This is designed to suggest that if Kerr had waited a few more days, Fraser would have lost his support and the Opposition would fold and pass supply. But, as we shall see, Kerr no longer had the luxury of waiting a few more days. It was Whitlam who set his tumbril in motion by requesting a meeting with Kerr on 11 November to advise a half-Senate election. It is true that Kerr said that if Whitlam had not initiated the meeting, Kerr would have had to send for him very shortly thereafter.

Kelly and Bramston note:

> It was extraordinary that so few people attached significance to the vice-regal notice published in the newspapers that morning, revealing two meetings the previous day between Kerr and Barwick. But Clarrie Harders, secretary of the Attorney General's Department was 'surprised'. Harders recalled: 'I noticed, as others also noticed,

---

[4] Kelly and Bramston, op.cit., p. 212.
[5] Ibid.

that Sir Garfield had called on the Governor-General.' Harders was not aware any such meeting had been planned. John Menadue, the Secretary of the Prime Minister's Department, also saw it. But no action was taken, no alarm was sounded. The Whitlam government was sunk in naivety.[6]

The fact that Whitlam, and apparently all his team, on discovering that Barwick had twice called on the Governor-General the previous day ignored the implicit warning that something was up, does not invalidate Kerr's fear that Whitlam might move against him. One interpretation for this apparent insouciance was, as I have suggested, that Whitlam well knew which way the wind was blowing and decided to sail with it, in order to draw the victim card in the election, which by this time was inevitable.

At about 9am on 11 November Fraser and his leadership team met with Whitlam and his. Whitlam again offered to delay a half-Senate election until close to 30 June (before which it must be held) if supply were granted. This would deny him the chance of getting a Senate majority for the next seven months. Fraser rejected this offer and agreed to grant supply if Whitlam agreed to an election of both Houses by mid-1976. Whitlam rejected this compromise and told them he would, in that case, advise a half-Senate election for 13 December. Fraser asked if he would be seeking supply to cover the election period. Whitlam said no. From *The Dismissal*:

> It was a decisive answer. Fraser felt sure that Whitlam had misjudged. 'You know, Prime Minister, the Governor-General can make up his own mind what to do,' Fraser said to Whitlam. 'You can't necessarily assume he will do just as you advise'. Recalling Whitlam's reply, Fraser said: 'He just wasn't disposed to listen.'[7]

Whitlam's version of this meeting omits any reference to Fraser's counteroffer. And the purported exchange relating to the Governor-General making up his own mind does not appear, which would be natural.[8]

---

[6] Ibid, pp. 211-212.
[7] Ibid., p. 212.
[8] Whitlam, *The Truth of the Matter*, pp. 104-105.

If that exchange did occur – and we only have Fraser's word that it did – then it lends credence to an almost insane lack of awareness, even obtuseness, on Whitlam's part. Whitlam observed that following this meeting 'Mr Crean commented somewhat reflectively, "They seem very cocky"'.[9]

By contrast, Kelly and Bramston report that:

> A number of people felt a sense of anticipation. The night before, 10 November, the lord mayor's banquet had been held in Melbourne. Whitlam attended, addressed the dinner and offered several opposition MPs a lift back to Canberra on the VIP flight. Andrew Peacock suspected something was afoot. 'On the plane on the way back, Malcolm and Phil [Lynch] had their heads together all the way,' he recalled. 'A couple of us sensed something was happening.' John Mant, Whitlam's office chief, was also on the plane. He said there was a heightened sense of things moving to a climax. 'You could feel it,' Mant said. Referring to Fraser and Lynch, Mant recalled: 'I said to Gough, "What are those two up to?" To my mind they knew.' Lynch's press secretary, Brian Buckley, said there was 'a change of mood' at this time towards a more 'optimistic' outlook. Lynch told his staff on the morning of 11 November that 'we should get a result today'.[10]

This passage, based mostly on quotes from interviews with the authors in 2015, gives the impression that Fraser and Lynch already knew that Kerr would dismiss Whitlam the next day. Mant's statement that 'to my mind they knew', strongly suggests this interpretation. Knew what? It could only be that Kerr would dismiss Whitlam. Whitlam, referring to the VIP flight, also intimated this:

> Mr Fraser and Mr Lynch were driven off together by Eric Kennedy. They spoke very quietly but at the end were relaxed enough to say, 'He doesn't seem to know anything about it. All we have to do now is hope the press doesn't get hold of it, because then it could all blow up in our faces.'[11]

This account, which appears at the beginning of Chapter Eight

---
[9] Ibid.
[10] Kelly and Bramston, op.cit., p. 213.
[11] Whitlam, op.cit., p. 104.

of *The Truth of the Matter,* titled 'Ambush', rings false. To begin with the wording sounds contrived. Is Whitlam saying he overheard this conversation, presumably carried out in the back of Fraser's Commonwealth car? Is he saying that Eric Kennedy reported it to him? If so, when? And if so, why did Kennedy not provide further detail? Or did Whitlam hear it while they were all still in the VIP aircraft?

This doubtful story, and Mant's observation on the VIP aircraft, accord with Kelly's and Bramston's claim, covered in Chapter Two, that Kerr tipped Fraser off. But that phone call to Fraser did not occur until the next morning. All that Fraser and Lynch knew on the evening of 10 November was what their intuition would have told them. Intuition that apparently deserted Whitlam and his entire team. And, anyway, why would Fraser and Lynch not be engrossed in conversation at this late stage of the crisis?

Kelly and Bramston then highlight another incident which should have sent a warning signal to Whitlam. The chief electoral officer, Mr Frank Ley, called Menadue and told him that Fraser had enquired about the timetable for holding an election for both Houses on 13 December. Ley told Menadue that he had confirmed for Fraser that the decision for an election on 13 December would have to be taken on 11, or at the latest, 12 November.[12] Whitlam claims, in *The Truth of the Matter*, he had this intelligence direct from Ley.[13] He apparently deduced nothing from it.

We now come to the critical phone calls. Kelly and Bramston say Fraser phoned Whitlam just after 10.00 am, following a personal meeting at 9.00 am, to tell him there was no deal. On Whitlam's instruction, Menadue phoned Government House to arrange an appointment for Whitlam to call on Kerr as soon as possible. Kerr told him it would be impossible at that time and that sometime after the Remembrance Day ceremony would be convenient. Whitlam then phoned Government House himself

---

[12] Kelly and Bramston, op.cit., pp. 213-214.
[13] Whitlam, op.cit., p. 106.

and was told that Kerr could not accept his call. Kerr was in fact talking to his daughter about his grandson who had been taken to hospital seriously ill. Whitlam then rang Kerr's direct number and spoke to Kerr. They agreed that they would meet during the Parliamentary luncheon adjournment at around 12.45 pm.

Kelly and Bramston then say:

> It is significant that Kerr asked Whitlam whether supply would be available for the campaign, and Whitlam confirmed that it would not be available. Kerr now understood there was no escape from a decision: 'I had either to let him have that [Senate] election without supply, with consequential financial chaos, or to act, so as to ensure full elections for both Houses with full supply ... Mr Whitlam had left his half-Senate election too late.[14]

The significance of Kerr's question is that it offered one more warning for Whitlam that things may not go according to his plan. By the way, the full quote from Kerr including the missing words is:

> I had either to let him have that election without supply, with consequential financial chaos, or to act, so as to ensure full elections for both Houses with full supply *produced at the last realistic moment before supply ran out.* Mr Whitlam had left his half-Senate lection too late.[15]

Presumably those few italicised words were excised from the Kelly and Bramston version because they make it clear that, in Kerr's mind, there was no scope for any further delay in resolving the crisis. Those words were not irrelevant to the context, and to leave them out was unprofessional at best.

There is some confusion about the timing of various phone calls. For example, Kelly and Bramston claim on page 215 that Fraser called Kerr just after 10.00 am (Kerr makes no mention of this call). On page 217 they say Kerr phoned Fraser at 9.55 am.

---

[14] Kelly and Bramston, op.cit., p. 216.
[15] Kerr, op.cit., p. 355.

This latter is the subject of the 'tip-off' claim:

> This call became a matter of high dispute between them. Fraser told Kerr there had been no resolution at his meeting with Whitlam that morning and there would be no temporary supply for the Senate election. Fraser says that Kerr then asked him a series of questions – relating to the terms and conditions he wanted Fraser to accept if commissioned as Prime Minister. It was tantamount to a tip-off of what Kerr was planning. Kerr, on the other hand, claimed he only raised these conditions at lunchtime when he was commissioning Fraser. An arrangement was made for Fraser to meet with Kerr also during the luncheon adjournment.[16]

This 'tip-off' is covered in detail in Chapter Two so I will not dwell on it here except to note that, if it occurred, it would only have been of value to Fraser if his troops were on the verge of revolt and he needed to pull them into line. As we have seen from Kelly's and Bramston's own accounts at the beginning of this chapter, that was not the case:

> Lynch's press secretary, Brian Buckley, said there was 'a change of mood' at this time towards a more 'optimistic' outlook.[17]

Given that everyone on the Coalition side believed the issue would come to a head on either 11 or 12 November, it would not have made sense for them to cave in at this point. Admittedly, Kerr could not know the state of mind of the Coalition party room with any certainty. He had to make a calculated guess and, as we shall see, there were other considerations to take into account. And even if Kerr's version of events were true i.e., that he didn't discuss terms and conditions with Fraser and merely arranged for him to come to Government House that afternoon, it would take a pretty dense Fraser not to put two and two together, particularly since he knew that Whitlam would be advising a half-Senate election, probably that day.

There follows some discussion about the Coalition party room meeting, which is neither here nor there as far as the events of the day are concerned and then the saga resumes with Sir

---

[16] Kelly and Bramston, op.cit., p. 217.
[17] Ibid., p. 213.

John and Lady Kerr arriving at the War Memorial for the Remembrance Day ceremony:

> Sir John and Lady Kerr arrived ... in a ceremonial Rolls-Royce. Sir John wore a tall black top hat, morning dress of grey pants and black jacket with tails. It was adorned with decorative medals. Kep Enderby, the attorney-general, was with the Kerrs at the ceremony that culminated at the eleventh hour on the eleventh day of the eleventh month.[18]

Is this a history of one of the major political controversies of our time or an article in the Women's Weekly society pages? Why are we not told what Lady Kerr and Kep Enderby were wearing? And 'decorative' medals? Are they suggesting Sir John found his decorations in the bottom of the vice-regal Corn Flakes packet? Certainly, we talk about 'highly decorated' persons (generally war heroes) but we do not refer to the emblems of their honours and awards as if they were fashion accessories. I may be being over-sensitive here and making a mountain out of a molehill. In other circumstances I would overlook this wording – decorative medals – as just being sloppy writing, but I know that Sir John Kerr was (rightly) proud of his honours and awards, and it seems to me this is just another, particularly petty, attempt to demean him – trying to liken him to some tin-pot third-world dictator. It is of a piece with the entirety of *The Dismissal*.

Having got that off my chest, I now return to the matter at hand. The House of Representatives session that morning concerned itself largely with duelling censure motions and broke for lunch at 12.55 pm. It was intended that Whitlam should arrive at Government House first and that Fraser would arrive while Whitlam was closeted with Kerr. In the event, Fraser arrived first and was ushered into an anteroom. Kelly and Bramston take up the tale:

> Whitlam arrived at Government House at about 1pm. The scene was set. Whitlam went straight into Kerr's study escorted by Chris Stephens, Kerr's aide-de-camp. Kerr knew his objective: he would

---

[18] Ibid., p. 219.

> not let Whitlam escape from Yarralumla without an election. What was Whitlam's mood as he walked into Kerr's study? He was supremely confident, yet he would have known this was a critical moment.[19]

It is encouraging to see the acknowledgement from the authors that Kerr's objective was not the dismissal of Whitlam but procuring an election. It might have been more accurate for them to say: 'he would not let Whitlam escape from Yarralumla *as Prime Minister* without an election'. They then continue with discussion of two differing versions of the interview – Whitlam's and Kerr's:

> Whitlam was asked to take a seat in front of the desk. Kerr's letter of dismissal was lying face down on his desk. 'I have a letter with the advice I gave you on the telephone this morning,' Whitlam said. According to Whitlam, Kerr then said: 'Before we go any further, I have to tell you that I have decided to terminate your commission. I have a letter for you giving my reasons.' Whitlam's response, having briefly scanned the letter, was: 'Have you discussed this with the Palace?' Kerr said, 'I don't have to and it's too late for you I have terminated your commission.'
>
> Kerr's version is as follows: 'Before you say anything, Prime Minister, I want to say something to you. You have told me this morning on the phone that your talks with the leaders on the other side have failed to produce any change and that things therefore remain the same. You intend to govern without parliamentary supply. He said "yes". I replied that in my view he had to have parliamentary supply to govern and as he had failed to obtain it and was not prepared to go to the people, I had decided to withdraw his commission.'
>
> In Kerr's account he claimed that on hearing the news of his dismissal, Whitlam 'jumped up, looked urgently around the room, looked at the telephone and said sharply, "I must get in touch with the Palace at once."' David Smith spoke to Kerr immediately after Whitlam left. Smith told the authors in an interview: 'The governor-general told me as they shook hands at the door, when Whitlam left the study, he said: "I must get in touch with the Palace."'[20]

---

[19] Ibid., p. 220.
[20] Ibid., pp. 220-221.

The versions above, particularly Kerr's, are not complete, although parts of Kerr's account are covered a little later. The narrative then becomes a little confusing because we return to Whitlam's account which contains a purported exchange between the two that Kerr's account did not include:

> According to Whitlam, he rose from his chair and Kerr did the same. 'The Chief Justice agrees with this course of action,' Kerr said. Whitlam responded: 'So that is why you had him to lunch yesterday. I advised you that you should not consult him on this matter.' It was done. Both men agreed on the final exchange. 'We shall both have to live with this,' Kerr said. Whitlam replied: 'You certainly will.' Kerr extended his hand to Whitlam and wished him luck. The deposed prime minister shook hands with the governor-general and then walked to the door of the office.[21]

It is probable that both men are gilding the lily a bit, knowing that there were no witnesses to their encounter.

Let's deal first with the claim that Whitlam jumped up and exclaimed that he must get in touch with the Palace at once. That is important from Kerr's point of view because fear of recall, or even having the Palace involved, was a driving factor in the tactics he used in resolving the crisis – tactics that Kelly and Bramston categorise as deceptive. To that extent, this claim could be an invention designed to corroborate his concern about the possibility of recall. Whitlam's response to this claim is:

> This is a concoction and an absurd one. ... I had no knowledge of the procedure for making calls. I did not know the number of the Palace. I had no staff with me. He had his aides, his secretaries, his telephonists, his police. I was trapped in an ambush; my sole instinct was to escape, to depart at once from the place where the deed had been done and the presence of the man who had done the deed. When he offered his hand and said 'Anyway, good luck' it was from ordinary habit and simple courtesy that I shook hands. ...
>
> To have imagined that I could have procured the dismissal of the Governor-General by a telephone call to Buckingham Palace in the middle of the night – it was 2a.m. in London – is preposterous; to

---

[21] Ibid., p. 221.

imagine that I would have tried to do so is ludicrous.²²

That rings true as far as it goes. But former Labor Minister, Clyde Cameron, no friend of Kerr, stated categorically in an interview with Sir Paul Hasluck, that Whitlam told the gathering at the Lodge after the dismissal: 'the bastard wouldn't let me get to the telephone. He said I'm no longer PM.' Cameron stated that this was before Whitlam had a chance to later revise his story for the history books, knowing that only Kerr and he knew exactly what had happened. In that same interview Cameron said, in relation to the 'race to the Palace' remark at the Tun Abdul Razak dinner: 'I knew Gough really well and no matter how much he might protest now, as he does, that it was made jocularly, it was a pretty pointed joke, and I knew it was more than a joke. He always kept that up his sleeve. If the Governor-General didn't do as he was told he would not hesitate to have him sacked'.²³ In the interests of objectivity, I should note here that Cameron was sacked as a Minister by Whitlam.

By making a call to the Palace, Whitlam did not need to procure the immediate dismissal of the Governor-General. It would suffice for his purposes to simply arrange a stay of execution. Had he done so the Palace would certainly have immediately called Kerr and 'suggested' he stay his hand. Kerr was as much exercised at the possibility of the Queen becoming embroiled in an Australian political crisis as he was about his own recall.

In fact, Whitlam did call the Palace in the middle of the night. He called Sir Martin Charteris at 4.15 am London time to advise him that his commission had been withdrawn. Charteris says Whitlam did not ask for anything. But why was it so urgent that a courtesy call of this nature had to be made in the middle of the night? By that time, no longer being Prime Minister, Whitlam had no official relationship with the Palace. He would have been aware that Government House would have advised

---

[22] Whitlam, op.cit., pp. 110-111.
[23] Clyde Cameron, (1985) Paul Hasluck in conversation with Clyde R. Cameron [sound recording].

the Palace almost as soon as the election had been called. (In fact, David Smith called the Palace at about 3.00 am London time.) Was Whitlam hoping that his friend would somehow intervene on his behalf? You be the judge. Here is Sir Martin Charteris's account of the call:

> Mr Whitlam prefaced his remarks by saying that he was speaking as a 'private citizen'; he rehearsed what had happened, the withdrawal of his commission, the passing of Supply and the vote of no confidence in Mr Fraser and the vote of confidence in the member for Werriwa, which had been passed in the House of Representatives, and said that now Supply had been passed, he should be recommissioned as Prime Minister so that he could choose his own time to call an election.
>
> He spoke calmly and did not ask me to make any approach to the Queen, or indeed to do anything other than the suggestion that I should speak to you to find out what was going on.[24]

On the other hand, Whitlam's account of the 11 November meeting does not ring true, almost in its entirety:

> Sir John asked me to take a seat, as usual on the other side of the desk. I said, 'I have a letter with the advice which I gave you on the telephone this morning.' He said,' Before we go any further I have to tell you that I have decided to terminate your commission. I have a letter for you giving my reasons.' He passed me a document. After glancing at it I said, 'Have you discussed this with the Palace?' He said, 'I don't have to and it's too late for you. I have terminated your commission'.
>
> I rose to leave. He also rose and added, 'The Chief Justice agrees with this course of action.' He did not tell me that he had a letter from the Chief Justice. I said, 'So that is why you had him to lunch yesterday. I advised you that you should not consult him on this matter.'
>
> He shrugged his shoulders. As he has written, he merely said, 'we shall all have to live with this' and I replied, 'You certainly will.' He wished me luck and extended his hand. I took it. I have never

---

[24] M Charteris, Letter to John Kerr, *The Palace Letters*, 17 November 1975, p. 36.

spoken to him since.[25]

We know that Kerr hoped for a compromise, as evidenced by his suggested wording of Sir Garfield Barwick's advice as discussed in the previous chapter. We know that Barwick believed that Kerr wished 'this cup might pass from him'. It is inconceivable that Kerr would have just presented Whitlam with a *fait accompli*. It just does not fit with what we know of Sir John's character. Whitlam's claim that Kerr never queried him on his resolve to govern without supply and did not delay formally tendering the withdrawal of Whitlam's commission until he had some time to consider his position just does not ring true.

Neither does the purported exchange about the Chief Justice. As a former salesman, one of my guiding principles was: once you have closed the deal, stop talking. As a lawyer, I'm sure Kerr would have understood that. Why would Kerr have offered this information when we know he had resolved, with Barwick, that he would not raise the matter unless Whitlam did. Kerr wanted to 'keep his powder dry' on this aspect. And, as a former NSW Chief Justice, he would never have been so inept as to say: 'the Chief Justice agrees with this *course of action.*' Kerr was at pains to restrict Barwick's advice to what legally could be done, not what should be done.

It seems to me that Whitlam's version has been constructed to negate Kerr's claim that Whitlam could have backed down and left Yarralumla as the Prime Minister if he had wanted to.

Kelly and Bramston argue that:

> The most contentious claim made by Kerr about this brief conversation is that he gave Whitlam the opportunity to save himself. Kerr said Whitlam was dismissed only when he was given the dismissal letter. He suggested that Whitlam could have negotiated then and there to save his prime ministership despite being told his commission had been terminated. 'He could still say, "Let us talk about this. If you are determined to have an election, I would rather go to

---

[25] Whitlam, op.cit., p. 110.

the people myself as Prime Minister." Had he done so I would have
agreed provided he committed himself by action there and then.'

> Kerr constructed this argument as a face-saving device. He pretended that at the precise moment of his planned political execution Whitlam could have remained prime minister. This claim was designed to rebut criticism that Kerr betrayed the conventions of the Crown by conducting a dismissal by ambush and without prior discussion of the situation with Whitlam. It is not believable.[26]

What is not believable is that Gough 'crash through or crash' Whitlam would have so meekly accepted his termination without any push back whatsoever, without even discussing the reasons Kerr offered him. Unless he was quite aware that that might be the outcome. And that he was not so convinced that the advantage of going to the election as Prime Minister would overcome his revulsion at capitulating to the demand of a man whom he, apparently, even then despised.

Whitlam was known to be a flamboyant character, a man who refused to suffer fools gladly, a man who, according to John Menadue who knew him better than most, 'would have taken [Kerr's] head off quickly' if he had known of Kerr's intention to dismiss him. Not a man noted for his reserve. A man who often spoke before thinking. Which account appears more believable? The one in which Whitlam displayed no emotion whatsoever, did not query or discuss the matter – other than a tangential reference to the Palace – but simply received his dismissal and 'rose to leave'? Or the one in which he displayed some emotion?

In the grand scheme of things, the claim that Kerr should have warned Whitlam is a semantic argument. The fact is that Kerr was going to have an election, whether Labor did it willingly or not. The government was going to be dismissed or forced to resign against its wishes. How placated would Labor and its supporters have been if the Whitlam government were forced to resign under duress – if Whitlam had effectively been told 'fall on your sword or I'll run you through'? And, in fact, the

---
[26] Kelly and Bramston, op.cit., pp. 222-223.

advantage of incumbency, as it turned, out was ephemeral at best. Fraser won a landslide victory. Again, I stress that Kerr's decision was not justified by the election result. The point I am making here is that whatever fault in this respect, if fault there is, that accrues to Kerr had no bearing on the outcome.

They continue:

> If Kerr had wanted to give Whitlam such an opportunity, he had days and weeks beforehand to raise it. The entire point of Kerr's strategy – as the governor-general kept arguing – was to deny Whitlam that opportunity. Kerr could not have it both ways. He deliberately hid his intentions from Whitlam over the previous month; he encouraged Whitlam to believe his proposed half-Senate election would be approved that morning; he flagged to Fraser what his intentions were at 9.55am; and he had Fraser waiting in another room to be commissioned within minutes.[27]

It was not within Kerr's remit, in the days and weeks beforehand, to offer Whitlam a choice between advising an election and attempting to govern without supply. The initiative rested with Whitlam. He could have advised an election at any time. Kerr could only respond to Whitlam's choice when he made it. Kerr could not advise him. Kelly and Bramston say that Kerr had a duty to warn Whitlam that he might be forced to terminate his commission. But again, we come to the fact that Kerr feared, not without reason, that Whitlam might involve the Palace if Kerr made clear to him that he would not rule out the use of the reserve powers. Whether or not Kerr's fear was justified to the extent that Whitlam would have sought to remove him is neither here nor there – and we have differing views on that from some of the major players. Kerr genuinely believed it was a possibility. Kerr's strategy was not to deny Whitlam the opportunity to go to an election as Prime Minister. It was to negate the possibility that Whitlam would move against him. The strategy, therefore, was to not provoke Whitlam while he was developing his own strategy but to give him the option at the latest possible moment. And that is what he did.

---

[27] Ibid., p. 223.

The claim that Kerr 'encouraged Whitlam to believe his proposed half-Senate election would be approved that morning' is false. Kerr was non-committal when he spoke to Whitlam on the morning of 11 November to arrange the appointment later in the day. He could hardly have been otherwise, because he had not received any formal legal advice from Whitlam, or the Law Officers, as to the legality or practicality of his proposed bank loan scheme.

Here is the Kerr version of the interview in full. It contains the portion in which Kerr claims Whitlam had the opportunity to reconsider his position:

> When Mr Whitlam entered my study he put his hand into his inside coat pocket and I said to him, 'Before you say anything, Prime Minister, I want to say something to you. You have told me this morning on the phone that your talks with the leaders on the other side have failed to produce any change and that things therefore remain the same. You intend to govern without parliamentary supply. He said "yes". I replied that in my view he had to have parliamentary supply to govern and as he had failed to obtain it and was not prepared to go to the people, I had decided to withdraw his commission.'
>
> Things then happened as I had foreseen. Mr Whitlam jumped up, looked urgently around the room, looked at the telephones and said sharply, 'I must get in touch with the Palace at once.' He did not interpret what I had so far said as an actual withdrawal of his commission and indeed it was not. He still had time in which to act, and he made it obvious what his action would be: not to seek to discuss with me any change of attitude, not to seek to go to the people in an election as Prime Minister, but to move at once for my dismissal by so advising the Queen.
>
> The documents, duly signed, were face down on my desk. I now knew there would be no changed advice, only the certainty of constitutional disruption if any time were to elapse. I therefore made my final decision to withdraw his commission. He could still say, 'Let us talk about this. If you are determined to have an election, I would rather go to the people myself as Prime Minister.' Had he done so I would have agreed provided he committed himself by action there and then.

> When he said, 'I must get in touch with the Palace at once', I replied, 'It is too late.' He said, 'Why?' and I told him, 'Because you are no longer Prime Minister. These documents tell you so and why'. I handed them to him and he took them. He did not read them. There was a short silence after which he said, 'I see' and stood up. He made no gesture towards discussion. He turned to the door and I came around my desk towards him. I said, 'I tried to get a compromise and failed.' I waited but still he said nothing. I said, 'We shall both have to live with this.' Mr Whitlam said, 'You certainly will.'[28]

That Kerr's account contains more detail does not, of itself, prove its veracity but, purely from the perspective of human nature it sounds more believable. That both accounts mention a reference to the Palace, both initiated by Whitlam, is curious. Whitlam claims that recourse to the Palace never entered his head, in which case why would he, on his own admission, have raised the matter and why would that be his first and only question of Kerr?

In fact, as Kerr points out in his memoir, Whitlam, at his press conference later in the day, intimated that, had he known of Kerr's proposed use of the dismissal power, he would have contacted the Palace:

> Journalist: Have you been in touch with Buckingham Palace or with London about the actions of the Governor-General?
>
> Whitlam: The Governor-General prevented me from getting in touch with the Queen by just withdrawing the Commission immediately. I was unable to communicate with the Queen, as I would have been entitled to do, if I'd had any warning of the course that he, the Governor-General, was to take.[29]

That exchange, perhaps not surprisingly, is one that Kelly and Bramston apparently judged as 'surplus to requirement' in their case against Kerr.

They say:

---

28 Kerr, op.cit., pp. 358-357.
29 'Gough Whitlam's Post Dismissal Press Conference', 11 November 1975.

Nothing was left to chance. The dismissal of Whitlam was devised in secrecy, in collusion with others, implemented by surprise and planned so that no recourse would undo it. Kerr's claim that he was giving a shocked Whitlam an opportunity to save himself – in the few seconds between being told he was dismissed and accepting the letter – is untenable.[30]

Even accepting that this characterisation is based on Whitlam's version of the interview, are we to believe that a man who was regarded as a formidable, even supreme, Parliamentary performer was so shocked that he could muster no response in his defence other than to ask if the Palace had been consulted? And, of course, nothing was left to chance – nothing within Sir John Kerr's power at any rate. That is as it should be.

I will pass over the commissioning of Fraser and come to the final observations in this chapter:

> When Whitlam left Yarralumla, he went to the Lodge for lunch ... [He] did not contest the legality of the dismissal, even though he thought it was unjustified. The truth is he was unprepared. He had given no prior consideration to managing a dismissal in Kerr's study and, now he had been dismissed, he had no contingency plan. He did not think quickly enough. Whitlam did not return to Parliament House to confer immediately with his staff, cabinet and Senate leadership.[31]

In fact, he returned to his official residence, the Lodge, and summoned the head of the Prime Minister's Department, John Menadue, his office chief, John Mant, ministers Frank Crean, Fred Daly and Kep Enderby as well as the Speaker of the House Gordon Scholes, speechwriter Graham Freudenberg and party secretary David Combe:

> The deposed prime minister drafted by hand a resolution that would form the basis of a censure motion against Fraser. It would declare confidence in the Whitlam government and inform the Queen the House had 'no confidence' in Fraser or any government he led. It was modified slightly and moved by Whitlam that afternoon.

---

30 Kelly and Bramston, op.cit., p. 223.
31 Ibid., pp. 225-226.

> Whitlam's strategy was to carry a 'no confidence' motion in Fraser and seek to be re-instated as prime minister. His hope was to overturn the dismissal within hours. Mant said: 'So we sat around and the focus of conversation was all about getting supply passed and moving a vote of "no confidence". Then Kerr would have to dismiss Fraser.' Mant said they expected that Whitlam could be re-instated later that day. 'There was still at that point the view that Kerr would behave properly,' he said. Mant called it a 'hammer blow' when this hope proved futile. The reality was that most Labor figures knew it was over. Once removed by Kerr, they sensed that there was no prospect of any reversal of their fortunes that day.[32]

This account prompts several observations. Firstly, the idea that the Queen would have had an official interest in the fact that the House had no confidence in Fraser, demonstrates that Whitlam and his brains trust had a fundamentally flawed understanding of our Constitution, in particular the roles of the Queen and the Governor-General. As I have noted elsewhere, the Governor-General is effectively a regent and he, and he (or his delegate) alone, exercises the prerogatives of the Crown. With the exception of the appointment and removal of the Governor-General, the Queen exercises no power in Australia.

Secondly, the reference to Whitlam's team being 'focussed on getting supply passed' is curious, since nothing had changed in this respect except that it would only be passed on the initiative of the new Prime Minister. That, in fact was the whole point of Kerr's actions. So, their strategy appears to have been that once supply was passed, they would rely on their vote of 'no confidence' to pressure Kerr to re-instate Whitlam.

Thirdly, there is a question mark surrounding the actions of John Menadue. As soon as he heard that Fraser was the new Prime Minister, Menadue had no business closeting himself with Whitlam and his team. His place was at his desk awaiting instructions from the new Prime Minister. I will let Sir David Smith tell this story:

> My first call was to John Menadue at his desk in the department, us-

---

[32] Ibid., p. 226.

ing his direct line. As soon as I had told him that the Governor-General had dismissed Whitlam as Prime Minister, Menadue's immediate response was a question – 'He's done it already?' I answered his question and went on to say that Fraser had been sworn in as Prime Minister, that he was now on his way back to his office at Parliament House, and that he wished to see him there right away.

Anyone who was aware of the speculation that was abroad at the time to the effect that Whitlam had been courting his own dismissal as his best prospect of winning the ensuing election with a sympathy vote, will recognise the significance of Menadue's immediate question to me on being told of Whitlam's dismissal. And if Menadue had been thinking about the possibility, and particularly, the timing of a dismissal, so had Whitlam ...

In his autobiography published in 1999, Menadue gives a slightly different account of my telephone call. He confirms that I telephoned him at about 1.45 pm ... However, he makes no mention of me telling him that his new Prime Minister wished to see him right away, which, of course, was the whole purpose of my call.

Menadue's failure to admit that I had told him that his new Prime Minister wished to see him right away is understandable given that his immediate action, according to his own account was to telephone Sir Frederick Wheeler, Secretary to the Treasury, and Alan Cooley, chairman of the Public Service Board, before going to see Whitlam at the Prime Minister's Lodge, apparently in response to a telephone call from Whitlam's driver.

While he was at the Lodge conferring with Whitlam, former Whitlam ministers, and staff from Whitlam's office, Menadue received a telephone call from his secretary to say that Fraser wanted to see him. He told her to say that she could not find him. About 15 minutes later she rang him again, this time with a more urgent message from his new Prime Minister. He finally took his leave of Whitlam and his parliamentary colleagues and staff and went to Parliament House.[33]

It seems clear that Menadue ignored his obligation to immediately place himself at the disposal of the Prime Minister,

---

[33] Smith, op.cit., pp. 252.

and that he participated in discussions designed to thwart his new boss. And yet, as we have seen, Fraser quickly threw Kerr overboard but rewarded Menadue by keeping him on as head of his Department and eventually appointing him Ambassador to Japan.

Although, this is a minor event in the grand scheme of things, it demonstrates the double standards of Kelly and Bramston. They make no criticism whatsoever of Menadue's clear dereliction of duty while giving no credence to Sir Garfield Barwick's assessment that he was unencumbered from giving advice to Kerr.

The final point I wish to make in this segment is in relation to the assertion that most Labor figures sensed that once removed from office by Kerr 'there was no prospect of any reversal of their fortune that day'. In that, as we shall see in the next chapter, they were entirely too fatalistic.

Kelly and Bramston note that Senate Leader, Ken Wriedt, was not invited to the Lodge for these tactical discussions. They see this as a fatal mistake, since it was in the Senate that the final act in this drama would play out. They tell us:

> Fraser knew he had to act quickly to fulfil the terms of his commission. On returning to Parliament House, he informed his staff, spoke to his parliamentary colleagues and ensured steps were in place to pass the budget. Unlike Whitlam, Fraser knew the critical issue was securing supply through the Senate. If he did not secure supply, Kerr's dismissal strategy would have been threatened. At 2.05 pm a press release was issued by Government House. It announced that the governor-general had terminated the prime minister's commission. The statement was delivered to the press gallery boxes at about the same time, producing confusion, shock and uproar.[34]

My only observation on this passage is that the reference to Kerr's 'dismissal strategy' being threatened again misses the crucial point. Kerr's strategy was the securing of supply. As

---

[34] Kelly and Bramston, op.cit., p. 227.

I will argue in the next chapter, Fraser's failure would not necessarily threaten that objective.

They conclude:

> During their subsequent late-night conversations, Kerr told Smith, he had no regrets. 'They left me with no alternative,' he said, blaming Whitlam. Kerr, in fact, had destroyed the sense of unity and impartiality for an incumbent in the office of governor-general.[35]

The only response to the last assertion is that Kerr did not accept that the office of Governor-General was a mere rubber-stamp. The unity Kerr was bound to uphold was constitutional unity, not political unity. Allowing one side of politics to remain in government by flouting the Constitution is hardly calculated to foster national unity.

---

[35] Ibid.

15

Death in the Afternoon: The Second Crisis

This chapter commences:

> The great myth of the dismissal story is that it was done and dusted at lunchtime on 11 November.[1]

Well, you might have believed that if all you had read so far was Kelly's and Bramston's narrative based on the assertion that the dismissal was what it was all about. As we have seen the dismissal was merely a necessary preamble to the main game – the securing of supply. They continue:

> The reality, however, is that Sir John Kerr had a worrying afternoon. His game plan prevailed due to crafty planning and good luck. But it was not guaranteed, and events could have turned ugly and unpredictable. The drama was conducted in public and in private at Yarralumla.[2]

Paradoxically, Kerr was guaranteed to get the result he wanted and yet he was on a hiding to nothing. Let me explain.

If Fraser had failed to secure supply that day, he would have had to return to Government House, eat humble pie and tender his resignation. He would have failed to have met the conditions under which he had been commissioned. Kerr would have had two options. The first of these would be a forced dissolution of the House of Representatives only, under Section 5 of the Constitution. That would have been highly contentious because

---

[1] Kelly and Bramston, *The Dismissal*, p. 229.
[2] Ibid.

it would have allowed the Senate, which had initiated the crisis, to avoid the consequences of its own actions. And it would have gifted Fraser the result he wanted – rewarded him for his own political failure. I'm sure Kerr would have relinquished his pension to avoid this outcome. The only other option he had would be to call for Whitlam and recommission him as Prime Minister. At that point, even if Fraser did not capitulate, enough of his senators would have broken ranks to give Labor supply. That is ultimately what Kerr was seeking, not – repeat not – the dismissal of Whitlam. So, from Kerr's point of view, that would have been mission accomplished.

Either way Kerr knew he would be excoriated by Labor and its supporters and much of the media. But from Kerr's personal perspective, Fraser's failure would have been an infinitely less desirable outcome, because he would have had no recourse other than to himself immediately resign under a cloud. So naturally he would have been worried for a very short time. His fate rested in Fraser's hands. But Fraser delivered by 2.24 pm that afternoon.

This chapter deals with how that played out:

> Having been outmanoeuvred in losing his commission, Whitlam was outmanoeuvred again in his efforts to regain his commission. It was a bad day that exposed his limits as a parliamentarian. Whitlam never grasped the essence of his dilemma – once sacked his only salvation was to deny Fraser supply, one of the conditions of his caretaker commission. Yet Labor voted for the supply bills in the Senate before 2.30 pm, thereby securing Fraser's position.[3]

The first point to note here is that Whitlam was not 'outmanoeuvred' in losing his commission. He lost it because he was unwilling to abandon a position which rendered his commission untenable. And the second point is that, if Whitlam 'never grasped that denying supply' to Fraser 'was his only salvation', then he must have suffered from something of a brain fade. Kerr recounted to the Palace, in a letter of 20 September 1975, a conversation he had with Whitlam during

---

[3] Ibid.

the Papua New Guinea independence celebrations:

> Another point of importance put to me by the Prime Minister in Port Moresby was that if I were, at the height of the crisis, contrary to his advice to decide to terminate his commission at the time when the public service, defence forces, police and so on were not being paid he would have to tell me that Mr Fraser would not be able to get supply either because new legislation would probably be necessary and it would not pass the House of Representatives. He was, however, frank in saying it may be legally possible for Mr Fraser to revive the bills which have passed the House and then have them passed in the Senate. We were, of course, talking on quite friendly terms in all of this.[4]

So, Whitlam was not quite so unaware as the authors would have you believe. They continue:

> The private drama came at Yarralumla that afternoon when Kerr faced a situation he had not anticipated. The House of Representatives had voted 'no confidence' in Fraser, the new prime minister and had called upon the governor-general to commission Whitlam to form a government. The issue for Kerr became: did he continue to exercise the reserve powers in the teeth of this demand or did he succumb to the House of Representatives resolution and reinstate Whitlam? The governor-general was determined to press ahead. But he was anxious to ensure the legal foundation for whatever he did – and herein lay the problem. The law officers began to query whether Kerr should revise his strategy. The political earth was briefly shaken by this new crisis.[5]

This overstates the case somewhat. Firstly, Kerr was quite alert to the possibility, indeed the probability, of a vote of 'no confidence' in Fraser:

> It was certain that there would be a vote of no confidence in [Fraser] in the House. This would in itself entitle him in the circumstances to ask for a dissolution to enable the whole issue to go to the people. It seemed to me unlikely he would be unable to get supply from the Senate and as it turned out, immediately after lunch, he succeeded. This put him in the position of being able to advise a double disso-

---

[4] Kerr, Letter to Martin Charteris, *The Palace Letters*, 20 September 1975, p. 15.
[5] Kelly and Bramston, op.cit., pp. 228-229.

lution, which he did by telephone as soon as supply was passed.[6]

He also wrote:

> There has been discussion of various tactics on the part of the Labor Party which might have resulted in the grant of supply being delayed or prevented. I thought such a development unlikely. Had there been problems they would have had to be faced, as they occurred, by the caretaker Government and perhaps by me.[7]

Kerr was alert to the possibility of Fraser failing to get supply and would no doubt have considered the implications of that, including what action he might be required to take. I'm sure that the scenario I outlined above occurred to him and he would have already decided what his decision would be. Knowing that one way or another supply would be granted that day, Kerr would have been, if not entirely relaxed, still comfortable with his decision of that morning. As I noted earlier, Kelly and Bramston claim that 'events could have turned ugly and unpredictable'. That overstates the case. Things could have turned ugly for Kerr personally but not constitutionally or politically. And they were not unpredictable.

This chapter covers two main issues. The first is the failure of Labor to prevent Fraser from getting supply. The second is a minor controversy surrounding the advice that Kerr sought and received from the law officers concerning his granting of the double dissolution to Fraser later that day.

As far as supply is concerned, this is a fascinating story from which it is difficult to extract a coherent interpretation of events. I will let Kelly and Bramston take up the story:

> The Senate had resumed at 2.00pm in a state of confusion. The government leader, Ken Wriedt, was not told of the dismissal. The Senate president, Justin O'Byrne, was not informed. Nor did the manager of government business, Doug McClelland, know. The opposition senators, led by Reg Withers, did know ... Having blocked the bills for a month, Withers now had to pass supply as

---

[6] Kerr, *Matters for Judgement*, pp. 367-368.
[7] Ibid., p. 368.

fast as possible for the Fraser government. 'How long will you take to get supply?' Fraser asked. 'Just leave it to me, Malcom,' Withers replied.

There was a touch of bravado in this remark. But Labor's ineptitude saw Withers deliver his pledge with astonishing speed. The Labor Senators were exceptionally unlucky.[8]

So, Labor goes from inept to merely unlucky in the space of two sentences. They continue:

News of Whitlam's dismissal swept around Kings Hall just a few minutes after they had walked into the Senate chamber. Veteran journalist, Alan Reid, who had just heard of the dismissal, saw McClelland and called out to him, but McClelland got diverted. He missed the moment when Reid would have told him. There must have been other such stories.[9]

No doubt there were other stories. The Senate is not a sealed chamber – people come and go all the time. And as the authors later reveal:

A note for file prepared by the Senate parliamentary liaison officer, MJ Hanson, dated 20 November 1975, described a pervading sense of 'confusion' in the Senate that afternoon. At 2 pm he had been phoned by his counterpart in the House with the news of the dismissal. He told Wriedt's office. They were to seek clarification from the prime minister's office. Hanson said he went to the Senate chamber and told McClelland. But he could not confirm the news. At about 2.00 pm, Hanson noted, clarification arrived from Whitlam's office that the government had been dismissed. This was conveyed to Wriedt and McClelland. Hanson said: 'At no stage had they received any communication from Mr Whitlam's office advising that Mr Fraser was now Prime Minister and that they were no longer Ministers.'[10]

So, by 2.10 pm both Wriedt and McClelland knew that Fraser was now the Prime Minister. The story continues:

Withers asked Wriedt: 'Are you going to move these bills or will

---

[8] Kelly and Bramston, op.cit., pp. 229-230.
[9] Ibid., p. 230.
[10] Ibid.

we?' Wriedt was in an impossible situation. Having had no contact with Whitlam or anybody from the lunchtime Lodge meeting, he was in ignorance of any agreed strategy and was still shaken by events. At 2.20 pm, Wriedt re-introduced the supply bills. The President of the Senate put the motion. In just four minutes, at 2.24 pm, the bills had passed with the support of both sides of the chamber, on the voices. Labor had voted for supply for Malcolm Fraser. The Senate was then suspended. Labor's only hope of thwarting Fraser had been extinguished.[11]

Try as I might, I cannot detect even a scintilla of bad luck in the foregoing sequence of events. In fact, according to Wriedt's own account to Paul Kelly in 1995:

> Withers told Wriedt the Coalition would pass the bills. Wriedt was astonished. He turned and spoke to his deputy, Don Willisee, and McClelland. 'There's something strange here,' he said. 'I can't understand why they've changed their minds.' Wriedt walked across to speak to John Button. 'There's a story going around that the government's been sacked,' Button told him. 'Don't be bloody ridiculous,' Wriedt said, 'Send someone to check it out.'[12]

So, Wriedt felt there was something strange going on and when offered the most logical explanation for it, his response was to say 'Don't be bloody ridiculous'?

Later, Kelly and Bramston say:

> If Wriedt had confirmation about the dismissal he would have asked the president, O'Byrne, to delay the vote. This would have given Labor time to consider an alternative strategy. But Wriedt doubted this would have made much difference.[13]

As we know, Wriedt did know, before moving to restore the supply bills, that Fraser was the new Prime Minister. And his doubt that delaying the vote would not have made much difference is obviously self-serving, and arguably wrong, as Kelly and Bramston go on to suggest:

---

[11] Ibid.
[12] Ibid.
[13] Ibid., p. 231.

Hanson, however, suggested in a later note, dated 24 November 1975, that all ALP senators knew Whitlam had been dismissed by 2.20 pm: 'Senator Wriedt went ahead with his motion without query from any Senator as to whether or not he should be moving such a motion on behalf of the new "government".'[14]

Hanson's contemporaneous note outlines how Kerr's dismissal action could have been thwarted in the Senate. 'Had Senator Wriedt not proceeded with his motion and had the initiative for passing the bills been left to the Liberal-National Country Party Senators, then it may have been possible for the Labor senators to have delayed passage of the bills until the following day,' Hanson wrote. 'This is because the restoration of the bills would be denied to the Liberal-National Country Party Senators as they would not have had an absolute majority in the Senate (assuming that Senators Steele Hall and [Cleaver] Bunton would have continued to vote with the Labor senators).' In this situation, surmised Hanson, 'The Speaker could then have informed the Governor-General not only of the want of confidence motion in the new prime minister but also the fact that supply had not been granted.'[15]

That seems to me to be a reasonable conclusion, although I am not sure why the tactic could not have continued indefinitely. But, either way, they only needed one day. Kerr would have had to recommission Whitlam if Fraser had not secured supply that day.

Returning to Wriedt, this extract from his entry in the Biographical Dictionary of the Australian Senate, might partly explain his easy acquiescence to passing the supply bills:

> Like some others in the Federal Parliamentary Labor Party, Wriedt was moving away from his earlier enthusiastic opinion of the Prime Minister, concerned at his leader's increasing failure to consult. In September 1974 Whitlam had given Wriedt no foreknowledge of

---

[14] Ibid.
[15] Ibid., p. 232.

the decision to devalue the currency. On 10 February 1975, following the retirement of Lionel Murphy, Wriedt was elected Leader of the Government in the Senate, with the Prime Minister's full support, defeating John Wheeldon. When Connor was removed as Minister for Minerals and Energy on 14 October, Wriedt took over the portfolio. When the Opposition in the Senate refused supply on 16 October, and the appropriation bills went back and forth between the two houses, Wriedt believed that Whitlam should have gone to the polls rather than engage in a stand-off. He was troubled by the prospect of the Government's financing breaking down if the crisis continued for much longer.[16] (emphases added)

As far as lack of consultation is concerned, Wriedt could not have cited a better example than what happened that day. Perhaps Whitlam saw his best opportunity of regaining his position to be by allowing supply to go through and then leveraging the constitutional weight of the vote of 'no confidence' to force Kerr to re-instate him. If this sounds far-fetched, is it any more so than the idea that the entire Labor machine was as totally inept as Kelly and Bramston have painted them? After all, we have that curious quote, covered in Chapter Fourteen, by Whitlam's secretary John Mant, regarding the conference at the Lodge earlier that day:

> So we sat around and the focus of conversation was all about getting supply passed and moving a vote of 'no confidence'.[17]

That – the vote of 'no confidence' – is the subject we now turn to:

> The trigger for the second crisis was the House 'no confidence' resolution in Fraser as prime minister. When the House resumed at 2 pm there was no mention of dismissal. Fraser did not inform the House that he had been commissioned as prime minister until 2.34pm, another astute move. By that time he had obtained supply in the Senate. The House was engulfed in shock and uproar. In a note for file dated 20 November, the House parliamentary liaison officer, AE Dyster, said there was 'disbelief of all "government"

---

[16] Roe M, 'Wriedt, Kenneth Shaw (1927–2010) Senator for Tasmania, 1968–80 (Australian Labor Party)', *The Biographical Dictionary of the Australian Senate*, 2010, https://biography.senate.gov.au/wriedt-kenneth-shaw/
[17] Kelly and Bramston, op.cit., p. 226.

members especially ministers' at news of the dismissal.[18]

Well not *all* government members and ministers would have expressed disbelief. Crean, Enderby and Daly already knew since they had been at the lunchtime conference at the Lodge. And Mr Speaker Scholes knew because he was also at the conference where they discussed 'getting supply passed and moving a vote of no confidence'. Immediately upon resumption, he recognised Mr Frank Crean, who held the floor for almost 34 minutes while he spoke on a censure motion against Fraser. If it was an *astute move* on Fraser's part – which offered him some tactical advantage – not to mention the dismissal, rather than just that he did not have an opportunity to do so, it was well within Whitlam's power to thwart it. He was in the Chamber.

> Fraser moved that the House adjourn and saw his motion defeated sixty-four to fifty-three. The Leader of the House, Fred Daly, then moved a suspension of standing orders to allow Whitlam to move a motion. That was carried sixty-four to fifty-three. Whitlam then moved a motion of 'no confidence' in the prime minister and demanded the governor-general recommission him. The Speaker, Gordon Scholes, announced he would convey the message of the House to the governor-general as soon as possible. The House was suspended at 3.15 until 5.30.

> Fraser had lost every division. These events demonstrated it was a gross violation of responsible government for a minority leader to have been made prime minister on the condition that he obtain supply.

The claim immediately above is a specious argument. A *non-sequitur*. 'Responsible government' is a nebulous term. It can be recruited, in various guises, to support whatever argument you wish to make. The Australian Parliament website defines it as:

> Responsible Government is the term used to describe a political system where the executive government, the Cabinet and Ministry,

---

[18] Ibid., p. 233.

is drawn from, and accountable to, the legislative branch.[19]

As we have seen, Barwick defined the legislative branch as comprising both the House of Representatives and the Senate and, indeed, for the purposes of 'responsible government', that must be so, because Ministers sit in both Houses. The events demonstrated only that Labor, understandably so, disagreed with Kerr's actions. Kelly and Bramston continue: "Nor was it necessarily achievable."

And yet it was achieved with ease.

> Kerr displayed contempt for the authority of the House of Representatives upon which majority democratic government in Australia depends.

Majority democratic government (an artificial term never heard before, as far as I am aware) in Australia depends as much on a government's ability to govern according to the Constitution as it does to numbers in the House of Representatives.

> There was no justification for him to commission a minority leader without exhausting every other option.[20]

We have heard of these other options from various sources, (Heseltine, Cutler etc) but no-one has ever spelled out what they might have been. Further delay? Both the tightness of the election timetable and the fact that Whitlam chose to present untenable advice on that very day precluded that option. I won't bother to recap the 'warn Whitlam' argument.

Meanwhile, Fraser had his staff fast track the supply bills to have them ready to present to the Governor-General that afternoon. And rather than rely on the Speaker to present his case, Whitlam intervened personally:

> An anxious governor-general, watching events unfold from Yarralumla, said he now took an important call – from the deposed prime minister. Kerr documented the call in a note for his papers

---

[19] 'Responsible Government', https://australianpolitics.com/democracy/key-terms/responsible-government
[20] Kelly and Bramston, op.cit., p. 234.

and in his memoirs. Supply had been granted and the House of Representatives had voted against Fraser.

> Kerr said: 'He [Whitlam] said that as supply had been granted I should terminate the prime minister's commission and recommission him. He wanted to attend upon me to put this point of view.' According to Kerr. Whitlam said, 'You saw Fraser before, so I suppose you will see me.' Kerr told Whitlam he would have to secure Fraser's approval for such a meeting. The tables had turned: 'I said I would speak to him and let Mr Whitlam know the position.' This was Kerr stalling Whitlam until the parliament was dissolved and it was too late to consider any alternate action. It was the method used with Scholes. A second meeting between Kerr and Whitlam on 11 November never took place. Whitlam never spoke to Kerr again.
>
> Whitlam later denied making the call. Yet Kerr made a note including details of the conversation. Whitlam's principal private secretary, John Mant, said it was entirely plausible that Whitlam rang. 'He could well have,' Mant said. 'It's a possibility, yes.'[21]

This incident is neither here nor there in the grand scheme of things. I include it merely to show that just because Whitlam denied something, doesn't mean it didn't happen. We now come to the advice that Kerr sought and received on the matter of the double dissolution.

Before presenting Kerr's version of events, I will cover the Kelly and Bramston version:

> The head of the Attorney-General's Department, a shocked and unhappy Clarrie Harders, arrived at Fraser's office at 3.45 pm. Fraser took Harders into an adjoining room and Harders made a note of their discussion: 'He [Fraser] said that it was possible that the Governor-General would wish to have advice regarding the resolution that had been adopted by the House of Representatives earlier in the afternoon expressing want of confidence in Mr Fraser.
>
> In short, Kerr had to negotiate his way around the House resolution. He had not anticipated the 'no confidence' motion against Fraser. We know that is not true (see above).

---

[21] Ibid., p. 235.

Fraser understood that Kerr needed to ensure a firm legal foundation for everything he was about to do. Fraser now said he wanted Harders to accompany him to Government House. Harders said that Solicitor-General Maurice Byers should come with them. But there wasn't sufficient time ...

In his note Harders recalled his discussion with Fraser en route: 'I spoke to the prime minister about the point he had raised with me. I said that it appeared that the Governor-General had acted on the basis that he had a reserve power, that the Governor-General had previously exercised a discretion that he regarded as residing in him and that the question whether he should change his decision in the light of the resolution adopted that afternoon by the House of Representatives was one for the Governor-General to consider, in the exercise of his discretion.'

In short, Harders was telling Fraser the transition of power was not a done deal. He was saying Kerr had to consider whether he 'should change his decision' given the 'no confidence' resolution in the House. Kerr, of course, had not the slightest intention of changing his decision. But he had to be careful.[22]

Harders' comment to Fraser seems to be little more than bureaucratic obfuscation.

Kerr says that he received a commitment from Fraser that, after he had obtained supply, he would recommend a double dissolution rather than a dissolution of the House of Representative. When he was discussing with Fraser the terms of his appointment, Kerr says:

> ... I told Mr Fraser that I assumed he would not get the confidence of the House and that he would advise an election. I pointed out that this would involve a dissolution and the question was whether it would be a dissolution of the House only or a double dissolution. He said he was prepared to advise a double dissolution.
>
> I next made the point that in my understanding the Parliament was deadlocked not only on supply but on twenty-one bills which the previous Government had passed and his parties had rejected in the

---

[22] Ibid., pp. 235-236.

Senate. It seemed to me that all deadlocks should be dealt with and go to the people ... Mr Fraser agreed that what I proposed was fair. He said he would immediately get legal advice and would, he felt sure, have the proper legal basis for advising a double dissolution both to resolve the twenty-one deadlocks and also to put to the people the issue involved in the dismissal and dissolution, as well as all the other general issues on which in his opinion the people should make their judgement. I asked him to give a formal undertaking to advise a double dissolution.

My fundamental reason for making this a condition was that I believed all outstanding deadlocks should go to the people, and that if Mr Whitlam won the election for the House and had the appropriate majority in both Houses or for a joint sitting thereafter, he should be immediately entitled, after the forced dissolution, to put his Bills through if he wanted to.[23]

That is eminently sensible and fair, but there was an element of practicality in Kerr's requirement. He knew Fraser would attract a vote of no confidence. But it seems to me, admittedly a non-lawyer, that would not of itself entitle Fraser to advise a dissolution. There would be two options open to Fraser, having passed supply but subject to a no-confidence motion: to tender his resignation or to advise an election. If there were a viable alternative government – as there was in this case – it would be highly contentious, if not untenable, for the Governor-General to send just the House of Representatives back to the people. But he could not engineer a situation in which, having appointed Fraser on the basis that he would approve supply, he would then be forced to abandon him. Section 57 resolved this dilemma. Section 57, under which the proposed double dissolution would be proclaimed, clearly gives the Governor-General discretion. It says:

> ... the Governor-General may dissolve the Senate and the House of Representatives simultaneously.

In these circumstances, the only constraint on the Governor-General was that the bills which would be the subject of the

---

[23] Kerr, op.cit., pp. 365-366.

dissolution satisfied the conditions of Section 57. That is the advice that Kerr was seeking. And that is the advice he got from Harders and Byers. When Fraser and Harders met Kerr:

> Kerr's first task was to give royal assent to the supply bills. He then turned his attention to the dissolution of both houses. ... Fraser advised Kerr the bills satisfied the constitutional requirements for a double dissolution election. In his note, however, Harders said he raised the consequences of the House of Representatives resolution.
>
> 'I stated the view that I had put to the Prime Minister during the journey to Government House,' Harders said. How hard did he press Kerr? In his note Harders did not provide any details of the words he actually used in cautioning the governor-general at such a momentous meeting. Harders said he and Byers had the same view. But Kerr's account is different and detailed.[24]

Let's look at Kerr's account:

> The proclamation dissolving the two Houses was then presented to me. It listed the twenty-one Bills which I was told satisfied the conditions of section 57. Mr Fraser told me that upon legal advice these Bills did satisfy section 57. Mr Harders repeated this advice to me and also said that in law I could act under section 57 on this oral advice which I had been given by the Prime Minister and him. I agreed with this. He said that it would be confirmed in writing as soon as possible but I need not wait for written confirmation. It was on the next day confirmed in writing.
>
> My Official Secretary was present during this conversation and he and I, as well as Mr Fraser, believed that Mr Harders had said that Mr Byers agreed with him not only about the validity of my continuing to carry out, under the reserve power, the 'forced dissolution' procedure, but also as to the availability of the twenty-one bills to support a double dissolution.
>
> However, both Mr Harders and Mr Byers have since said that it was only on the first point about the continued use of the reserve power that Mr Harders had My Byers' agreement, the latter feeling the need to check the position as to the Bills. He did so and I received

---

[24] Kelly and Bramston, op.cit., p. 237.

the confirmatory advice the next day. The facts are that Mr Harders brought out, when he came with the Prime Minister, a Proclamation for a double dissolution based on the twenty-one Bills and he as Secretary of the Department advised Mr Fraser in my presence that all satisfied the requirements of Section 57 of the Constitution. We all thought at the time that Mr Byers concurred at that time as he did the next day ...

I then referred to my conversation with Mr Whitlam after the no-confidence vote, to the resolution of the House and to Mr Scholes' desire to see me. I asked whether Mr Byers and Mr Harders saw any legal or constitutional problems, arising from the passing of supply in the Senate and the resolution of the House, standing in the way of my carrying out the decision I had made before lunch. Mr Harders said he had spoken to Mr Byers and both of them were of the view that, as I had exercised a reserve power in the morning, I could complete its exercise and could accept the advice of the Prime Minister in favour of a double dissolution. I could in the existing circumstances dissolve both Houses. I was in effect being told that I did have a reserve power to exercise which would justify a dissolution.

If I had no power to do what I had done in dismissing the previous government it would have been the duty of Mr Byers and Mr Harders to advise the Prime Minister and me that what I had done before lunch was invalid and, in those circumstances, as supply had been granted and Mr Whitlam had the confidence of the House, my duty would have been to undo my invalid act, withdraw Mr Fraser's commission and send for Mr Whitlam. This they did not do.[25]

Kelly and Bramston say:

This is pure sophistry: even if Harders and Byers had said this, Kerr would have proceeded anyway. His memoirs make plain he was not asking the law officers whether they agreed with his decision – but merely for their views about the validity of the powers he was exercising.

Interviewed later Harders said: 'I didn't doubt that the Governor-General had such a discretion. The problem was the way it was

---

[25] Kerr, op.cit., pp. 369-371.

done.' But Kerr was not interested in any Harders view about the way it was done. He cared only for the legal advice on the powers.[26]

No, it is not sophistry. Whether or not, in their estimation, Kerr would have proceeded anyway would not excuse the law officers from expressing their opinion for the record. What Kerr wanted was advice that the Prime Minister, from whom he was accepting advice for a double dissolution, was a person validly in a position to offer such advice. All that Kerr needed was their opinion that he had appointed Fraser under a discretion that he did, in fact, possess. Harders confirmed that. No doubt Kerr felt that the advice he received from Barwick was sound, but having the law officers agree, at least on the point of the existence of the power, added further support for his position. It is not unnatural that he would want this. Indeed, it was incumbent upon him, for the sake of his office, to dot every 'i' and cross every 't' that he could.

They continue:

> At 4 pm Kerr signed the proclamation dissolving both houses of parliament on the basis of the twenty-one bills ... Any idea that Kerr at that time would have recommissioned Whitlam was nonsense. Whitlam's argument to this effect is unconvincing. That would have constituted a betrayal of Fraser. Having commissioned Fraser as a caretaker prime minister subject to obtaining supply and advising an election, Kerr could not then turn around and dismiss Fraser after he had fulfilled the terms of his commission as set down by Kerr. The Senate had passed supply only because Fraser was prime minister. The House vote had demonstrated what Kerr had known – that Whitlam had its confidence. Kerr knew he was commissioning Fraser as a minority prime minister to advise an election. If Kerr had reversed his position, he would have had no option but to resign. No governor-general could betray two prime ministers on the same day and still survive.[27]

In other words, the dismissal of Whitlam, commissioning of Fraser and the double dissolution were a 'package deal'. As Kerr said: 'Mr Harders said he had spoken to Mr Byers

---

[26] Kelly and Bramston, op.cit., p. 238.
[27] Ibid., pp. 238-239.

and both of them were of the view that, as I had exercised a reserve power in the morning, I could complete its exercise and could accept the advice of the Prime Minister in favour of a double dissolution.' Once Kerr invoked the reserve powers with a particular outcome in mind, he would not, as a matter of logic anyway, be constrained from executing every step of the process.

A later controversy arose when Byers' draft opinion became public and was misinterpreted. Kelly and Bramston point out that:

> The report was highly misleading and gave the impression that Byers advised the powers did not exist. Kerr was immediately concerned. At his initiative the attorney-general in the caretaker government, Senator Ivor Greenwood, convened a meeting on Monday 17 November ... it involved Kerr, Greenwood, Harders and Byers. The focus was the legal foundation for Kerr's action and, beyond that, his reputation and historical standing.
>
> That afternoon Harders told Kerr his termination of Whitlam's government had not been justified. Accounts of this meeting indicate it was highly charged.
>
> Kerr's notes suggest his motive: he wanted to clarify that Harders and Byers accepted the legal basis for the dismissal, and to 'lock' them into his action, as far as possible. But with the deed a week old, Harders and Byers were firm: they accepted the legality but not the justification for the dismissal.[28]

That's that then. They confirmed the advice that Kerr believed they had tendered on 11 November.

Following this there is a lengthy examination of the arguments between the protagonists as to the justification of the dismissal. But as the opinion of the law officers on this question is irrelevant, I will not trouble to look at this minor controversy. Harders was a bureaucrat, and I do not mean this in any pejorative sense. But his natural inclination would be to support the *status quo* and to abhor any radical action.

---

[28] Ibid., p. 241.

On 12 November, the Speaker of the House, Gordon Scholes, wrote to the Queen asking her to restore Whitlam to the Prime Ministership:

> It was an understandable but extremely embarrassing letter. Scholes tried to draw the Queen into the crisis. 'I wrote to the Queen to tell her she should reconsider the action of the Governor-General,' Scholes recalled in 2015. 'We were trying very clearly to reverse the decision. We wanted her to act.' Scholes said there was a belief that the Queen could 'override' a governor-general. This was soon proven to be nonsense.[29]

That a senior Parliamentarian held this view is astonishing and just adds weight to Kerr's reluctance to telegraph his intentions until the last possible moment. If Labor were prepared to 'draw the Queen into the crisis' after it was too late to do anything, why would they not do the same before the event, had they been forewarned, at a time when they could effect the recall of the Governor-General. It is a nonsense to suggest they would not have. The Palace politely rejected Scholes' request.

Whitlam also wrote to the Palace on 16 December, after the election:

> 'In no way,' he argued, 'do the elections resolve the legal and constitutional questions raised by the conduct of the Crown's representative on and before 11 November. Nor could the election result of itself legitimize that conduct.' Whitlam's concern was 'the manner in which the Governor-General chose to invoke and exercise the reserve powers' which have 'put in jeopardy the future of the Crown in Australia.' He said confidence in the monarchy was undermined by 'any intervention, or appearance of intervention, on behalf of the contending political parties'. Whitlam detailed what he believed were Kerr's 'political decisions' to assist the Coalition parties. His accusation was that Kerr's actions 'have been such as to call into question on the part of many millions of Australians, particularly the younger majority, not merely the limits of the powers of the Crown, but its whole future role in Australia.[30]

---

[29] Ibid., p. 245.
[30] Ibid., p. 246.

Since Whitlam was the principal aggrieved party, we can expect him to have that view. But it was one not, by any means, universally shared. And as we have seen, apart from personal attacks on Sir John Kerr, the strength of the Monarchy was unaffected, even in the immediate aftermath of November 1975. It remains strong today, and if its popularity has waned somewhat, that is not due to Sir John Kerr. Whitlam's letter did not elicit the response he might have hoped:

> On 12 January 1976, Whitlam received a reply from Charteris. He said the Queen had read the letter, thanked him for it and 'taken note' of the views. 'I am sure you will neither wish nor expect me to enter into argument about the constitutional propriety of Sir John Kerr's actions,' Charteris wrote. 'I hope, however, you will allow me to make one comment on what you say. It is this. The constitutional role of the Governor-General and his reserve powers stem not from his position as the Queen's personal representative, to which he is appointed on the advice of the Prime Minister, but rather from what is written in the Constitution Act as applicable constitutionally. This point has, I think, particular relevance to the position of the Queen as Queen of Australia.' The Palace was washing its hands of the dismissal.[31]

The Palace was not washing its hands of the dismissal. The point Charteris was making was that it never had any role to play in the first place. The roles of the Queen and the Governor-General are defined in the Australian Constitution. As I have argued, the Governor-General is analogous to a Regent, and the Queen herself does not have any power that she may exercise in Australia other than to appoint and dismiss the Governor-General on the advice of the Prime Minister. In particular, the Queen could not suggest, let alone demand, any changes to either the wording or the working of our Constitution. She is literally a figurehead. The Governor-General is not.

As to Whitlam's strategy, it seems to me that allowing supply to be passed may well not have been a misstep, but a deliberate decision linked to a belief that, once supply had been passed, Kerr, confronted with the vote of 'no confidence', would have

---

[31] Ibid., p. 247.

no choice but to reinstate him. This was wishful thinking. The most obvious ploy would have been to deny Fraser supply in the hope that Kerr, again confronted with a vote of 'no confidence', would withdraw his commission and that, having failed, the Coalition would then fold and pass supply. That Whitlam did not choose this option is a mystery.

Conclusion

The Dismissal continues with chapters on the British View (irrelevant), The Liberal and Labor Views (partisan) and the CIA Myth (debunked, not least by Paul Kelly). I don't intend to examine them in detail, but I will include a couple of relevant points in this Conclusion.

The back cover of *The Dismissal* tells the reader:

> Forty years on, the dismissal remains one of the most damaging and controversial events in Australian politics. This ground-breaking book by two of our leading journalists provides a startling reinterpretation of events. It tells the story of the clash between extraordinary personalities: two political giants – Gough Whitlam and Malcolm Fraser – and an ambitious and calculating governor-general, Sir John Kerr.
>
> Drawing on a range of new sources, some of which have never before been made public – including hundreds of pages from Kerr's archives – this remarkable account is dispassionate in its analysis, vivid in its narrative and brutal in its conclusions. It exposes the true motivations, the extent of the deceit and the scale of the collusion.

Almost everything in the above blurb is wrong. Forty years on from the events of 1975 almost nobody cares about it any longer. It was controversial at the time but any damage it caused to our nation is indiscernible to any but a few diehard ideologues. And that is the real lesson we should take from the 'dismissal'. Furthermore, neither Whitlam nor Fraser were political giants. Whitlam's prime ministership lasted three years, was an unmitigated disaster and revealed him as merely a showman. Fraser's three terms in office, largely built upon the reputational damage Whitlam inflicted on Labor, were undistinguished. He was followed by two figures, Hawke and Howard, both of whom could more justly be described as political giants. Kerr may have been ambitious and calculating. But the first is a virtue we encourage in our children and the second is just a pejorative way in which to say that Kerr acted deliberately and not reactively. In the hands of this pair, 'saintly' could be made to sound derogatory. And it is notable that 'being ambitious' does not appear in the rap sheets of either Whitlam or Fraser, which causes one to wonder – by what serendipitous chance did they both become Prime Minister? *The Dismissal* is certainly vivid in its narrative and brutal in its conclusions, but it is by no means dispassionate, as I hope I have demonstrated.

My book is not a hagiography, and I accept that Sir John Kerr made some mistakes. But as his self-appointed 'defence counsel', I did not see it necessary to dwell on them. Kerr kept copious notes and documentation, and so all his thoughts and concerns have been laid bare for Kelly and Bramston, including, as they say, 'hundreds of pages from Kerr's archives'. They have made good use of them, but it is telling that neither Whitlam nor Fraser left behind such detailed personal documentation that might have provided more insight into their motivations. That puts Kerr at a distinct disadvantage in this show trial. Author Gerard Henderson also makes this point:

> Paul Kelly and Troy Bramston have written a scholarly book. But they overlook the fact that, according to the extant evidence, only John Kerr and Garfield Barwick left contemporaneous notes about their involvement in The Dismissal. Kelly/Bramston rely on the recall of Fraser and Withers and Liberal MP Vic Garland along with that of Fraser staffers David Kemp and Dale Budd. All this group, living or dead, left memories but not contemporaneous notes. The same appears to be the case with respect to Sir Anthony Mason. Memory is a very unreliable historical tool.[1]

To summarise, if you strip away the legion of *ad hominem* attacks and the peripheral issues (such as taking advice from Barwick and Mason) only one substantive criticism can be made of Sir John Kerr – that he failed to warn Whitlam that he risked dismissal and that this failure encouraged Whitlam to remain obdurate. Kerr effectively warned Whitlam by giving

---

[1] G. Henderson, 'Evidence, Memory and the Dismissal', *The Sydney Institute*, 2 February 2016.

Conclusion

him an opportunity to back down at the last minute. Given that both Fraser and Whitlam had been engaged in a war of brinkmanship, it is beyond belief that Whitlam would not have had the nous to seize this opportunity to go to the election as Prime Minister had he been so inclined. As to Kerr's failure to warn Whitlam earlier, we have evidence that Kerr (encouraged by Whitlam himself) believed that had he done so Whitlam would have moved to have him recalled. Kelly and Bramston downplay this defence on the grounds that it is doubtful Whitlam would have 'called the Palace'. But they cannot deny it was a possibility. Kerr had to balance the odds (however slim) that it might happen, against the almost incalculable harm, discussed in Chapter Nine, had it occurred. And Whitlam was certainly aware he risked being dismissed.

All the other charges against Kerr are subjective judgements which, in hindsight, are easy to make by people who did not have the responsibility that he had and the pressure under which he was operating. Kerr addresses all these criticisms in *Matters for Judgement*, as do I in earlier chapters.

The fact is that many prominent people supported Sir John Kerr's decision, but they don't get much of a run in *The Dismissal*.

Dr David Butler, a distinguished British political scientist wrote:

> In retrospect various alternative courses of action have been prescribed for the Governor-General. The most obvious is that on November 11, he should have done nothing beyond acceding to Mr Whitlam's request for a half-Senate election on December 13. But it was very doubtful whether that election would have by itself solved the crisis, and by December 13 Supply would have run out if the Senate remained obdurate. Of course, many argue that the Senate would not have remained obdurate – a weakening on the part of only one of the four or five Liberal senators who had indicated reluctance over the blocking of Supply would have ruined the Opposition's strategy. Yet the Governor-General could hardly gamble on such a weakening. If the Opposition senators stood firm, then

Supply would have run out by early December.²

Or to put it more prosaically, if a parent sees two children playing some dangerous game of chicken, they will step in before the harm is done. Butler continues:

> Many have contended that the Governor-General should, after pressing Mr Whitlam harder to call the election himself, have given him time to consult his colleagues about the ultimatum. But that ignores the possibility that Mr Whitlam would instantly have asked the Queen to replace the Governor-General with a more complaisant appointee. Such a request would have put the Queen in an impossible dilemma: acceptance, or refusal, or even delay in answering, would only have heightened the crisis.³

We have seen that both Whitlam and the Speaker, Gordon Scholes, did approach the Palace *post hoc* suggesting that Whitlam should be re-instated. Can we doubt that they would have done the same in order to prevent the dismissal in the first place, had they been given any inkling?

Canadian Senator Eugene Forsey was an eminent constitutional scholar with an international reputation as an expert in the Westminster system. He wrote the epilogue to Kerr's *Matter's for Judgement*:

> Never for a moment did I doubt the correctness of the action of Sir John Kerr. For the life of me, I could not see, and still cannot see, what else he could have done in the circumstances. The constitutional right of the Senate to refuse, or defer, supply, seems to me incontestable. Perhaps it should never have been given that right. But it was; and the result of its exercise of that right, and of Mr Whitlam's response to that exercise, was that, but for Sir John's action, the Government of Australia would have been left for some months with no funds to meet some 40 per cent of its expenses, except by the use of measures of very doubtful legal validity and even more doubtful effectiveness.
>
> The duty of a Prime Minister denied supply by an Upper House is either to resign, or to advise a dissolution of the Lower House. Mr

---

² Kerr, *Matters for Judgement*, p. 392.
³ Ibid., p. 393.

Whitlam declined to do either.[4]

Admittedly, the two foregoing opinions are just that. They carry no more weight than the contrary opinions of other experts. But they do carry equal weight. Yet these, and other similar opinions, are conspicuous by their absence from *The Dismissal*. That hardly suggests a dispassionate or balanced coverage.

Kelly and Bramston note in their Epilogue:

> Until his death, in March 1991, Kerr looked for reassurance, just as he did during the 1975 crisis. The authors have had access to hundreds of pages of Kerr's documents, memos, diaries and handwritten notes available from the National Archives. They reveal a man forever obsessed about the dismissal and its justification.[5]

Obsessed about the dismissal? Maybe, but, in this respect, he was not unlike Kelly who has written four books and numerous essays on the subject. Kerr's quest for vindication is probably in direct proportion to the vilification heaped upon him by the likes of Kelly and Bramston.

Sir David Smith in his own book, *Head of State*, laments the state of journalism, certainly as it applies to November 1975:

> The late Philip Graham, former publisher of Newsweek and the Washington Post, once said that good journalism should aim to be 'the first rough draft of history'.[6]

He goes on to detail three examples published shortly after the event which fall well short of this lofty aim. I am sure he would be mightily discouraged to see that things have not improved in the meantime. If *The Dismissal* represents a second draft of history, journalism still has a long way to go to deliver justice to Sir John Kerr and more importantly to the people of Australia.

We should be able to agree to disagree on whether or not Kerr made some misjudgements without vilifying him personally. Professor Geoffrey Sawyer – who believed that Kerr had acted

---

[4] Ibid., pp. 440-441.
[5] Kelly and Bramston, *The Dismissal*, p. 296.
[6] Smith, *Head of State*, p. 286.

prematurely and should not have consulted Barwick –quoted in the *Canberra Times* said that:

> 'the Governor-General, unlike the Queen or any State Governors, operated in terrible isolation' and it was unreasonable to criticize him personally.[7]

But I will leave the last word on this subject to former Treasurer, Opposition Leader and Governor-General, Bill Hayden, quoted, to the credit of the authors, in *The Dismissal*:

> In retrospect, Hayden thought Kerr deserved to be 'looked upon in a kinder and less subjective light'. Hayden wrote: 'There may have been weaknesses in his character and defects in his judgement, which is to say he was human, but I have no evidence that his motives were sinister. I believe John Kerr was a good man who, at worst, erred on this occasion; it would be a mark of maturity if more of us would acknowledge that he was far from an evil man.' It is an assessment remarkable for its generosity.[8]

Bravo Bill Hayden, whose judgement – as one who was directly affected by Kerr's decision – deserves more than to be dismissed as merely 'remarkably generous'.

Which brings me to my final point – the reserve powers themselves. Kelly and Bramston reveal a conversation that Kerr had with Sir Morrice James, the British High Commissioner to Australia, a week after the election:

> 'Sir J Kerr thought it no bad thing that the public in Australia (and perhaps those in other monarchical Commonwealth, not excluding Britain) should have been reminded that the crown possessed reserve powers.,' James wrote. The use of such extraordinary powers, Kerr argued, was a good thing and should be seen throughout the Commonwealth as a sign of the Crown's authority.
>
> Kerr was undeterred by the reaction to his exercise of the dismissal power as the Queen's representative. Indeed he was recommending that voters need 'a reminder' that the powers exist and he suggested

---

[7] G Sawyer, 'Professor Sawyer Criticizes Sir John's Actions', *The Canberra Times*, 20 November 1975.
[8] Kelly and Bramston, op.cit., p. 285.

Conclusion

> they be used perhaps 'every twenty-five or fifty years'. Invoking the royal prerogative would reinforce the point that 'the Crown's functions were not merely titular or ceremonial' ... Here was Kerr, one month after the dismissal, arguing to British government representatives that each generation needed reminding about these unique powers. It seemed more than slightly mad.[9]

It was probably somewhat indiscreet for Kerr for to have expressed this thought to the British High Commissioner, but I suspect it was no more than a throwaway line – a touch of defiant bravado in the face of the vitriolic criticism he was enduring. Nonetheless, in essence, he was correct. The Crown, in the person of the Governor-General, does have certain prerogatives and they are powerful. And for this reason, as Kerr himself acknowledged, they should only be used rarely, viz., in extreme circumstances. And therein lies a problem. The infrequency of their use renders them vulnerable to the claim or perception that they no longer exist. This argument was invoked by some against Kerr, despite the fact that Sir Philip Game had dismissed Jack Lang a mere forty odd years earlier. Now, I am not suggesting that a reserve power should be dusted off and taken for a spin every twenty-five or fifty years, as Kerr is alleged to have said. I have not been able to access that letter and we have only fragments of a conversation from which it is difficult to extract the full context and any nuances that might be inferred. For example, did Kerr really suggest that they be used perhaps 'every twenty-five or fifty years'? Only part of that claim is in quotation marks, so it is a paraphrase – and we have already seen the liberties Kelly and Bramston take with paraphrasing. Did Kelly and Bramston paraphrase Kerr accurately or fairly? It is possible that what Kerr meant was, that it would be *no bad thing* if the powers were called upon every twenty-five or fifty years, assuming their use was justified, but that it would indicate the system was broken if they were called upon more often than that. And I would agree with that proposition.

But beyond that, what those of us who believe that the reserve

---

[9] Ibid, p. 252.

powers are a real and valuable feature of the Westminster system of government, can do is to rebut the argument that these powers, although they undoubtedly exist, should never be used. Which is essentially what Kelly and Bramston argue. And, as I have argued earlier, one of the ways in which they are prosecuting this campaign is by vilifying Sir John Kerr so thoroughly that future Governors-General will shrink from employing the reserve powers even though the circumstances may justify such action. In support of this point I return to their Introduction:

> [This story] is a reminder that institutions cannot be abused and constitutional powers cannot be pushed to their limits. Political leaders must recognise this and governors-general must live with the obligation to rectify Sir John Kerr's legacy.[10]

In other words, the reserve powers are to be relegated to history in some bizarre attempt to symbolically undo the events of November 1975. A sort of Vice-Regal hairshirt.

Why are these powers important? I cannot outline a particular set of circumstances in which their use may be called upon. But I do look at recent developments, such as the increasing influence of supra-national organizations that threaten national sovereignty. This suggests to me that we should not lightly abandon one of the last lines of defence in our constitutional democracy. The Westminster system is not a 'one size fits' all model. We are a federation with a bi-cameral parliament and a written constitution. What applies in Britain does not necessarily apply here.

At the beginning of this book, I stated that the Australian Constitution is largely a written constitution. I pointed out that we also inherited some conventions from Britain. But there is another unwritten element to our Constitution that is fundamental to everything. And that is the collection of our rights as individuals. The right to freedom of religion, to free speech, to free association, to equality before the law and so on. These are not explicit as they are in the US Constitution

---

[10] Ibid., p. xv.

by virtue of its Bill of Rights. We do not get our individual human rights from UN covenants. We inherited them from the common law of Britain and they are therefore not beyond the reach of Parliaments, which increasingly seem to embrace a predominantly collectivist view of society.

At the time of writing, a left-wing activist government, led by a supposedly charismatic prime minister, is stealthily and unaccountably remaking the unwritten constitution of New Zealand. New Zealand citizens are being presented with *fait accompli* legislative and administrative decisions that they never voted for. This is being done on the specious and incorrect basis that the Treaty of Waitangi, which forms the basis of New Zealand's nationhood, was not actually a cession of sovereignty on the part of the warring Maori tribes, but a 'partnership agreement'. The same logic they are using is also being employed by activists here to push the idea of a separate Aboriginal sovereignty and to achieve the same break-up of Australia as is already well advanced in New Zealand.

And the actions of various State premiers in accreting to themselves, under the guise of 'keeping us safe', pandemic powers that put them above the scrutiny of their own parliaments is also a cause for concern. As are the actions of Canadian Prime Minister Trudeau in invoking anti-terrorism measures against legitimate and peaceful anti-vaccine mandate protestors. If it can happen in Canada of all places, why should it not happen here?

We can no longer trust a modern High Court to disallow legislation that offends against fundamental human rights, constitutional provisions or even basic common sense. One protection we have is the reserve power of the Governor-General to refuse assent to a Bill or to delay assent in order to receive advice from, for example, the Chief Justice, or to propose some amendment. To be clear, I am not advocating that a Governor-General should be able to refuse assent to a bill because he doesn't like it or thinks it is bad policy. The power should only be invoked when a non-justiciable bill threatens to infringe our fundamental rights as individuals. The actions of Canadian Prime Minister Trudeau referred to earlier, in my view, come perilously close to infringing fundamental individual rights. These are rights that are, or should be, protected by the Crown. Indeed, it could be argued that this is a primary function of the Crown – to ensure that Parliament, which is ultimately responsible to the people, does not exceed its authority in this respect. Just as Sir John Kerr acted to ensure that the government of the day did not exceed its authority in relation to the Parliament.

I have used royal assent as an example of the way in which the Governor-General's reserve powers may be necessary to protect our rights, because it is easy to postulate, as I have done, occasions under which its use might be called for. But employment of the Crown's discretion may not even be an action as drastic as refusing assent to a bill. A Governor-General could refuse advice to sign an Executive Council minute that, for example, contemplated actions such as those of Trudeau.

True it would take a courageous and sensible Governor-General to invoke these powers. It may well even be a long shot, but we should not disarm ourselves by eliminating the possibility altogether.

Critics may claim that the right to refuse assent has become moribund, pointing out that, in the United Kingdom it was last used, by Queen Anne, in 1707. But Professor Anne Twomey, in Chapter Nine of her comprehensive text *The Veiled Sceptre,* identifies numerous occasions in which it has been used, or contemplated, for various reasons, and in various Westminster jurisdictions, since then. One of those reasons is to protect fundamental rights. She notes that delay, rather than outright rejection, might be an appropriate option. And that considerations which might constrain intervention by the Governor-General on this basis would include the justiciability of the bill and/or the possibility of correction at a subsequent election.[11]

Here is a question for the Australian Republican Movement. What would have happened in November 1975 in the absence of a Governor-General (or President) who did not have the power (or the nous to use it) to resolve the political deadlock? The only way in which Whitlam could have been prevented from acting unconstitutionally would be by means of an appeal to the High Court. That would have taken considerable time, during which immense damage would have been done. And in the end Whitlam would have been forced to an election anyway. Sir John Kerr solved the problem in just one day by exercising a power which he undoubtedly had, and which has only been used once in over 120 years. We are told the reserve powers should be used only very rarely. Tick.

Let me return to a point I made in my Introduction. When we go to the polls, we do not elect a government. We elect a Parliament. That is what the Constitution says. This is a fine, but critical, distinction. Sir John Kerr did not dismiss an 'elected government'. That is just emotive click-bait. Certainly, voters give guidance to the Governor-General as to how he should appoint his Ministry, and it would be a foolish Governor-General who ignored this advice on a whim. But, in Australia, there is no such thing as an elected government whose tenure is sacrosanct. If there were, we would have no need of House of Representative by-elections. A casual vacancy would be filled by the nominee of the incumbent party, just as it is in the Senate.

Sir John Kerr satisfied himself that, in 1974, the voters had presented his predecessor with a Parliament that, by 1975, had become unworkable. What he did was to offer voters the chance to rectify that situation. That people so fundamentally misunderstood our Constitution was not Sir John Kerr's fault. It was the fault of our lack of education in civics, and it continues to this day.

Thank God we have a written Constitution. We may end

---

[11] A. Twomey. (2018) *The Veiled Sceptre: Reserve Powers of Heads of State in Westminster Systems.* London: Cambridge University Press, pp. 668-670.

up being grateful for its 'last line of defence' – the reserve powers. But integral to their effectiveness is the presence of an informed, disinterested and resolute Governor-General. One who has not been indoctrinated or intimidated by polemics such as *The Dismissal*.

I will leave the last word on this to Sir Kenneth Bailey, a former Solicitor General who died in 1972, writing the Introduction to the first edition of Evatt's *The King and His Dominion Governors*:

> It is not too much to say the whole future of the British constitutional system is likely to depend on the extent to which in the next few years, it is demonstrated that the reserve powers of the Crown are not the antithesis but the corollary of the democratic principle that political authority is derived from the people.[12] (emphasis added)

The people spoke on 13 December 1975 and, indirectly, gave the thumbs up to Sir John Kerr.

---

[12] H. V. Evatt (1935). *The King and His Dominion Governors*, London: Oxford University Press, p. xxxv.

APPENDIX

MEMORANDUM OF SIR PAUL HASLUCK
DATED 10 AUGUST 1977

This is a complete and verbatim transcription of the Memorandum written as a private note by Sir Paul Hasluck and not intended for publication during his lifetime. The original is held in trust by his executor, Nicholas Hasluck, who has authorised the publication of this transcription by the author for the purposes of this book only.

I am writing this note following the public announcement of the retirement of Sir John Kerr from the office of Governor-General.

I was aware that this retirement was going to happen and knew from conversations with Sir Martin Charteris that, on the last day of The Queen's visit to Australia, on board the Britannia at Fremantle on March 30, 1977, the audience The Queen gave to Sir John Kerr had brought the matter to a head. From that day his retirement was certain and only the question of timing was left open.

In a long conversation at Buckingham Palace on August 1, 1977, Charteris canvassed my opinion on whether they had been right in deferring any question of retirement until after The Queen's visit to Australia. I said that it was only fair to Kerr that they should have done so. Charteris added that Kerr had also wanted to have the visit to London for the Silver Jubilee and he thought (and I agreed) that it was fair to him and gave the right public appearance to let him do so. From my conversations with Charteris on the Britannia at Fremantle and at the Palace in London, I gained the impression that the Palace had brought pressure to bear on Kerr to retire although of course I have no knowledge of what passed between The Queen and the Governor-General either in conversation or in correspondence. One remark which Charteris made explicitly in talking with me in London was that in the talk on board the Britannia at Fremantle "we" (presumably The Queen in the presence of Charteris) obtained the assurance from Kerr that after his retirement he would not publish any of his dispatches or other communications to The Queen or Her communications to him concerning the dismissal of the Whitlam Government. He was told that these were The Queen's property.

This point arose because, in London on August 1, one part of the conversation between Charteris and myself concerned reports in Australian newspapers to the effect that Kerr was going out of office with a book ready written under his arm and that very high bids were being made for the right to publish it. Charteris said the Palace had been in touch with Kerr about this and had reminded him of his assurance and the position of The Queen in respect of any communications to and from Her. They would not judge him, Charteris said to me, until he gave any reason to doubt that he would act properly and discreetly but the offers were reported to be very high and of course Kerr was rather "greedy" and "the lady in the case" much more so. "We will wait and see", said Charteris. He also said that he heard that the " Fairfax offer" to Kerr had not been high enough yet to tempt him. I said that Kerr would know what was discreet and proper and I did not think he would wish to appear to act dishonourably even for a good price. He had shown some weakness for "self-justification" but his experience as a judge should have taught him that there are some positions in which one had to forego the pleasures of self-justification. The Governor-Generalship was one of them. I thought that self-justification might be his strongest temptation. I had noticed on two occasions at social functions at Government House, Perth, at a time when the controversy over Whitlam's dismissal was keen, that Kerr was going from guest to guest asking in effect "Did I do the right thing?"

Charteris asked my opinion whether Kerr was "a politician". I misunderstood his question and answered at first to the effect that Kerr had always been interested in politics and had political ambitions without being ready to make firm political commitments but he had not had much first-hand experience in the practice of politics and the management of political situations. Charteris then made his question more direct by asking my opinion whether when Kerr "sacked Whitlam" he acted as a politician or as a judge. After reflection I said I thought his thinking was more political than judicial at that time. Charteris was inclined to the view that he had acted judicially on the facts. We then moved to a discussion of the crisis. I said at one stage that there was no doubt in my mind that the Governor-General had the power to act as he did and the success of his action was the final

Appendix

proof of that fact.

If one assumed that Mr Whitlam was in a frame of mind that was unreasonable, arrogant and, indeed, close to defiant of any persuasion to conventional courses of action, then undoubtedly the Governor-General was right to use that power.

I did not know what had passed between Mr Whitlam and the Governor-General or what the frame of mind of Mr Whitlam was. I offered the opinion that Kerr had acted politically because I thought he may have helped to produce the situation in which it was possible for him to act "judicially".

The remaining doubt in my mind about the Governor-General's action did not concern the moment of crisis but the events leading up to it. Again I did not know all the material facts but it seemed to me that in the period leading up to crisis the Governor-General had either acted politically or had been neglectful. Of course this view arose from my view that in a constitutional monarchy the wisdom is to avoid confrontation and never let an issue come to a crisis in the political sense.

Charteris was in general agreement with my doctrine and we recalled the words about "counsel, advice and warning". I said I had always found Whitlam an intelligent man and one conscious of the judgment of history as well as immediate advantage.

Charteris interrupted: "Yes, you got on very well with Whitlam".

We then agreed that part of the situation was that Whitlam had a poor opinion of Kerr. I recalled remarks Whitlam made to me about Kerr at the time he was recommending his appointment. Neither of us was quite sure whether or not Whitlam intended Kerr to be his puppet but it was clear that he had a poor opinion of him and consequently this lessened any influence that Kerr might have had in the role of Governor-General as counsellor and one able to give advice and warning to the Prime Minister. I said that I myself had found Whitlam very responsive to a question or a cautionary word. (We returned to this point a little later).

Unfortunately, as we both agreed, Whitlam had publicly expressed his low opinion of Kerr. He was also reported to have said as the crisis was approaching, "The Governor-General will do what I tell him." This would understandably have stiffened Kerr and possibly put him into a frame of mind - political rather than judicial - of showing the Prime Minister who was master and perhaps (again with a motive that was political rather than judicial) of trying to outwit him by producing the situation in which he could dismiss him.

In answer to Charteris, I then developed further the theme that the wisdom of a constitutional monarchy is to avoid confrontation. If at the time of the "loans crisis" Kerr had been diligent and attentive to the duties of his office, if he had been available at all times instead of travelling abroad, and if he had called Whitlam to see him more frequently and, in doing this had established in Whitlam's mind some greater respect for the office of Governor-General and some greater confidence in his (Kerr's) own trustworthiness and wisdom, there never would have been a crisis.

Charteris agreed with this view of the role of Governor-General. He then posed a theoretical question. Supposing that Whitlam had proposed to The Queen that She should dismiss the Governor-General, what did I think The Queen could have done?

I shrugged and, before I could say anything, Charteris said that I had probably heard the remark attributed to Whitlam, perhaps not with truth, that it was a case of "who got to the telephone first". He then said that the first he (Charteris) heard of the crisis was in fact a telephone call from Whitlam. He had been away from the Palace and on his return was told that there was a telephone caller from Australia. When he took the telephone, a voice said, "Mr Whitlam is calling" and while he was still wondering why it was announced to him as "Mr Whitlam" and not as "the Prime Minister of Australia", Mr Whitlam came on the line and said: "This is the member for Werriwa speaking". He then told him that he had been dismissed by the Governor-General. Charteris was able to reply in complete honesty that this was the first he had heard of it. At that stage Kerr had not "got to the telephone first". Charteris told me nothing of his conversation with Whitlam but said: "Supposing that, having got to the telephone first, the Prime Minister of Australia, had recommended that The Queen dismiss the Governor-General, what would you have done if you had been me?" I replied that, if one assumed that the Prime Minister was Whitlam and the situation was much the same as the one that we knew in November, 1975, then I would have said in effect that this was not the sort of matter in which action could be taken on a telephone call and that in fairness to The Queen and

Appendix

to himself, the Prime Minister should make a formal submission in writing and transmit it to be placed before The Queen. As it clearly involved constitutional issues it would probably be advisable to have the submission supported by opinion by the Crown's legal advisers and both documents should be prepared in a form that would allow them to be published as giving sound reasons for the action. In the meantime no other measures should be taken either by Governor-General or Prime Minister.

In my view a man such as Whitlam would have enough intelligence to consider his next step very soberly and only to persist with his recommendation if there were good and defensible reasons for it. I also remarked on the oddity of the situation that apparently a Governor-General could "sack" a Prime Minister without further consideration but a Prime Minister had no power to "sack" a Governor-General without recourse to The Queen. It appeared to me from our conversation that The Queen had not been involved in any way in Kerr's action in dismissing Whitlam. Charteris concurred.

We discussed the Kerrs, both man and wife, the conclusion being that it was "a good thing" that they were going, that up to date it was a relief to know that his resignation was being handled smoothly, and that the Palace was fervently hoping that at the time he left office or immediately thereafter he did not do anything that was improper, either in publication or in public activities. It was apparent that at the Palace the chief fear arose from a belief that the Kerrs and, especially Lady Kerr, were "very greedy". It was also apparent that at some stage some pressure had been applied from the Palace to bring about his resignation.

Charteris – and by implication the Queen – had a poor opinion of the Kerrs.

INDEX

Alternative financial arrangement 202-203, 229, 241, 249-251, 261-264, 271, 276-280, 319

Anthony D 80

Australian Parliamentary Education Office 93

Australian republic 16, 131, 202, 356

Ayres P 68, 71

Bagehot W 269

Bailey Sir K 358

Bank loan scheme 202-203, 229, 241, 249-251, 261-264, 271, 276-280, 319

Barwick Sir G 21, 69, 82, 89-102, 106-107, 122-126, 137-139, 142, 157, 222, 231, 234, 244-246, 285-302, 305-306, 323, 335, 342, 348

Blamey Sir T 109

Brennan Sir G 89-90

Bjelke-Petersen Sir J 150, 154-156

Buckley B 307, 310

Budd D 67-68, 70, 348

Bunton C 154-155, 157, 259, 333

Butler D 349

Byers Sir M 167, 170-173, 178, 183, 216, 221, 225-229, 263, 338, 340-343,

Cameron C 41, 87, 125, 175, 314

Cameron R 251

Cairns J 168, 170, 183-184

Carleton R 217

Charteris Sir M 30-35, 37-39, 41-61, 80-82, 193, 198, 200-201, 203, 205, 207-208, 219, 237, 314-315, 345, 359-363

CIA 35, 347

Colston M 155

Cook Sir J 147

Combe D 251, 321

Conlon A 108-109

Connor M 69, 99

Connor RFX 10-11, 158-159, 168, 170, 179, 183-184, 186, 334

Constitution, Australian

General 7, 11-17, 20, 23, 26 49, 63, 78, 90, 96-97, 101, 128-129, 130-131, 146, 157, 160, 161-163, 200, 202, 214-215, 290, 345, 354, 357

Reserve powers 7, 14, 20, 26, 127-129, 134, 137, 143, 345

Section 5 7, 126, 228, 327

Section 51 215

Section 57 7, 126, 147, 153, 167, 226-227, 339-341

Section 58 7, 126

Section 61

Section 62 20, 169

Section 64 7, 126-127

Separation of powers 90, 93-95, 99

Cooley A 323

Cowan Sir Z 36, 142

Cowper Sir N 253-255

Crean F 307, 321, 335

Cutler Sir R 103, 116-119, 199-200, 271-272, 282, 336

Daly F 321, 335

Deakin Sir A 147
Democratic Labor Party 111, 115, 149, 153
Double dissolution
 1914 100, 147
 1951 147-148
 1974 9, 152, 166-167, 210
 1975 18, 65, 72, 153, 187, 189, 241, 260, 330, 337-343
Dyster A 334
Ellicott R 46-47, 85-86, 151, 177-178, 183, 196, 207, 215-216, 223-227, 237, 240, 244-246, 264, 271, 290-291, 297, 301
Enderby K 130, 216, 225, 229, 263-264, 311, 321, 335
Evatt H 105-107, 109-110, 115, 123-126, 130, 132-134, 137-138, 142, 221, 224, 245, 246, 302, 358
Executive Council
 General 10, 12, 77-78, 125, 158, 254, 356
 13 December 1974 168-184
Field A 155-157, 259
Flint D 69, 72, 209
Forsey E 50-51, 228, 246, 302, 350
Fraser J M
 Blocking supply 11, 18, 64, 79, 83, 145-161, 238
 Granting supply 65, 306, 328, 330-335
 Meetings with Kerr 195-198, 203-206, 256-258, 264, 272-275,
French R 90, 94
Freudenberg G 321
Gair V 153, 156

Game Sir P 98, 119, 137, 254, 266-268, 353
Garland V 65, 69, 348
Gibbs Sir H 95, 138, 302
Gleeson M 90, 101
Glorious Revolution of 1688 127
Gorton J 40, 149, 151
Greenwood I 343
Griffith Sir S 100, 163
Hall S 154, 156
Hamer R 264
Hanson M 331, 333
Harders Sir C 171, 176, 184-185, 217-218, 225, 305-306, 337-338, 340-343
Hasluck Memorandum 30-39, 208, 359-363
Hasluck Sir P 9, 30-41, 44, 47, 88, 119, 125, 153, 166-168, 174-176, 179, 201, 208-210, 221, 314, 359-363
Hayden W 159, 252, 261, 263, 277-278, 352
Henderson G 234, 348
Herron Sir L 117
Heseltine Sir W 18, 41-44, 207, 336
Heydon Justice D 17
High Court of Australia
 General 21, 23, 89-101, 124, 138, 154, 156-157, 167-168, 183, 191-192, 215, 256, 287, 290-292, 300, 302, 355, 357
 Mabo decision 99
Hocking J 199
Jacobs Sir K 95, 100
James Sir M 352
Jennings Sir I 128

Index

Justiciability 94-95, 97, 167, 172-173, 178, 355-356

Kane J 111, 149

Kemp D 36, 273, 348

Kennedy E 307-308

Kerr Lady A 31, 114, 195, 288, 311, 363

Khemlani T 10, 150, 158, 168, 178, 196

King George V 133

Kirby M 100

Lane P 221

Lang J 98, 106, 119, 141, 228, 254, 353

Lewis T 154-155

Ley F 308

Lindell G 140

Loans Affair 10, 41, 65, 70, 72, 150, 158, 168-169, 177, 189, 196, 238

Loans Council 10, -216172

Thoms v The Commonwealth of Australia 215

Lynch P 73, 307-308, 310

Mant J 193-194, 207, 215, 307-308, 321-322, 334, 337

Marr D 39

Mason Sir A 69, 75-76, 82, 89, 95, 98-100, 135-136, 138-139, 231-247, 274, 276, 285-292, 297-298, 302, 348

McAuley J 120-121

McClelland D 330-332

McClelland J 84, 159, 207, 256, 258

McDonald R 133-134

McDonald T 44-45

McKell Sir W 105, 148

McMahon W 40

McManus F 153, 156

McTiernan E 95

Menadue J 44, 51, 54, 60, 83, 176, 178, 193, 207, 214, 217-219, 306, 308, 317, 321-324

Menzies Sir R 91, 110-111, 147, 292

Milliner B 155

Murphy L 95, 148-149, 154-156, 167-168, 170-171, 178-179, 184-185, 192, 245, 287, 301, 334

Myer K 119

O'Byrne J 330, 332

Palace Letters 31, 33, 37-38, 43, 46-60, 80-81, 199, 203-205, 219, 238, 263, 267, 315, 329

Peacock A 307

Prince Charles 39, 198

Queen Anne 356

Queen Elizabeth II 19, 29-30, 32-33, 35, 37-38, 41-43, 45, 51, 53-54, 56-57, 61, 79-81, 191-192, 197, 200, 207-208, 270, 314, 322, 344-345, 350

Reid A 72, 168, 189, 331

Responsible government 49, 161-163, 187, 222, 335-336

Rudd K 227

Sawyer G 139-140, 174-175, 181, 351

Scholes G 321, 335, 337, 341, 344, 350

Scullin J 147

Senate

    Casual vacancies 154-157, 357

    Convention against blocking supply 146-148, 161, 225-226, 228, 242

    Half-Senate election 11, 18, 22, 63-62, 73, 78, 118, 152-153, 157, 220,

229, 241, 249, 251-252, 256, 258-261, 263-264, 271-272, 276-277, 279, 304-306, 309-310, 318-319, 349

Sexton M 95, 225

Short L 110

Smith Sir D 36, 41-43, 53, 67-69, 149, 170, 195, 200, 210, 223, 235, 281, 303-304, 312, 315, 322, 325, 351

Snedden B 112, 132, 151, 154

Spender Sir P 107

Staley T 36, 275

Stephens C 311

Stewart F 169, 171

Stone J 168, 185

Street Sir L 103, 119

Taylor G 128, 129

Thornton E 110

Tun Abdul Razak dinner 195-196, 299, 314

Twomey A 60, 100, 356

Ward E 109

Wheeldon J 84, 554

Wheeler Sir F 168, 185, 323

Willisee D 332

Wilson Sir H 83, 186-187, 191-192, 210

Winneke Sir H 271-272

Withers R 65-66, 69, 125, 156, 279, 330-332, 348

Wriedt K 186, 324, 330-334

www.ingramcontent.com/pod-product-compliance
Lightning Source LLC
Chambersburg PA
CBHW022008300426
44117CB00005B/85